Phantoms Afoot

Books by Mary Summer Rain

Nonfiction

Spirit Song
Phoenix Rising
Dreamwalker
Phantoms Afoot
Earthway
Daybreak
Soul Sounds
Whispered Wisdom
Ancient Echoes

Children's

Mountains, Meadows and Moonbeams

Phantoms Afoot
Helping The Spirits Among Us

**Mary
Summer Rain**

HAMPTONROADS
PUBLISHING COMPANY, INC.

Hampton Roads Publishing Co., Inc.
891 Norfolk Square
Norfolk, VA 23502

If you are unable to order this book from your local bookseller,
you may order directly from the publisher. Call 1-800-766-8009.

Library of Congress Cataloging in Publication Data

Summer Rain, Mary, 1945-
Phantoms afoot: journeys into the night/by Mary Summer
Rain.
Sequel to: Dreamwalker.

1.No-Eyes, 1892?-1984. 2.Summer Rain, Mary, 1945-. 3.New
Age movement. 4.Spiritual life. 5.Prophecies. 6.Ojibwa In-
dians—Biography. 7.Shamans—Colorado—Biography. 8.Ojibwa
Indians—Religion and mythology. 9.Indians of North
America—Colorado—Religion and mythology. 1.Title.
BP605.N48S863 1989 89-30299
133. 1'09788-dc 19 CIP
ISBN 1-878901-64-8

Contents

Preface to the 1993 Edition 11

Author's Foreword 13

THE PROMPTINGS

Springtime—The Rebirth of
   Dormant Memories 16

THE ENCOUNTERS

In the Dark of Black Wolf Canyon 64

A Sound of Crying on Thunder Mountain . . 101

Eternal Nightwatch in Sweetwater 136

Moon of the Nightstalker 188

Axe Man of Miner's Creek 213

Madness in Bogan Flats 247

Psychic Inferno and Hell Demons 271

Through Owl Eyes 306

Afterword 325

For the two Dreamwalkers in my life—
The wise Brian Many Heart bestowed upon me
the acute awareness of additional spiritual
obligations of the highest order.
The sweet No-Eyes gently took my hand and
guided me through the many lost memories
that served to shatter my fears and replace
them with the strength of dedication.
And for Bill, my very best friend, whose continued
love provides me with the strong support of
tandem power required to show the wandering
souls their final pathway home.

The existence of finer dimensions of reality is not a matter of debate for the learned men of physical science. The related issue that is frequently considered is the possibility of what exactly these delineating dimensions consist of, and what precise manner of altered forms constitute the vast realms of differing vibrational rates.

However, such considerations were no great ponderable dilemma for the wise No-Eyes. Her statement was as clear and as simple as the fact itself. It interpreted as the following:

The existence of spirits cannot be stupidly ignored or eradicated by skepticism or atheism, for spirits are not affected by either, but continue to exist in spite of them both.

Preface to the
1993 Edition

Following the initial publication of *Phantoms Afoot*, I received hundreds of letters from readers who found the book extremely helpful in coming to terms with the death of a loved one. One the other hand, I also received many letters from readers who apologized for *not* having read it. . .out of fear. The latter both surprised and disturbed me because a spirit is really nothing more than the mind of a once-living person, only now it has a spirit form of energy essence instead of flesh and blood. There are no diabolical monsters depicted in *Phantoms Afoot*. There are no screaming banshees hiding between the pages. What *is* found here are simply good people who have gotten lost after physical death, and each one—caught in differing situations—desperately needs to be shown love and understanding.

If you found yourself in a completely foreign country and couldn't speak the language and felt totally alone and lost, wouldn't you welcome the helping hand of a familiar face. . .a friend?

This then is really what *Phantoms Afoot* is all about—helping another individual to feel comfortable in a new environment—helping with directions. We are not so different after physical death. We retain our personalities and thoughts. We can become confused. We can welcome assistance. And we can appreciate being shown which way Home is. Therefore, readers shouldn't shy away from this book out of fear, for there is not one thing to be fearful of unless it is Understanding or Compassion or Love—and I've yet to come across anyone who was afraid of those beautiful attributes. Yet these are precisely what this book are all about. . .Understanding death. . .having Compassion for a confused mind and. . .giving all the Love you can in order to help someone find his way out of the darkness and into the brilliance of the Light that shines from the opened doorway of Home.

This book was never written with the intent to sensationalize the negative side of spirit manifestations. It was written as a chronicle of events that document the simple mechanics of a person's life/death transition and, ultimately, the survival of one's mind and personality. This is a book of problematical situations...all resolved. This is a book of Endings...all happy.

Mary Summer Rain
January, 1993

Author's Foreword

There are myriad books attesting to the vast array of spirit manifestations witnessed throughout the State of Colorado. Grimacing and grinning goblins, screaming and moaning ghosts, and flitting specters all float their haunting ways into more than a few of the spooky pages that comprise each town's historical society's books of record.

There are dozens of spine-tingling tales that each region can attest to. Mysterious cemetery lights, eerie train whistles heard from long-abandoned trestles, miners' talk of the unseen Tommyknockers, strange noises, and vanishing apparitions; all duly recorded, told, and retold in all their hair-raising glory. Therefore, I have no intention of being redundant by rehashing or rearranging that which has already been heavily detailed. What I have managed to do here is to set aside my reluctance to publish this volume in deference to the importance of emphasizing the bare spiritual aspects of the misunderstood subject.

I have endeavored to approach the issue in a spiritually logical and mature manner in order to dispel the "spookiness" of it and to dissipate the readers' general conception of such matters as being mysterious or highly esoteric.

What you will read within the following pages will not be a simple recounting of various manifestations as written in books or historical records, nor will they merely be the descriptive sightings of obscure eyewitnesses; rather, they will be accounts that bring you into the beating heart of the manifestation itself, and keep you beside Bill and me as we encounter the entity, confront it, and interact with it to make it think rationally about its present situation.

Spirits are a fact of life. Spirits who are unfortunately caught between dimensions cannot be logically disputed. And the most beautiful and emotionally-moving experience one could have is being actively instrumental in freeing a confused and lost soul.

I have foregone delving into any previously recorded cases. I deal strictly with those manifestations No-Eyes enlightened me about and with those I've self-discovered through my own sensitivities. I do not become involved with what some erroneously term 'poltergeist' activity (psychokinetic manifestations of the mind) nor do I work with unexplained activity evidenced within private homes (usually generated by extreme psychic energy within the minds of the emotionally-troubled occupants, which I personally consider a serious matter for a psychologist or psychiatrist). And I do not deal with alleged possession cases.

Bill and I are oftentimes away from our home base so that we can quietly and anonymously assist yet another wayward soul to reach its intended ultimate destination. It is highly exacting work and we frequently return home mentally, psychically, and physically exhausted; yet, spiritually speaking, there is nothing more uplifting than when we've attended to a manifestation obligation and have it conclude with reasonable success.

The following encounter experiences represent eight such renderings of actual "clearing" endeavors throughout various regions of Colorado. Four of these encounters detailed are precise in their geographical locale. Four had to be adequately altered in an effort to protect those living individuals involved who desire to maintain anonymity for themselves and their peaceful towns or mountain region. Out of high regard and deep appreciation to them, I have duly respected their wishes by altering all proper names and personal characteristics of those four cases. Three of the four altered cases have been given totally fictitious regional names; however, the fourth one was given an actual Colorado town name. There is such a place as Sweetwater, Colorado, yet that town is in no way connected with the geographical location of the actual case. I simply chose the name because it is so typical of the colorful names throughout the state of Colorado and because it so aptly maintains the reminiscent tone and mood of the "Old West" that so permeated the actual location.

In the final analysis, I have come to realize that the only important issue here is not "where" the encounter took place or even those individuals who were remotely involved to make it possible. The real meat of the matter rests solely in the isolated event itself—the sequence of thought, applied logic to an operable plan, eventual action taken, and the ultimate end result—the spiritual beauty of freeing a lost soul from its earthly confines of self-imposed bounds.

The Promptings

Springtime— The Rebirth of Dormant Memories

When given the Master Key, all the rusted padlocks of the mind are sprung wide. All the closed windows and doors open to the sunny Light of Day. . .and the sweet freshness of awareness, Understanding and Freedom rush in.

After a long and bitter winter, the gentle thought of early May would normally conjure up technicolor visions of multi-colored tulips, saffron daffodils, delicate magnolias and sweetly-scented morning air. Early May would ordinarily present all of these sensual delights to me except for the cold hard fact that I live in the high Colorado mountains, where Mother Nature frequently tickles her fancy by playing jokes on the mountain folk.

Springtime in the Rockies sounds a bit melodic—it has a certain romantic ring to it; however, for those in-the-know, springtime in the Rockies merely interprets as "snow"—occasionally, days and days of heavy, wet snowfall. And dear ol' Mother Nature was staying true to her traditional humor as I prepared for my weekly journey out to No-Eyes' place this early May morn.

The family was still sound asleep while I quietly dressed and tiptoed about the silent house. While I was brushing my hair, Rainbow drowsily sauntered around the bathroom doorway and padded softly in to greet me. She put her large paws up on the edge of the sink, wagged her bushy tail and gently nosed my elbow. Without speaking to her, I looked down into the anxiously pleading eyes. I knew what she wanted. I patted her silky head and ran the cold water for her to drink from. She lapped for a long while before nudging my side to say that she was finished. I hugged the sweet four-legged person and whispered to her that it wasn't time for her to be up yet. She gave me one of her pitiful soulful looks and reluctantly moseyed back through the silent house to curl up on the bottom of the girls' bed.

While I finished getting ready, I entertained humorous thoughts about our ever-faithful canine that was half coyote. She was so much like a real person. She understood so much of what we said to her it was just like she could almost read our minds for, many times, words weren't necessary for our communications and she would simply respond to certain looks or gestures and, in return, Rainbow communicated her own sensitive feelings just as effectively as the spoken word.

An amused grin mischievously crept up my face as I thought of how ferociously she protected us whenever strangers came around—even the neighbors and some of our more infrequent visitors wouldn't come through the front door unless "that wild killer" was put into the confinement of the backyard. If they only knew how incredibly sensitive and loving she was toward each family member, if they only could see her ecstatic joy as she leaps onto our bed each morning and pleads to be petted and snuggled. And I thought of how she loves games, especially Hide and Seek, where she tries to find where the girls are hiding within the house. Yes, she certainly could be vicious toward strangers, yet, with us, she was simply another member of the family. And I inwardly chuckled over her apparent Jekell and Hyde nature.

With growing concern, I spun my fingers around in the moisture of the kitchen window and peered out. The dripping circlet revealed a harsh exterior world. It was snowing heavily. Blowing winds were whipping and gusting down out of a dark and menacing sky.

I sighed. It'd be nice to romp in an alpine meadow full of wildflowers today instead of having to don my heavy blanket serape and knee-high moccasins. Then again, no place is perfect. Springtime in the Rockies was something I was used to. The May snowstorm was not unexpected.

When I slowly backed the Chevy pickup down alongside our cabin, a sudden movement in a window caught my eye, almost subliminally. Rainbow, warm nose pressed firmly up against a cold windowpane, had parted the curtains to say goodbye. She'd gotten up on Jenny's bed to get her head on the window sill. She would guard the silent house and protect the slumbering occupants until they awoke and she could happily greet them with a wagging tail, wet kisses, and whimpers of pure joy.

My progress through town was tediously slow. The snow-fall had gained its momentum—it had decided to transform itself into a full-fledged blizzard, complete with frequent blinding white-outs. I was the only traveler to boldly venture out on the roads this cold spring morning, and the massive snowplows were just beginning to warm up their frigid innards and belch out their smokey reluctance into the opaque atmosphere.

Once I managed to clear the limits of Woodland Park, I silently plowed through an enchanted land of fantasy. The mountains were mystically touched by an adept alchemist who had metamorphosed the forest greenery into a magical shimmering fairyland of whiteness. Perhaps I did miss out on seeing the crisp, white magnolias, the pink cherry blossoms and the multicolored tulips of the East, but my mountain wonderland also possessed a dazzling beauty that electrified and stunned the senses. I was satisfied and contented with my total acceptance of it. Nature was indeed a fickle Lady, and I liked that spontaneous aspect of her fascinating unpredictable personality.

Just as I had anticipated, No-Eyes had a roaring fire raging within her fireplace—she had stoked it red hot. The thick roiling smoke billowed up out of the ancient stone chimney and was immediately whisked away by the blustering force of the wind.

I remained within the warm confines of the pickup for a few sweet revelling minutes while a gentle melancholia drifted over my consciousness.

I surveyed the wild scene of nature that ranted through my friend's vast backyard of wooded mountains. The tall jack pines and the spired firs were being tortuously bent this way and that. A spectral whiteness swirled in a whipping circle dance around and through the bending sentinels that were reluctantly forced to join in the wild dervish that nature was choreographing.

I peered through the windshield up at the nearly invisible cabin-on-the-hill that was bravely holding its own—standing in direct defiance of the relentless assaults of the blizzard. And the mountains that towered behind the cabin served to emphasize the small dwelling's strength of character.

A sudden force of wind gusted against the truck and rocked

it, pelting the windshield with a blast of snow that sounded ominously like sleet. I had to get out and be about my business before I found myself permanently entombed in the vehicle.

I turned the engine off, snuggled my head down beneath the hood of the serape, and attempted to open the door. It wouldn't budge. The powerful might of the wind was pushing against it with an incredible counter force. Finally, by exerting all the energy I could muster, I managed to push it open just wide enough to inch out. The door slammed back with a great force.

All the way up the old woman's hillside, the Entity of the Storm gnashed its jagged teeth at me as it tested my strength by trying to blow me off my feet and whip away my serape. I lost my precarious balance several times while leaning forward into the wind, and when it suddenly decided to trip me up by teasingly switching directions, I'd fall off-balance onto my face. Eventually I reached the snow-drifted steps and pushed open the frosted pine door. A blast of snow blustered in with me into the toasty warm living room. Immediately the waiting incense of burning juniper wood and pine weighed heavily on my receiving senses. The scent was good—so good.

The old one was well prepared for me. She deftly whipped off my wet serape and lovingly placed a warmed blanket over my head. Tenderly, she tucked it in around my shoulders as she led me to the crackling fire. The visionary then shook out my sodden wrap and carefully spread it out by the hearth. Steam began rising from the woven fabric. A hot mug of freshly-steeped herbs was gently placed in my hands, and I silently watched while my teacher scooted her rocker up to me. She spoke not a word as her coal black eyes bored deep into my soul.

I slipped the warmed blanket down and off my head and rearranged it about my shoulders as the pitch in the pine logs popped and exploded behind me. I fanned out my hair and combed my ringers through the damp strands so the blaze would dry it quicker. The room was alive with the fluttering reflections of the dancing fire, and the flickering oil lamp that burned brightly on her kitchen table radiated additional beams of golden serenity throughout the tiny cabin. All was protectively mellow and serenely calm within my small schoolroom as the saber-sharp jaws of Nature angrily clamped again and again at the cabin's exterior. It was deeply comforting. It was incredibly full of an encompassing peace. . .a breathing, touchable peace.

No-Eyes remained staring into her contented student. Then the eyes twinkled impishly. She spoke. "Spirit of spring be havin' one good time out there, huh Summer?"

A soft smile tipped the corners of my lips. "That's one way of putting it." That was not exactly how I would've described the tempest that raged outside but, then again, the visionary always characterized the Spirit of Nature in a most favorable light.

The old one made no reply to my statement. A long, extended silence filled more than several minutes before the impaired rocker began to speak as the woman mentally prepared to begin today's lesson.

"Summer, this day we gonna speak 'bout some special kind of spirits. No-Eyes gonna be speakin' bout spirits who be stupid dumb."

Some obscure subliminal warning signal pricked up and down along my spine. I frowned slightly.

"What do you mean, dumb?" Then, before she could reply, I changed the subject rather abruptly after sipping a taste of the flavorful tea blend. "What's in this? It's really tasty."

Her wide eyes danced and rolled beneath slitted lids. "No-Eyes put some blackberry in with other stuff," she cleverly replied, not bothering to define the nebulous "other stuff."

I lowered my head and suspiciously squinted back up at her. It was a teasing sort of gesture of admonishment and trusting acceptance all rolled into one. I gingerly sipped again and playfully licked my lips at the faint underlying taste of the mysterious ingredient.

I lifted my head and, when our intense eyes met, it was clear that our moment of light bantering had passed. I returned to the subject of the lesson.

"You were speaking about the dumb spirits. Dumb in what way?"

The old one leaned back into the rocker and gently allowed the corners of her mouth to lift before becoming serious once more.

"As you already know, all peoples' spirits survive physical death. All spirits return to spirit place of remembering and learning. But Summer," she reminded softly, "some spirits be stupid dumb. They not do what they know be right stuff to do. They not listen to other spirits who come to guide them through passageway into reality of light and truth." She then paused.

I had been thinking while she spoke. I knew exactly what

she was saying. "No-Eyes, do you think that those spirits would've done the right thing if their physical minds were more aware of how things really are while they were alive?"

She outwardly balked at the idea and shook her head in clear denial of the theory.

I went deeper with my line of thought. "But if people were truly cognizant of the realities of the spirit dimension, why wouldn't they then be prepared for the afterlife when it came?"

I had been under the impression that conscious awareness in the physical automatically insured the spirit's quick and natural rite of passage after death. I told her of my thoughts on it.

A soft sigh escaped from between her thin lips as she closed her eyes and then slowly opened them wide at me.

"Not always, Summer. That always depend on *manner* of physical death. See?"

"Not really," I admitted.

Suddenly the aged visionary mysteriously shifted her sightless gaze to the fogged windows. She appeared to be intently listening for something.

In the new eerie stillness, I strained my ears. I thought I picked up a slight whispering sort of murmur emitting from somewhere within our silent cabin.

The wind was creating havoc with the ancient wooden dwelling; the windows rattled, the rafters creaked and groaned, and the massive pines surrounding the cabin were being viciously bent low against it. The terrible din confused my efforts of concentration and compounded my purpose. And as I watched my teacher intently center on the ambiguous sound, I found myself tensing to strain harder and harder to hear.

I watched as No-Eyes cryptically turned her head in my direction to slowly bend forward and peer at me while her ear remained attentive to the spectral voice.

My spine tingled with the high intensity of the frozen moment. I involuntarily quivered as though I had been struck by a sudden gush of arctic air, though no such entity brushed against me. My higher sensors detected no negative force within our aura of reality. My eyes remained hopelessly magnetized to her black pools that widened into onyx saucers of expectancy.

Skin crawled.

I couldn't stand the strain. I dared to snap the tension with my whispered inquiry. "What is it? Who's here?"

A knobby finger slowly raised to pursed lips.

I anxiously waited while cautiously sliding my eyes away from those of No-Eyes. I let them perceptively pan the room full of writhing shadows. We were assuredly not alone any more.

Someone had joined us.

A slight movement from the rocker brought my attention back to the woman. She had inclined her head further toward the sound. I looked to her side and discerned a faint wavering motion within the darkened shadows on the far wall. Something I couldn't quite distinguish was interrupting the shadows cast by the firelight.

There was a definitive outline of a form.

While No-Eyes was concentrating on the audio facet of the unexpected manifestation, I shifted mental gears to cue in on the video aspect. I intently watched the area directly beside her. My altered perception was working—the form appeared to gain additional substance, although this substance was not due to an actual material solidification, but rather from my own increased rate of awareness.

My physical tenseness relaxed as recognition of the form registered within my consciousness. It was tall and possessed a formidable and commanding character, yet it also appeared to exhibit a sublime quality of sensitivity.

I began to comprehend more and more of the form's details. It was the spirit of a man, an Indian man. My initial thought was that he was Two Trees, No-Eyes' father. Then, I was certain of the direct relationship when he bent down and placed a loving kiss on the woman's forehead.

My gaze went to No-Eyes' face. The countenance was most serene, and the glint of tears began to fill her eyes. I looked away, feeling as though I was intruding on their private moment of touching. Closing my eyes and leaning contentedly back against the warm fireplace stones, I revelled within my happy heart that No-Eyes was adept enough to experience such a mystically beautiful touching with her wise father. My heart was glad for them. And I became lost within the soft tranquility of the esoteric feat's beautiful mood.

Suddenly, a sharp creak rent the downy fabric of my restful reverie. My eyes shot open to see No-Eyes timing the meter of her rocker, a satisfied smile on her creviced face. She was alone. She was staring into the bright flames that illuminated her face.

I relaxed. Again I closed my eyes until the old one's mood

was ready to accept the spoken word. I didn't have long to wait.

In a soft voice, she asked, "Why Summer not stay with us?"

"Stay? Oh no, No-Eyes. I felt like some kind of voyeur. I didn't want to intrude upon such a beautifully tender moment—it was way too personal."

She turned her head slightly to squint down at me out of the sharp corner of her eyes. "Tsk-tsk," she admonished playfully. "No-Eyes have many, many times like that. If it been so private, he not even come now when Summer be here."

Her mischievous smile widened. "Peoples think No-Eyes be so all 'lone up here in this old cabin, but I got many visitors they not even *see!*" The black opals twinkled at the thought of what people didn't know.

I grinned at her childlike mirth, then returned to the subject of her father's visit with more seriousness. "No-Eyes?"

Her gaze had returned to the dancing flames. She stared deep into the blaze. "Mmmm?"

"Can I ask a question about what just happened?"

The chair began to rock, then it stopped. "Summer sure she want to ask this?"

"Yes."

The woman's head eerily rotated in my direction. The firelight limelighted the stray hairs of her head like a glowing silver halo. "Summer can always ask, but Summer not always like answer."

The visionary's mood had greatly altered. Now she was being gravely cryptic. I had to carry it through.

"Why did he choose this time to come? I mean, while I'm here?"

"Don't you know?" came the soft whisper.

My spine tingled. My head was full of a million splintered ideas and thoughts. . .none of them gave me any comfort at all. Over and over the same scene kept replaying a flashback in my head. For some crazy reason, I kept seeing Brian Many Heart sitting in front of the fire instead of the old woman. That day I spent with him in this very room left a sour taste in my mouth and a sinking feeling in the pit of my stomach. It was the day he tried to talk me into helping lost spirits and I'd have none of it. I closed my ears and mind to it. I'd even gotten up and closed the door on him. Now that same old sour taste and sinking feeling was back, because I'd just remembered he'd said that No-Eyes would one day change my mind on the subject. And I had the awful sensation that my hour of reckoning had just arrived.

My eyes slid up to meet hers. "No-Eyes?"

"Mmmm."

"Did the visitation of your father have anything to do with me?"

"Should it?"

"I don't know, that's why I'm asking."

Silence.

Waiting.

"What so! He been here many times before."

"But never when I've been here with you."

Silence.

"Are you going to answer me?"

"Yup."

"Well?"

"No-Eyes gonna answer."

I patiently waited for more to come. Nothing followed. I sighed and looked to the fire, wondering just what exactly all this senseless verbal circling was about. The silent moments ticked endlessly on as the flames drew my full attention into their hypnotic movements and the totality of my consciousness became completely absorbed within the warm entity of the fire. I was completely at peace.

"Summer gonna walk out on No-Eyes?"

The softly spoken words crept into my peace. They answered my question. They confirmed the reason for my former sensations of warning. I continued to stare into the licking tongues of orange.

"No, No-Eyes, I won't slam the door on you." Then I turned. Our eyes met. "It's time for that talk, isn't it."

"Yep, it be that time now, Summer. Two Trees say it be right time to tell Summer 'bout those dumb spirits she an' her man gonna see—gonna help be on way."

At her words, the blood drained from my face. I had been secretly dreading this moment since the day Many Heart said it would one day come. My first impulse was to balk, to place my usual objections in my usual animated manner, but somehow I knew I wouldn't do that anymore. Deep inside, I knew those sudden outbursts were over.

I allowed a heavy sigh to escape as I defeatedly slouched back against the fireplace stones. Outside I could hear the cruel wind laughing at me—the wild heart within me had been finally tamed.

The wind banged and pounded uproariously at the frail windows in its characteristic expression of humiliating ridicule. I listened to the raging tempest outside and I listened to the soothing calm within. And I allowed the mellow sounds within to quell the angered ones. The radiating warmth of the snapping fire sparked subliminal visions in my mind. Again the fragmentary scenes of that other time in this room began to replay vividly as they gained in strength and form. I reviewed the incident and thought long and hard on it.

While the old rocking chair creaked in the background, I entered the memory of that former time when I sat before the cabin's blazing fire with Brian Many Heart, the Dreamwalker—my friend and part-time mentor. That distant day had a direct connection with what No-Eyes and I were presently approaching. Recalling his grave words about it being a Dreamwalker's duty to assist wayward spirits brought on feelings of shame for how I'd reacted that fateful day with him.

He'd said that the old one would one day convince me of the validity of the work and that it was high spiritual business—more important than any other an enlightened person could ever do. At the time, I'd refused to listen. At the time, I hadn't even stayed to listen. At the time, I walked out on the subject. . .and him. Now I realized that the time had come when the visionary was going to do her level best to change my thinking on the subject. She was going to work her magic on me and ease me into seeing reason. This was going to be the biggest hurdle I'd have to clear—it was the highest. . .and the last.

I didn't want to be difficult anymore. I didn't want to make things so hard for my beloved teacher, but I always utilized my free will and, in direct respect to that aspect, I also needed to logically weigh every facet of spiritual input she offered me. Things had to set right. They had to feel damn right. I had to experience the feeling and the knowing of rightness in order to be perfectly comfortable with everything I did—or was expected to do.

Considering how powerfully adept the visionary had proven herself to be in the past, I now had no doubts that she would also pull this one off just as smoothly as she had everything else previously attempted. Even though we'd frequently experienced the clashing of minds, I was ultimately no match for her incredible wisdom and indisputable logic. However, that fact alone wouldn't keep me from holding my own now because I didn't like the premise of the subject. I didn't like the idea of fooling around with spirits—wayward or otherwise. I didn't see how I could do it or why I had to. The very idea literally scared the hell out of me and, to be perfectly honest, I didn't want anything to do with spirits. I didn't see the need. In fact, I didn't see so much about the subject, I suppose you could say I was downright blind to it. Maybe that was my problem. Regardless, I resigned myself to remain calm.

"Okay," I whispered. "I'm ready to listen."

The lady's eyes were soft. Her voice was full of compassion. "No-Eyes know Summer not want to hear 'bout this but it must be spoken 'bout. It not gonna go away, but it not gonna be so bad either. Summer see."

I managed a weak smile. "No-Eyes?"

"Mmm."

"I really do want to feel comfortable with this. I really want to feel good about it."

"No-Eyes know that. We gonna get into it now."

The rocker began to gently creak and thud.

I had resigned myself to the lesson material. I would be good. She had my full attention as she began speaking.

"No-Eyes know how many times Summer an' Bill go 'round in mountains. You go here, go there, go all over even. Summer an' Bill ever feel stuff when you be goin' through some mountains?"

"We love these mountains, No-Eyes. We feel the bond of unity with them." I hesitated then because she already knew that and was clearly searching for a different type of "feeling." I took another trail with it.

"Some areas have stronger vibrations than others; some are good, some bad. And," I reluctantly admitted, "some regions are downright spooky."

Her expression remained unchanged, but the rocking motion of her chair paused a split second while she inquired, "Spooky?"

"Yeah, you know, areas that give you that sudden case of goosebumps or prickles in your hair."

"And what those mean, Summer?"

"That there's a powerful force of energy within the area."

The rhythmic meter of the rocker began again. "Force from what? Magnet force of earth? What?"

I grinned at her simplistic silliness. "You're toying with me. Of course it's not from the magnetic field. This force is of a psychic nature, from lasting impressions or from the lingering presence of living spirits." And, before I had even finished out the sentence, I realized that I had just talked myself right into the swirling vortex of my lesson. Consequently, my mental light bulb flashed on and off like a blinking barricade beacon in the middle of a dark, deserted country road.

"That's it, isn't it. You're talking about the geographical areas where lingering spirits choose to be earthbound, aren't you."

Although she tried, the old one couldn't manage to contain her grin. "Yup, Summer, No-Eyes mean those stupid ones all right."

I gave her a questioning sideglance. "Well then," I asked suspiciously, "what did you mean about the *helping* part we're supposed to be going to do?"

She clearly avoided the implied skepticism behind my doubtful glance and continued speaking in a clipped yet cheerful manner.

"Listen now. There be many areas in mountains where these stupid spirits stay and stay and stay. They not listen to guides—to those smart spirits who try to tell them they not belong on earth any more. They stay and waste much time anyway. They need Summer an' Bill to push on their way, to show how dumb they been actin'." My teacher was grinning from ear-to-ear with her good news.

But the news wasn't good and I wasn't grinning back. I think I was in a state of shock.

Her mirthful grin slackened as the wispy brows wrinkled her forehead. "What the matter now? No-Eyes give Summer an' Bill good way to use spirit sight, good way to help out dumb, lost spirits. That be part of what you both be here to do!" She peered inquisitively down at me. "What so! Summer maybe be scared?"

A sudden icy shudder rippled through me. "I'm not sure. No-Eyes, I'm not sure we can do this wonderful thing."

"*Can't*? Or, don't *want* to?" she corrected calmly.

She had me there. "Probably both," I admitted, knowing full well what the woman's forthcoming reaction was going to be. I cringed as I steeled myself in anticipation of its forceful onslaught.

Her foot stamped, her arms flailed the air and she shouted, "*Who* be stupid one here? Great Spirit say we gotta *use* gifts of spirit! He *not* say to let them *rot* like fallen leafs on forest floor!" She bent forward, placing her face low, nose-to-nose with mine, and softly whispered, "*Now*, tell No-Eyes *again* why Summer an' Bill no can do this good spirit helpin' stuff."

I attempted to focus on her eyes, but she was too close—too close for comfort. I looked down at my hands.

"*Look* at No-Eyes!" she ordered.

Again I looked up into the obsidian eyes. "I don't think we're ready for that stuff yet," I boldly reiterated.

Without further comment, she rested back into the old rickety chair and stared hard past me into the fire.

I felt ashamed to have verbally doubted our gifts' effectiveness—to have doubted her wise evaluated judgment of them, and I bowed my head to study my fingers.

The next words from her lips were filled with a wise tenderness that exemplified her deep understanding of the situation.

"Summer, No-Eyes know what be up in Summer's head, what be up in Bill's, what spirit level you both be at. No-Eyes know many things 'bout stuff you both be ready for. . .even if Summer an' Bill not know yet. I not gonna say you be ready if you not be."

Her sensitive mood served to effectively file down the rough edges of my defensive embarrassment.

"I said I couldn't do that wayward spirit stuff because I think we're not psychically strong enough, and also. . .also because I think I'd be scared to death."

The old one gracefully accepted my honesty in stride. "We gonna get all that scared stuff straight here. First, why Summer feel she not have spirit that not be equal to dumb spirit's power?"

"Actually," I immediately replied, "to tell you the truth, I never really considered whether my spirit had equal or greater power than another's because I never considered the possibility of becoming a psychic or spiritual adversary to anyone—anyone living *or* dead."

A bony finger rose in quick interruption as her bear-trap mind clamped down on my unintentional contradiction.

"Well then, Summer *had* to think 'bout this stuff anyway—without a conscious thought—how else Summer think she be so frightened? Summer *must* have some *hidden* thoughts that she maybe have less powerful spirit than another. Huh?"

I thought on that logic. "Well, I suppose you're right. But now that we *are* consciously giving this some concrete attention, would it be illogical to attribute more psychic power to a spirit on the premise that they don't have any of their energies wasted on the physical—the energies expended to operate the physical vehicle (body)? Aren't spirits all spirit force?"

Her hands flipped back and forth to mime irrelevancy.

"That be illogical, all right. All peoples spirit forces be all spirit energy. *Physical* energy be for physical only. See? Beside," she beamed with a chuckle, "Summer's protection be most strong medicine."

I weakly attempted to veer onto another trail of reasoning. I kept trying to wheedle out of this wonderful future work. "Well yes, but if the spirit guides and helpers on the other side have failed to effectively convince the wayward spirits, then I don't see how a physical person can accomplish what they couldn't."

She clearly saw through my flimsy ruse. "That be big cop-out! These lost spirits not *listen* to other spirits, they need a *physical* helper to prove how *different* they really be—that they *really* be dead!"

She blew one of her powerful "humphs" at me and raised one wispy brow above a peering eye. "No-Eyes think Summer be tryin' to find holes to worm out of stuff here."

Our eyes locked.

"Maybe I am," I admitted without hesitation. "Maybe I'm just plain scared of this thing. Maybe I don't want to get anywhere near it because the entire idea of having a face-off with an unhappy or angered ghost scares me to death."

"Ahhh," she sighed with the confession, "now we gettin' down to some of those big roots called truth. Why Summer think she be so scared to face spirits? Summer did good once before, she can do good again. . .and again."

She was a marksman that shot straight from the hip. She was shooting down every excuse I flung at her, and I was beginning to become upset at her for it. I was losing pitifully and I didn't like it one bit. I didn't generally expect to win our mental battles, but she was so adept at anticipating every mental move before it was made, it ultimately turned out to be very frustrating. Consequently, now it was my turn to become animated with a last-ditch effort to save myself and Bill from the terrifying spiritual job she said we had. Although I had planned on keeping my cool. . .I lost it anyway.

I flung off the blanket, jumped to my feet and paced the floor. "Look! Aren't we doing enough already? I've literally gone through hell because of my lessons. I've done everything you've asked of me. I promised I'd write about my times with you—the lessons, even though some people will probably think I'm absolutely Looney Tunes. I've been humiliated, embarrassed, and scared out of my wits by you with the lessons!

I've promised to correspond with the seekers and to help them in any way I can. Isn't that quite *enough?*"

Silence.

"Well, No-Eyes?"

Silence.

"Will you please *answer* me!"

Deeper silence.

I wasn't going to allow her to psychologically manipulate me this time. I exasperatedly strode around to her side, knelt down and attempted to look her square in the eye.

She quickly snapped her head away.

"*Look* at me!" I demanded.

And ever so slowly did the head turn.

My heart sank with a hard thud. The firelight sent sparkles of reflections along the stream of tears that coursed jaggedly down the deeply creviced face.

I was mortified. "Oh God, No-Eyes, I'm sorry. I didn't mean it, I really didn't."

A thin-skinned hand gently settled over mine. "Summer mean each word she say 'cause each word be truth. Summer done all those things. No-Eyes done all those things to Summer. It all be truth."

That didn't serve to explain the cause of her tears. "Then why are you crying?"

She smiled and compassionately patted my hand. "Summer, go back by fire and sit down now. We gonna speak more 'bout this stuff."

When I arose from beside the old one's chair, I noticed that the fire needed replenishing. And I returned to my place on the hearth only after restocking it with fresh juniper.

Heartsick inside, I waited.

Her face had been wiped dry while my back was turned. She was again the composed teacher who was prepared to continue with her words of wisdom and logic. I was never to find out the cause of her tears because she avoided the matter and continued with the lesson instead.

"Why Summer feel she done 'nough here?"

Since the heat of my former rage had cooled, I simply managed a deflated shrug.

"That not be very good answer comin' from someone who be aware."

"I suppose I just didn't think I had more to do—additional types of spiritual work, I mean."

The rocker became activated. "Summer know she got more

to do." Her voice was barely above a whisper. "Who you tryin'
to fool here?"

"Fool? Nobody. I'm not trying to fool you. . .or myself. I
simply never thought that there would be spiritual things like
this for us to be involved in."

Silence.

I ran my fingers through the hair that kept falling into my
face and, wrapping my arms around my legs, I rested my chin
on them.

The constant snapping of the logs sent flares of sparks
exploding in the fireplace. Shapeless entities danced upon the
uneven surface of the log walls. And I resigned myself to the
conversation at hand, but not without some meager effort at
raising further objections/excuses.

"Well. . .you're going to have to do a heck of a lot of convincing to make me feel comfortable with this thing. Guides
are one thing when it comes to face-to-face encounters, but
coercing unwilling, rebellious spirits is quite another story."

The rocker slowly tipped back and forth. The metered creak
and thud ticked off the seconds like the swinging pendulum
of a grandfather clock. The atmosphere was heavily tranquil.
Her voice was soft.

"No-Eyes not gonna try to *convince* Summer of no thing.
Summer use wrong word here 'cause Summer not need to be
convinced of no stuff. What Summer need, be a tiny bit of push
behind mind—in memory. No-Eyes gonna do a little bit of that
prompting 'cause that all Summer gonna need here."

I chuckled with a hint of mild disbelief in my voice. "Is that
a fact? Just a little bit of prompting and I'll be ready to chase
right out into the rolling fog of the woods and into dark,
haunted houses to face all those moaning, menacing ghosts
who are lurking around and terrorizing everyone who ven-
tures innocently across their paths." I skeptically shook my
head. "I don't think so, No-Eyes. I don't think so."

The smart-mouthed student left the teacher undaunted. She
simply let that cunning, knowing smile of hers lift the corners
of her mouth. The old one didn't think my smugness deserved
a response.

I hated that type of clever display because it always meant
that I would ultimately end up eating my words. We were at
opposite poles once again. We were at odds, and the psychic
sound of our horns clashing was drowning out the ferocity of
the blizzard that raged outside the drawn perimeter of our
battleground.

No-Eyes then comically sniffed at the air. "What that strange smell comin' from Summer's blanket wrap?" she asked as she wrinkled her nose and bent down toward the still-steaming serape.

I hadn't the faintest idea of what she was talking about and I leaned over on my elbow to take a quick whiff of the drying material. I didn't smell anything particular. I looked up at the sniffing woman. "I don't smell anything."

Her head moved from side to side as the nose wrinkled more. "There be some strange smell all right an' it be comin' from that blanket."

Now I put my nose into the fabric. And now I grinned. "That's frankincense and myrrh, No-Eyes. It's one of the scents I burn at home." I shrugged. "I guess my serape has absorbed some of it. Do you like the fragrance?"

She pursed her lips and gave a definitive nod. "It be one heavy fragrance. Why that one?" she asked with a raised brow which clearly indicated that she already knew.

I shrugged. "I just feel at ease with it—sort of homey, if you know what I mean. It gives me a certain sense of inner peace."

"That 'cause it make Summer's spirit content—'cause of lifetime lived so long, long ago, huh."

"Yeah," I admitted, "but we're getting way off track, No-Eyes."

The visionary rolled her eyes to the smoky ceiling before lowering them back to bore hard into mine. "Maybe so. Maybe we get a tiny bit off track. We just went too far back, that all. But you gonna need to do some of this backtrackin' anyways. Not back to that ancient life, just back into childhood and adulthood of present lifetime. Okay?"

"Sure. If that's what's needed, but what does that have to do with prompting me? I don't see any connection with my childhood and my working with wayward spirits."

"Summer be blind student. That why No-Eyes be here to help."

"Still, what's the. . ."

A deep rush of exhaled breath broke off my sentence. She sighed over her student's constant questions. "Summer say she be so scared of wayward and rebellious spirits?"

"Well. . .yes, but only because they're an unknown factor to me, only because I haven't had any actual physical experience in the matter. Dealing with them will be an entirely new type of encounter—one that should be handled with the delicacy of highly knowledgeable and thoroughly trained adepts," I snuck in, trying a vain effort to weigh down my side of the ongoing controversy.

"BLAH!" She threw out her arms and then wagged a crooked finger at me. "*That* what *Summer* think! That thinkin' be all slithery like snake winding 'round behind prey. Summer still tryin' to avoid issue here—still tryin' to sneak away from subject!"

Then the wise one leered down into my face. "But No-Eyes be too *old* for Summer's young tricks. No-Eyes gonna take Summer way back into childhood to prod out old buried memories that hide deep in mind. We gonna go *see* how inexperienced you *really* be!" And, settling confidently back into her chair, she spoke softly. "Now. . .lay down an' close eyes. You not gonna sleep here. You not even gonna make spirit journey either. You just gonna be peaceful. See?"

"All right." I did as I was directed and waited for further instructions. This appeared to be an entirely new experience for me—something we hadn't ever done before. I relaxed on the worn braided rug and allowed the warming fire to comfort and calm my senses.

No-Eyes was sharp. She was observing not only the physical calmness of my bodily systems, but was also acutely aware of my mental attitude that had altered from Expectancy to Acceptance and Openness.

"Now," she began as she gently rocked, "journey way, way back. Summer be 'round three years old, maybe three and a half even. It be time when you be livin' in upstairs of grandmother's house by big church. Remember that house?"

"Yes," I answered quietly.

"Good. Summer inside that house yet?"

"Yes."

"Good. Now downstairs, in back bedroom, is your sick grandmother. Little Summer be peekin' 'round bedroom doorway. Then. . .then little Summer see somebody else in that room. Tell No-Eyes who that somebody be."

My eyes shot open and I began to rise in my excitement.

"Lay *down*!" she quickly barked. "Go *back*!"

I followed orders but couldn't contain the curiosity that had risen to the surface. "How'd you know about something that I didn't even remember? How'd you *see* that?"

The voice was gentle, yet was patronizing and held whole notes of exasperation. "It be there for *all* to see. Just 'cause *you* be blind, it not mean teacher also be blind." She quietly chuckled to herself before continuing. "So! What that tiny little girl see beside sick grandmother's bed that afternoon?"

"A ghost! Well. . .I mean that's the only thing I knew it to be way back then. Now I know that what I saw was a spirit form."

Through closed lids I saw through the eyes of my childhood—I relived the vision again.

"The spirit had his hand on my grandmother's head. He smiled at me. I remember it now. It's all so clear. I can recall how I froze in that doorway, unable to move a muscle or twitch an eye. Then, when I finally gathered up enough nerve, I turned and fled like the devil himself was chasing me. I ran all the way back upstairs to our own place where my mother was. I can even see her standing at the ironing board."

I paused for a second or two. "You know something, No-Eyes? I never told a soul about what I saw in my grandma's room."

"Why you not tell? Huh?"

Now it was my turn to "humph." "That answer is rather clear, isn't it? I mean, who the hell's going to believe a little three-year-old kid when she says that she's just seen a ghost standing next to her grandma."

"Then what happened to little Summer?"

The new question drew a complete blank. Maybe because I was so excited to have actually remembered about my grandmother's incident, my mind wasn't clear enough—settled enough for clear thinking.

"No-Eyes gonna do some of that prompting here to help Summer out now. No-Eyes gonna shake many dusty cobwebs out of mind. We gonna bring dark rooms out into fresh sunshine now."

"Okay," I readily agreed. I was excited with the prospect of continuing this new type of exercise. Then I frowned as a dark thought overshadowed the mood. "I don't have anything to hide. . .do I?" Although my eyes were closed, I could well imagine the mirthful grin that crossed her face. I could hear the muffled snicker she tried to stifle.

"We gonna go find that stuff out, huh. Now, go back again to the night of that first spirit sighting. That little girl be in her bed. A tiny light be on in room, but little girl not see it 'cause she be hiding under many hot blankets. Why little girl be doing that hiding stuff?"

Spontaneously it all came back to me in a flood of vividly clear flashbacks. Memories that had been long ago forgotten and locked securely away within the attic of my mind suddenly became as crystal clear as if they had occurred just yesterday.

"Yes, I remember! I can see it so clear! I was in my bed. I can actually feel how terribly hot I was. I was sweating and I couldn't breathe good because of the heavy covers I'd pulled over my head. My parents were in the room next to mine—the dining room. And they were talking in low tones. *No-Eyes!* This is incredible! I can even *see* those old fashioned rough-textured walls!"

"Go on," came the gentle urging.

"Well, I was hiding under all those blankets because I was too scared to move. I was terrified because I could hear somebody *breathing* in my room!"

No-Eyes' pink gums showed with her expressed glee. "So! Summer be only three years old, and in one day she see *and* hear spirit stuff."

Silence. Deep thinking going on. Then my eyes lit up like a pair of klieg lights. "Yeah! Yeah, I did, didn't I!"

"Yup," she chirped, "that be first time. What else Summer remember 'bout that time?"

"Oh, I recall all sorts of lost things, particularly when our pet parakeet, Tommy, died. It was raining out and. . ."

"Summer can think 'bout all stuff like that some other day. Now we gonna move on to new family house when little Summer share room with sister, when little Summer have feet stuck out of blankets at night."

This exercise of hers was not only amazing, it was downright eerie. This thing we were doing, this experience in deep recall, wasn't scary because she knew all that I had ever done; it was scary simply because I was actually remembering it all in its vivid totality. I wasn't cognizant of the particular specifics of her mechanics of the thing—nor did I really care about them; what pleased me was the simple fact of the matter that she was somehow pulling out long forgotten memories into the forefront of my present-day consciousness. It was nothing like hypnotic regression because I was totally awake. Yet she was achieving the same results. It was just incredible.

Now she was unearthing another buried incident out of my murky memory and I grinned.

"I know exactly what you're getting at. You're referring to the times when I'd stick my feet out of the blankets and they'd be tickled!

"No-Eyes, that was so weird. After the initial fright went away, I'd purposely stick those little feet out the bottom of my

35

bed just to see if they were going to be tickled—they usually were. It was a strange, yet great, childhood game."

I paused then. "Funny thing though, even when the game occasionally involved the blankets being slowly pulled down off of me, it never bothered me not knowing *who* was playing with me—it never really mattered at all. I was simply having fun and that's all that seemed to matter. It became a great secret between me and my invisible playmate. I say 'invisible' because he certainly wasn't imaginary. No imaginary playmate could actually tickle feet and pull down your blankets.

"Anyway, after a while, the game abruptly stopped, but, instead, I frequently felt a soft whisper-like kiss placed firmly upon my brow after I got into bed. Maybe by then I was getting too old for the footsie games."

My wise teacher kept the meter of my memory gears turning non-stop. She had me on a winning roll. "Now little girl be 'bout eight. She sleep on top bunk now. What little Summer see then?"

That one was easy. "The face on my bedroom ceiling just over my bed. I recall that, at first, I thought it was just an odd design made by the dust. I stood up on my bed and brushed at the spot—it wasn't dust.

"The following day, I scrubbed the entire area with hand soap. When it dried, the area was clear. But the next morning, when I awoke, the thing was back—looking down at me. It was an area of only five inches or so, but I kept scrubbing that spot with every type of cleanser I could get my hands on and. . .it kept returning.

"Finally, I bugged my father until he moved the bunk beds to the opposite side of the room where the ceiling was clear. I never told him the real reason why I wanted the room rearranged.

"I remember that that first night I slept real sound knowing I was out from under the constant stare of that face. In the morning though, it greeted me as usual. I jumped out of bed, ran to where the beds used to be and searched the old spot for the impression—it was gone. It had moved! How could an image move? It actually followed me all around the room-no matter *where* we put those beds."

Silence.

Remembering.

"Summer, that just be way of spirit signs, that all. They not always be easy to read—to explain."

That was illogical. By my way of thinking, her explanation

made no sense at all. "But what's the point of spirits giving someone signs if they don't even comprehend the sign's significance?" I sighed. "Just seems so pointless."

"Spirits know what they be doing. They know that one sign gonna lead into another and another and more and more to make many. They be like drops of rainwater dripping into big rain barrel. One drop at a time make full barrel. Spirits give little signs here an' there like a painter an' his colors. Pretty soon all colors make the total picture. Signs be understood one day. They serve as guideposts for awareness along one's trail through life. They all mean some important thing. They show little girl reality to life, that there be strange, unexplainable stuff that be truth to life."

As usual, the wisdom of my teacher delicately untangled the philosophical knots within my head. She took the most confusing enigmas and made them simple and clear.

"I guess that's pretty logical after all." Then I was pensive for a bit. "No-Eyes?"

"Mmmm."

"I never told anyone about any of those unusual things."

"So?"

"So I suppose it was for the best—keeping them to myself, I mean."

She smiled sympathetically. "Summer always been secretive child. That just pave way for when she be grown up. See? See how it all been pavin' way?"

I did.

Creak-thud. Creak-thud.

The fire crackled and snapped behind me. Outside, the wind howled as it whipped around our little sturdy fortress. The rafters groaned. An orange glow radiated throughout the room. And I was very peaceful.

"Summer?"

"Yes?"

"This remembered stuff be scary?"

I smiled. "You have a way of making it all right, No-Eyes. What scared me as a kid isn't frightening anymore—the emotions are different now."

Then, the soft voice that came through the tranquil surround was deeply solemn. "There be many kinds of scared, Summer. Some turn to peace through understanding an' some never turn to that good peace."

Her statement was understood, but I didn't see how it related to what we were talking about. "Are you referring to the leftover emotions that can remain even though complete understanding has been gained?"

She nodded.

I spent a few minutes thinking that over. "But my emotions have changed regarding these old incidents."

Our eyes locked.

"We not be done yet," came the cryptic statement. "Close eyes again."

I stared at her. My eyes lingered on hers just long enough to realize that now I was going to be unearthing memories that were supposed to remain interred within the weed-choked cemetery of my mind. Now I'd be opening up the mausoleum gates that I'd hoped had rusted closed. I was about to ask her if this next phase was necessary, but the seriousness in her eyes made my question unnecessary.

I closed my eyes as bid.

Through the serene atmosphere of the cozy room, the old one's voice whispered, "Now Summer go back couple years from before. Little girl be 'bout six. She wants to go across street to neighbor's house to visit childless couple. Summer's mother no want her little daughter to go there this day 'cause she got real bad feelings 'bout it. She not know why, she just got bad, bad feelings. But she not listen to them. She let little girl go anyway."

The visionary paused. "You over there yet, Summer?"

"Yes," I said, seeing the rooms just as they were as I relived the event that had taken place over thirty years ago. "The couple are so happy to see me. I'm having fun trying to pick out the pennies they'd wedged in all the window sills. They're always brand new pennies and the sunlight made them so shiny. I managed to get a few pulled out and I showed them to the woman. Helen said I could keep them, and I put them safely into my pocket.

"Harry was roughhousing with the big German shepherd. He was teasing it with a glove and making it viciously growl and attack it. The dog frightened me because he sounded so mean."

I stopped.

"Go on, Summer. What else?" came the faraway voice.

"Harry. . .Harry set the leather glove down and got up to leave the room. Helen was in the kitchen baking cookies for me. I walked over to Harry's chair and spied some *National Geographics* on the table and wanted to took through them. I loved looking at those magazines.

"The dog was sitting in front of the chair, and I looked into its eyes. 'Nice doggie,' I said to it while inching by him so I could climb in the chair. I picked up the glove that'd been left on the seat and when I turned to sit down, the dog went for it. He got my face instead. I let him have the glove, but he didn't play with it because he was immediately shoved into a closet. Helen was screaming and screaming for Harry while she grabbed a kitchen towel and rushed over to me.

"I didn't know what all the sudden commotion was about because I was looking at a beautiful man surrounded by bright light. I just stared at him and felt so peaceful. The couple's voices were like hearing them in a dream—they were muffled. . .distant.

"Then Helen had me right against her breast. She was holding the towel over my face. I remember that I felt like she was suffocating me, but it wasn't an important feeling at the time. . .nothing was important but the Man of Light. It was like everything happening around me was some far-off dream. The only reality was me and the beautiful man that kept smiling at me. My total consciousness was with him.

"Suddenly I heard sirens and two policemen charged in through the front door. My dad was their boss and had sent them over when the call came into the precinct. 'His little girl was seriously hurt,' they'd said. I didn't know I was hurt. Were they talking about one of my older sisters? But when one of the policemen picked me up, I saw that Helen's beautiful blue dress was covered with blood. I can see the material so clearly. It was a shiny material, something like jersey, and the entire front was glistening with a soaked darkness. I looked to my shining Friend. He nodded and I wasn't scared.

"The ride in the police car was fun. The sirens were going and all the cars in front of us pulled aside to let us through. The policeman's voice was soothing as he held me against his chest and stroked my hair. In the emergency room, I was whisked under bright lights and heard talk of something called rabies. 'Did they have the dog?' someone asked. A sheet with a hole in it was placed over my face and the stitching began. 'Isn't Mary a good little girl, Doctor Demitroff?' I heard the nurse say over and over again from beneath the sheet.

"When the operation was over, I sat up on the gurney and my father came in and saw me for the first time. All he said was, 'Oh my God!' After I got home I looked in a mirror. Fifty-six stitches were holding on my left cheek that only a couple hours before had been hanging by a slivered piece of skin at my mouth."

I opened my eyes. I was deep in the memory as I spoke to the old one looking down at me. "I never cried, No-Eyes, not once. I never even knew the dog had ripped off half my face. I had no pain—not even a prick of it. When I saw the mess on Helen's pretty dress, nothing connected—my mind didn't even transmit that the blood was mine. And. . .and of all the times I've thought back on that ugly childhood incident, the entire thing was very fuzzy. . .today was the first time I ever remembered seeing the beautiful Man of Light. He was why I felt no fear, no pain, wasn't he?"

She closed her eyes and nodded.

I stared up at the dancing firelight that reflected on the low hand-hewn beams. "I remember people around me commenting about my lack of fear, the lack of panic and tears, of pain. Someone thought I was in shock."

The visionary shook her head.

"What was I in, No-Eyes?"

"Peace. The spirit drew up your consciousness into the greatest Peace there is. All else existed outside its protective circle."

"But why? I mean, why me? These things happen every day to children all over the world."

"So does the Peace."

"And, like me, they forget."

"Yes," she said sadly, "so many forget the true reality that saves them pain and anguish."

We were silent for several meaningful minutes.

"What Summer smiling 'bout?" she asked.

"Oh nothing, really. It's just nice to have remembered the doctor's name, that's all. He was so big, yet so gentle. I remember how dark he was. Black, black hair, hairy hands, and very dark eyes." I grinned up at my teacher. "No-Eyes, I was only six and I looked like a freak in a horror show. Those ugly black stitches all over my face were really hard to look at, yet the handsome Dr. Demitroff's eyes always lit up when I saw him for my checkups. At six, as ugly as I had become, he made me feel pretty. I was in love. I had someone to ease the emotional pain." Then my warm smile downturned.

"What the frown for?"

"My mysterious anesthesiologist. . .the spirit. He never got so much as a thank-you. Now I feel bad about that."

Her eyes narrowed. "That be comin'. That hoop gonna close

soon an' all thanks gonna be said. All deeds gonna be balanced."

"Oh? How?"

"No-Eyes tell that stuff later. We still not be finished yet. Now," she said, wriggling a finger down at me, "close eyes again."

I did.

She waited.

"I'm ready," I said.

Silence.

"I'm ready, No-Eyes."

"Nope, not yet. Just rest, Summer. Just relax and breathe slow an' even."

Minutes passed as the fire crackled and its warmth washed over me. I heard the woman sigh.

"Now little girl be 'bout ten. It be summer season. She be standing on stairway in big house. She be hearing her older sister out in middle of street. Sister be screamin' for somebody to call police. Father be. . .father be killin' mother. Little girl standing lookin' down at what be happening on stairs in house."

"Yes," I coldly answered. "My stomach's churning. My father's bent over my mother on the stairs below me. He's wrapping the vacuum cord around her neck. She's trying to fight him off. I feel sick. Oh God, I'm going to throw up. Ohhh, I feel so sick!

"I can't watch anymore and I scramble up the landing. Tears are blurring my vision. I trip but manage to reach my room where I race into the closet and crouch in a corner under the hanging clothes. My hands are clamped tight over my ears. I think I hear a siren. My head is buried in my knees. I can still hear the screaming coming from the stairs. Then. . .nothing, nothing but the kind, soft Voice and the warm Light."

My eyes opened at the new recalled memory. "Always the soothing Voice and warming Light came to vanish my terrors. Oh No-Eyes, why haven't I ever remembered that?"

"That never been important 'til now. What be most important back then was for little girl to survive without emotional damage."

"But that seems so unfair."

The visionary cocked her head. "Unfair?"

"Yes. For a spirit to be helping like that all the time and never really be appreciated or even remembered for it."

"That be spirit's job, Summer. He be like guardian angel who help whenever he can. Spirits *always* help."

There was an inflection in her voice that gave clear indication that her statement had a double intention. The "spirits always help" part struck a familiar chord—one she was presently trying to hit me with. And since she didn't elaborate on it, I let it pass. Her voice jarred my attention back.

"One more experience we gonna speak 'bout when Summer be young. Now it be night. Summer be walkin' dog when car come from round corner—out of nowhere. Remember, Summer?"

I wished that I hadn't. "No-Eyes, these are painful memories. This is an especially sad one for me."

"Yup, but not all be remembered 'bout it. Summer been too sad at time to remember most important part. Go on, tell No-Eyes 'bout that night."

"Okay, but this *new* stuff had better be something worthwhile."

Her eyes danced with the knowledge I was about to self-discover.

I sucked in a deep breath and let it out slowly before I began the mystical process of reliving forgotten and buried events that had been locked away because of their pain.

I again closed my eyes and journeyed back through time to the precise point of departure. I stepped out into a clear autumn night. "I remember that it was a beautifully clear evening. I was walking Mitzy down our quiet neighborhood. We came to a streetlight on a corner and, as I stepped off the curb, a car suddenly came out of nowhere, took the corner on two wheels and somehow I let go of the leash. When the car had disappeared down the street, Mitzy was sprawled in the middle of the street. I ran to her. I called her name as I smoothed my hand over her shiny black coat. I whispered her name. The neighborhood was silent except for the rustling of the leaves and the sounds of my crying.

"I managed to pick up the limp animal and approach the corner house. I told the lady that someone had just killed my dog and could I please leave the animal on her porch until the authorities came to remove her in the morning. The woman became tearful and readily agreed. I walked the rest of the way home alone, sobbing, heartbroken for the pet that'd given me so much love and comfort during my lonely childhood."

The old one was clearly sympathetic.

"No-Eyes be so sorry too 'bout good pet. No-Eyes see why

Summer not remember most important part of happening—girl just be too, too sad. Her heart be dropped on ground. But sometimes great emotions block stuff out. We gonna go fix that now. Summer say 'somehow' she let go of leash. Think deeper on that one action. Think hard. "

I mentally went back and replayed the scene. "All I know is that I wasn't holding onto it anymore."

That was no good.

She stared hard at me with powerful eyes. She glared into me. "Think deeper. Go deeper. Summer, *deeper*! *Live* it *again*!"

As reluctant as I was to relive the grief-filled incident, I did as bid. This time I put all I had into it. The sights were exceptionally clear. The crisp sound of the maple leaves were rustling in my ears. The roar of a racing engine from out of the silence of the night, a sudden bark, a leash jerking, a push. . .a push?

My teacher's stare relaxed. She visibly drew back in her powerful energy used to catapult my mental efforts. She closed her eyes to rest a moment.

"No-Eyes! I was *pushed* back from that curb. That's when I let go of the leash! I was *forced* to!"

Silence.

It was time to contemplate upon the freshness of all the old mildewed memories that No-Eyes had gently lifted out of my rusty cedar chest. She was such a powerful psychic catalyst that she was years, centuries, eons ahead of man's present brain research. Her mere presence was enough.

As I thought about all the things that were newly-revealed, the most amazing aspect was that the old wise one never *planted* anything within my mind; she had simply brought me up to the precise point where I myself would pull out the hidden events through my own efforts of total recall.

I listened to the blizzard rant and rage on. And I suddenly had the sinking feeling that there would be no way for me to get home this evening, for surely my truck was snowed in by now.

I went over to the window, rubbed a circlet in the foggy moisture and anxiously peered out—nothing but white all around.

· "Nope," came the confirming voice from behind me. "No-Eyes gonna have company tonight. Bill get Summer dug out in morning."

I stared at the high rounded mound of snow that shrouded

the old pickup. "But you don't have a phone. He'll be frantic with worry."

When I turned to her, a wispy brow was raised in question of my concern.

"Yeah," I sighed, "he'll know I'm safe." I returned to my fireside position. "Well?"

"Well!" she exclaimed back with a sharp slap to her lap. "It be long past lunchtime. Summer be hungry?"

"No, but you go ahead. Can I fix you something?"

"No-Eyes not be cripple! Besides," she softened, "I not be hungry anyways."

I settled back down onto the blanket. "Good. Let's get on with it then."

Her wide grin creased the corners of her elfin eyes. "No-Eyes hopin' you say that. Summer, see how all this forgotten stuff fit in with new spirit work yet?"

I really was getting the subliminal drift of it but was reticent to voice the fact. "Not exactly, but it does show my early exposure to the spirit realities, exposure that I had completely forgotten about."

"Not only *early* ones. We gonna finish up this exposure stuff now. Summer gonna talk 'bout strange stuff that happen when she be teenager and after she marry Bill."

"All right. Is there anything left in the cedar chest though?"

"Nope. First we gonna start with that little person."

"We already talked about that, No-Eyes. Still, seeing that tiny woman in the grass was a real shocker."

"Yup. That be real beginning to conscious awareness. We gonna go on to the day Summer and girlfriend be walkin' down busy downtown street."

I grinned and nodded as I rested back into my expected position.

"I've never forgotten that one. It was on a Friday night after work, around ten after five. We had a long walk to our bus station on Michigan Avenue. Rush hour in downtown Detroit can be disastrous.

"Anyway, we were busily chatting about our boyfriends when we approached a corner. Just as we were about to step off the curb, I heard someone behind me loudly whisper my name in my ear. I halted in midstep and spun around to see who it was. My friend saw me turn and she looked back to see what had caught my attention. Nobody was there! But, as I turned to the mysterious voice, a city bus sped past the curb.

"My friend felt weak in the knees as she exclaimed that if I hadn't turned at that exact moment, we both would've been run down by that speeding bus. She yakked about it all during our bus ride home.

"No-Eyes, that loud whisper saved my life, I know that. I've heard it twice since then."

The obsidian eyes twinkled. "It save life those times too?" she inquired knowingly.

"Yes," I admitted gratefully.

"Ever wonder 'bout that? 'Bout why?"

"Not really. After I learned about the true realities of the spirit, I merely chalked it up to the work of my guide."

"That be true," she chuckled. "That be why he got so many white hairs!"

We both laughed over that, although there was probably a lot more truth to it than I'd like to openly admit to.

"Now we gonna move up to time after Bill and Summer be married. Remember first place you got?"

"Oh my! How could I ever forget?"

"Tell No-Eyes 'bout scary stuff that gone on in there."

I looked at her teasingly through my narrowed eyes. "I'm doing an awfully lot of telling here. How about I tell No-Eyes what she wants to hear about these spooky happenings if No-Eyes promises to tell me the *causes* of them when I'm finished."

Silence. Thinking that one over.

I craned my neck to squint up at her. "No-Eyes?"

"Okay," she acquiesced, "No-Eyes do that for Summer."

"Don't forget you made a promise."

Her brows shot down in a hard vee. "No-Eyes *ever* forget *anything*?" she barked playfully.

I grinned and shook my head. Then, closing my eyes again, I began by recalling my past.

"At that time, it was a real battle trying to get a firm hold on a decent apartment or flat to rent. We saw an ad for an upper flat in a middle-class section of Detroit.

"We were supposed to meet with the landlord at eight that evening. When we pulled up in front of the house, four other couples were in their cars waiting too. We weren't going to wait, so we rang the bell of the lower flat. The woman invited us in to wait. We immediately hit it off like old friends and, when the landlord came, we were already there—we got the upper flat.

"Of course we were ecstatic to have our very first place. We both worked at the time. He was a crew leader for a gas company and I worked for a big printing company doing all their composition and lay-out work. In the evenings, we got together and visited with our new friends who lived downstairs.

"Everything was fine, except for the basement which gave me the creeps. It was old, damp, and dark with one bare bulb hanging over the washer. I hated it whenever I had to do my laundry because there was a room down there with a big locked padlock on it. I asked Marie if she had ever been in the room, and her eyes widened with fear. She said that she hated the basement too, and that no, she'd never been in that room and didn't think she ever wanted to either. So, our first bad feelings came from the mere existence of that secret room with the mysterious padlock.

"Then the time came for Bill to do his yearly two weeks in the Army Reserve. He was an instructor for rifles and map reading. While he was away, I spent my evenings downstairs with Marie after her youngsters were in bed. We were all alone because her husband worked nights.

"One evening, when we were sitting in her living room chatting about my work, we heard the basement light click on. She had a basement entrance through her kitchen, but kept the door securely bolted. On the basement side of the door was the light switch.

"We immediately stopped talking and froze in place. Since her husband was at work and her kids were sleeping, we were all alone—at least we should've been.

"Without speaking, we softly crept into the kitchen and peered under the door—the basement stairway light was on. We looked at each other with fear in our wide eyes. I silently reached into her kitchen drawer and grabbed a heavy cleaver. And quietly pulling it out, I motioned a plan to her. At the given count of three, she soundlessly slipped back the bolt and threw open the door while I raised the cumbersome cleaver. . .nothing! I called down into the basement. No answer came. We flipped off the light switch and closed the door, re-locking it against the darkness below.

"Returning to the living room, we began chatting once more and we were somewhat at ease again. Marie was busily telling me that during the day she had organized all of her extra pots and pans on the shelf ledge of the basement stairwell. She began telling me about a new recipe she had tried that day, when a sudden loud racket caused us to jump out of our skins. It sounded just as if all her pots and pans had been angrily flung down the basement stairs. Then. . .silence. Then. . .the light switch.

"We were both sweating from sheer terror, yet we were young and foolish enough to re-enact our first investigative attempt. Her, operating the bolt and door; me, wielding the cleaver. The door was whipped open again, the cleaver poised to swing. . .nothing!

"The light was on again. The switch had been flipped up to the ON position and all the pots and pans were *untouched!* Our hair prickled as we quickly slammed the door and bolted it. The remainder of the evening was inactive as far as the basement went, but we were on edge and perplexed over the two bizarre incidents.

"During future nights, we were to experience the same occurrences over and over again. Even after Marie removed all her cooking utensils from the basement shelf, the clattering racket persisted without any physical evidence of logical cause. After a while we never even bothered to check it out because we knew nobody would be there.

"Then, one evening when my downstairs friends were away on a vacation, and Bill was back from his military duty, the house was eerily quiet. We were reading in our upstairs flat when our cat suddenly became extremely agitated. It began hissing at our inside door which led down to the first level flat and continued further down into the basement. The cat then tore under our bed. This was very aberrant behavior for her as we had never seen her do anything like this before—she was definitely frightened into a heightened state of sheer terror.

"We exchanged casual comments about the incident and returned to our individual reading material. But while I read, a barely audible rhythm invaded my consciousness. I listened for it. It sounded just like the muted footfalls of someone walking through the empty darkness of the unoccupied apartment below us. Then Bill looked over the top of his book to peer over at me. He had heard it too. My scalp pricked and my hands became clammy. We listened together as our eyes locked and our muscles tensed tighter at each passing second.

"Simultaneously, we both rose and silently tip-toed over to the stairway door, all the while, breaking out in a cold sweat as we strained to distinguish the footfalls that shouldn't have been there.

"I whispered, 'Oh my GOD, Bill! Someone's *down* there!' He got his revolver and silently inched the door open. He called out as he stealthily descended into the darkness. No answer came. The footfalls continued. He approached the closed door leading to the bottom flat and listened. Someone was walking about in the darkness. He peered further down the landing into the basement then looked up at me. I was having silent animated fits for him to get his behind back upstairs. Again he pressed his ear to our friend's door and I was ready to faint. Finally he backed up to our door, locked it and called two of his friends to come over with their shotguns.

"The three of them thoroughly searched the house from top to bottom; in closets, cupboards, under furniture, behind shower curtains and. . .in the dreaded basement. All exit doors were bolted from the inside, so naturally the intruder hadn't gotten out. All windows were likewise latched. Whoever caused those stealthy footfalls was still in the house. The three men searched everything once again. . .nothing!

"That evening, when we were safe in bed with all our doors securely bolted, just as we were finally drifting off to sleep, the muted rhythm began again. The mysterious footfalls were still with us.

"I don't know how we ever slept that terrifying night, but soon afterward, both the upstairs and the downstairs tenants of that house moved out. We both moved away without ever discovering what lay behind the foreboding padlocked door in the basement."

I was finished with the telling.

No-Eyes had been listening intently all through my long story. "Forgot 'bout fire," she calmly reminded.

I frowned and thought back. "Yeah, guess I did. Anyway, that happened while Bill was working nights too. Marie and I were sitting down in her flat watching television and she had this sudden urge to go into her kids' bedroom to check on them. Then I heard her scream, 'FIRE! FIRE!' I ran through the house to help carry out the kids to the front porch while she quickly dialed the emergency number.

"After the fire department left, we put the kids into the parents' bedroom. The fire had damaged part of the back porch and the children's room. There was no way a fire could've started. It was all very baffling to the firemen. . .and, to us.

"Well?" I asked. "Who flipped on the basement light all the time and who made the crashing noises? Who was walking around downstairs?"

Very matter of factly, she simply said, "Old dead owner who hung himself in that basement room."

A shiver rippled down my spine. "Why was he doing those things to us?"

"He not want others living in house. He got house taken away, so he try to scare tenants so landlord not be able to make monies from house."

"Well he certainly scared us plenty!" I was almost afraid to voice my next question. "Is he still there?"

She simply nodded.

I looked into the fire. "What a waste. What a pitiful waste."

"We gonna move on now, Summer. We gonna move up a few more years to when you an' Bill be in bed at his mother's house. It be a summer night and some strange feeling come to Summer. Remember that? Summer know what No-Eyes be talkin 'bout?"

"Yes, although I've never even told Bill about that one. We were lying in bed, just about to fall asleep, when I felt him rest his hand on my shoulder like he often does. I smiled and reached up to hold it, but touched my skin instead of the hand I was expecting. I quickly turned to him, but he was sound asleep with his *back* to me.

"No-Eyes, I wasn't *asleep*. I *wasn't* dreaming. I definitely felt a hand placed firmly on my bare shoulder!"

The visionary's eyes rounded. "Who you tryin' to convince? No-Eyes know that be true."

"Well. . .I suppose I was just emphasizing it."

She shrugged the incident off. "That been Summer's guide, that all. Now we move up in time to when Bill and Summer finally be lookin' for own house to buy. Tell No-Eyes 'bout those feelings."

"There's not much of anything to tell really. Just that when the real estate agent walked us through certain houses, I'd get an unexplainable eerie feeling. Sometimes I'd break out in a cold sweat. Sometimes I'd get a chill down my spine and, other times, I'd be overcome with a terrible feeling of oppressive heaviness—like a blackness closing in on me. There were actually houses that we never even bothered to enter because just seeing their exterior gave me a frightening feeling and I'd immediately say that it wasn't at all what I was looking for."

The old one quickly moved ahead. "Now we gonna move up to time after Bill an' Summer be in new house, new farmhouse. How Summer's night be then?"

I couldn't contain the smile that brightened my face. "Oh, No-Eyes, I loved that old house. When we first saw it, it was very decrepit. It had paint peeling on the walls and there was water covering the basement floor. It smelled real musty and was a total mess. But all I saw was its charming character and how it'd look after I finished with it. There was an extra lot with the property that was left to go fallow with tall weeds. But I wanted it. . .I wanted that house. My family nearly cried when they saw what we'd actually bought.

"Then, after wallpapering, panelling, and having the basement waterproofed, the house was miraculously transformed. Bill had some of his work-crew friends bring out their bulldozers and we leveled the extra lot and planted seed. Soon the property looked like a country showcase. The grass was green and looked like sod. The apple and pear trees were in blossom, I planted all sorts of flowers, and eventually we sold it for double what we paid for it."

The visionary held up her hand and clicked her tongue. "That not what No-Eyes mean for Summer to remember. How Summer's *nights* been there?"

I smiled again. "Still, the place was good medicine. The place was peaceful enough for me to finally begin meditating regularly, and this brought on the side benefit of the dreams, dreams that. . ."

"Dreams?" she said curiously.

"Yes, dreams of premonitions. . .the first I'd ever had. I'd dream of disasters that became realities just a few days later. I'd dream of all sorts of future events and then I eventually began dreaming of my relatives' death dates—dates which later became realities."

"And then?" she prodded further.

"And then one night, during the early morning hours, I awoke to see my grandmother standing at the foot of our bed. She had died just a couple months earlier. I remember that I was terribly frightened, yet I also simultaneously felt a peaceful wave wash over the room. She didn't actually speak; it was more of a mental or psychic hearing on my part. It was the first time I'd heard my Indian name spoken. She had been foretelling my future, giving hints to its true heritage of spirit and suggesting our move to Colorado. At the time, we were planning on moving to North Dakota near the Canada border. Her mention of Colorado seemed confusing."

The old one leaned toward me and spoke softly. "Summer an' Bill go to North Dakota?"

"Yes, but when we got there, things didn't feel right. We talked about our uncomfortableness over dinner, and the next morning we packed our little girls into the truck and pulled the tiny U-Haul down to Colorado. As we crossed the state line and approached the WELCOME TO COLORFUL COLORADO sign, the radio played 'Back Home Again.' It was very significant. Its meaning didn't slip by us."

The visionary closed her eyes and slowly nodded. When she opened them, they were full of shining wisdom. "All those special times in Summer's life give spirit experience. You *still* gonna claim you not got any spirit experience? Summer *still* gonna tell No-Eyes that?"

Silence. She had gotten the best of me. She *had* made me eat my words.

My teacher was not going to rub it in though. She knew she had been successful, and, more than that, she knew that I also realized it. She tactfully changed the subject. "We gonna go eat some supper now. It gettin' pretty late an' we got many stuff to talk 'bout yet."

I crossed the room and stood by the windows. The blizzard had finally exhausted itself and left a glistening world in its wake. The fire crackled behind me. A warm glow filled the toasty room and I felt a great peace infiltrate my being and gently settle there.

We ate at her kitchen table with the old oil lamp burning brightly between us. We spoke of the suddenness of the snowstorm and laughingly joked about how quickly it'd probably melt away after a few hours of our Rocky Mountain sunshine tomorrow. The old one reminisced about her girlhood winters and how the Minnesota snows would never seem to leave.

After supper, I stoked our fire and built it up again. Clouds remained thick and dark until nightfall silently draped her massive velvet cloak about the cabin. We were snug and warm, for Nature had tucked us in for the night.

No-Eyes pulled her chair over to face the couch while I curled up on the sofa to finish the evening out by listening to my teacher's further words on the subject of spirit inhabitations. A gentle rocking began.

"We got long trail to walk this night," the old one said. "Summer got any questions before we start?"

She surprised me with the question and off the top of my head I had only one. "That promise I made you, the one about the books, is this material included?"

"What Summer think?"

"If I knew for sure I wouldn't be asking now. I'm sure that when the time comes for me to sit down with pen in hand there will be experiences that I won't feel right about exposing. I don't know. Maybe this sort of dilemma can only be resolved when the time comes and I'll go with my inner instincts on it."

Silence.

"Well?"

"Summer already got big conflict in head 'bout this spirit stuff. Maybe it never gonna be decided what to do 'bout it."

"I'm not with you, No-Eyes. What are you talking about?" Her brow rose.

It was clearly thinking time. After a few minutes I found my voice. "This subject is very obscure. I'll want to write about concrete experiences, ones that were beautiful and described our unique relationship."

"What be obscure?"

"Things that are untouchable. Concepts that cannot necessarily be proven. Obscure is undefined. . .something without true boundaries."

"Like Many Heart's magic?"

"Yes, like that."

"Like Summer's vision quest and dreams?"

"Uh-huh. You got the idea."

"Like Summer's journeys an' Corridor of Time? Like trip to mesa with Many Heart and visit to hell? Time with Joe Red Sky? Future sight? Visions? Summer's Man of Light?"

Silence.

"Huh, Summer? All that stuff got no borders. What left to write 'bout?"

"The truths. How spiritual things really are. . .their realities."

"What so. There be no boundaries to truths. . .only finer realities. Truths exist in those. And truths exist in trail between them. . .trail spirit travels on. Where this trail be? What highway it called? See? It be *obscure* in simple three-dimension reality!"

I understood it all. What *would* be left to write about? I tried to sort it out. "Then I guess I'll just go ahead and describe most of my experiences like they happened."

"Summer gonna pick an' choose?"

"Yes."

"That answer come awful fast. You sure?"

"Yes I'm sure. Some of the things we've done together are far too private and sacred. Many Heart too—I'll tone those times down. No-Eyes, some things are just too sacred."

"So! Now we follow path in circle back to beginning. You gonna write 'bout the spirit stuff?"

"I said I'll go with my feelings when the time comes. Right now I wouldn't know where to start or what to include. I'll probably make a real mess of it."

"It gonna iron out. Maybe it gonna be that mess in beginning cause Summer gonna have so much in head to get out, but it gonna be some good stuff after you learn how to sort it all out."

I eyed her. "If you know all that then you must also know if I'll write about the spirit material."

"Maybe No-Eyes know that."

"I won't, will I."

"Blah."

"I will."

She shrugged the thin shoulders.

"Maybe? What kind of answer is that?"

"Right answer."

"Well for heaven's sake, will I or won't I?"

"Summer gonna do both."

"That's not possible."

"Summer *seen* stuff *happen* that not be possible. No-Eyes only sayin' what be in future. Summer gonna write 'bout spirit stuff then she gonna not know if peoples be ready for it. . .then Summer gonna tear up whole book."

"Wait a minute. You say I'll spend hours writing and typing and then I'm going to tear up an entire book?"

"Yup! That what No-Eyes say."

"Then I *don't* write about the subject."

"That not what No-Eyes say."

Silence.

Creak—thud. Creak—thud.

"I rewrite it."

She grinned.

"What's going to be behind all this nonsense?"

"Summer not gonna think peoples be ready for spirit stuff, remember? Summer gonna write it an' then not feel right with it—gonna spend many nights being awake over it. Then it gonna get torn up."

"What makes me redo it?"

"Truths be truths. Summer gonna realize that an' be strong with determination to tell 'bout that spirit stuff."

"Well then," I smiled, "now that I know how the story ends, I can save myself a lot of trouble and time by doing the book just once!"

The visionary's eyes twinkled above a knowing grin.

(Being aware of the future does not necessarily alter the foreseen events. I *did* write the book. I *did* spend sleepless nights over it. I *did* tear it to pieces. And, obviously, I did *rewrite* it. And to this day, I'm still not totally convinced people are ready for it but, like the old one said, "Truths are truths" and damn the torpedoes if people can't believe.)

"I think I know why I'll have trouble with this subject," I said after giving it some thought.

"Tell No-Eyes what Summer be thinkin'."

"I know a lady who says she's a Christian but then she says that she doesn't believe in a spirit world. I found that very upsetting."

"Why?"

"Isn't that rather obvious?"

"Guess it not be so obvious to her. Why it be so obvious to you?"

"Well, because the statement is totally illogical."

"How it be so illogical?"

"Because it contradicts itself."

"How?"

I frowned at the woman sitting across from me. "Come on, you know as well as I do. Here we have a person who swears that there's a Heaven, Hell and even a Purgatory and she has the ignorance to disbelieve in a spirit realm. Honestly, No-Eyes, where does she think these concepts exist? Especially the Purgatory. Does she think it's down the street? In the next city?

The visionary snickered.

"No. It's not funny. . .not funny at all. I get so irritated with this type of illogical and irrational thought process. Then she says she doesn't believe in spirits or guides. What the hell are the guardian angels then? She taught her kids about those. She believes in guardian angels. Where does she think they exist? Around the corner in their house? What *are* these angels she believes in? They're *spirits!* Oh, but there's *no* spirit realm. She doesn't even think deep enough to realize that all the angels she believes in; Angels, Archangels, Principalities, Powers, Cherubim, Seraphim and the rest have to exist *somewhere!*"

"Settle down, calm down now."

I shut up and seethed.

"Why that upset you so bad?"

I sighed. "Because I hate illogical thought. I detest narrow-mindedness and adamant tunnel vision. Closed minds are primitive to me. They make me feel this entire planet is populated by hairy-brained Neanderthals."

"By what?"

"Cave men!"

The snicker came again.

My brows went down at her.

"No-Eyes be sorry. Summer thinkin' lot like No-Eyes, that all."

And that definitely made me smile wide. It was a compliment of the highest degree. "Well," I said, "I suppose it'll be something like that sort of situation that'll keep me up nights after I write the book." I hesitated before going on. "But I guess I finally get it all sorted out and resolved in my head, huh?"

"Yup. Summer gonna get angry and decide that truths be truths after all."

I noticed the fire was down to glowing embers and got up to stoke and restock it. After sitting down again, my teacher didn't waste any time getting back into the matter at hand.

"We first gonna go over some simple spirit stuff."

"Okay. A refresher course wouldn't be a bad idea."

The rocker tipped back and forth.

"What Summer know 'bout wayward spirits?"

"Well, I know that upon physical death they didn't continue on to where they belong. They remained within the third dimension for personal reasons."

"What they called?"

"I thought we were talking about 'wayward' spirits."

"Yup. What it called when they appear?"

"A haunting. They're apparitions that do the act of haunting." I paused. "Now I know what you're getting at. Some people confuse the basic terms."

"Yup."

"Well, I hate to differ with the parapsychologists, but they do mix the terms of different concepts. They call a 'psychic imprint' a 'haunting.' That's all wrong. The very word is a verb which expresses action, and action is caused by a true living spirit. A 'haunting' is the active manifestation of an apparitional spirit and. . ."

"Summer!"

"What!"

"Slow down."

I stopped.

"Summer be right. What this 'psychic imprint' be?"

"I'm sorry. That's a lasting impression of visuals or other

sensory manifestations resulting from an energy surge generated from a past event."

Then I realized that maybe my explanation wasn't really an explanation at all. I reworded the concept.

"A psychic imprint isn't real. It has no living force behind it. People seen in an imprint aren't real. It's like a replay of a movie film, a clip. It reenacts the same action over and over. . .nothing varies—ever."

The visionary nodded. "Yup, that not be real spirit stuff. That only be crossover dimension that still hold energy of event."

I smiled. "I couldn't have said it better myself."

"What 'bout mind energy spirit stuff?"

I tilted my head to squint at her. "You trying to trip me up?"

"Nope."

"Well. . .the mind energy spirit stuff isn't 'spirit' stuff at all. It has nothing to do with living spirits. It's simply excessive brain energy without adequate outlets for constructive release; therefore it shoots out to affect inanimates around the perpetrator." Again, I caught myself. "It's only someone's strong mental energies that make objects around them move. Some people think this type of manifestation is from a poltergeist, from a playful or noisy spirit, but it's not. People are really confused on all these terms, No-Eyes. It's really been all mucked up."

"No-Eyes know."

"So. . .what else do you want to know?"

"Summer done talkin'. No-Eyes just makin' sure Summer not have spirit stuff 'mucked up' in head before we get into important part."

I grinned. "I'm not mucked up?"

"Nope."

"That's good news for a change."

The visionary eyed me. "Summer bein' smart mouth again?"

"Nope."

Creak—thud. Creak—thud.

Waiting.

"This gonna be serious stuff, Summer."

"It's always serious, No-Eyes."

"This gonna be *most serious.*"

"I'm ready. I'm most serious."

The rocker's vocal chords had the floor for a full two minutes before the visionary sensed the right mood.

"Summer, our People know all 'bout living spirits. They know for years an' years 'bout spirit stuff. They no doubt like some stupid others do. This be real to the People."

"Yes, I know."

"Other peoples know too. Other peoples see stuff. They hear an' feel even. They experience stuff of spirits an' they believe."

"Yes."

"But we not gonna spend time now on people. We gotta speak 'bout them spirits. . .them dumb ones who be wayward."

"I'm with you."

A peculiar stillness settled over the room. The atmosphere became heavy with the woman's seriousness. Even the fire stopped crackling as if it were actually listening with held breath.

"Spirits who be dumb, be dumb. No-Eyes mean they got no logic, that why they be dumb."

"But they retain intelligence."

"Yup. They got minds to think with but they no think good, that why they be so dumb. That why they hang 'round wrong place, wrong time even."

"These spirits always have a cause, don't they?"

"Mmmm. It always be illogical one, but it seem right to them. Strong emotions can make them stay 'round. Hate, Love, Greed. Revenge. Stuff like that keep them here."

"How about unfinished business?"

"Yup. That too."

"And that's illogical because they're pure spirits and they need to be where they belong so they can spiritually advance themselves."

"That be right."

I didn't have another comment ready and my teacher allowed silence to dominate the space between us.

I thought about all we had discussed so far and wondered what more there was to talk through. The subject seemed clear enough. The facts were simple and uncomplicated. . .at least I thought they were until my mentor spoke again. Her words sent an icy chill down my spine. I should've known it was all too simple.

"Spirits kill," came the frigid words. "Spirits got great power of energy. They got strong power to move stuff. They got power to control stuff." Her eyes widened as they locked onto mine. "Summer, never trust a spirit. If Summer do that dumb stuff, maybe it be last stupid thing Summer ever do."

The old one had me as mesmerized as a rabbit before a snake. My scalp crawled and the hair on my neck tingled. All I could do was to listen. . .and learn.

"Wayward spirits be 'round 'cause they not be thinkin' right. They never act like people think they should. They be so, so unpredictable. One minute they gonna be calm an' then next minute they gonna be in great anger. Angry ones got most powerful energy. . .'nough to kill."

The sinking feeling filled my stomach again. "No-Eyes. . ."

"Shhh. You gonna listen now."

I sighed.

"You not be some dummy here. You know in heart what be right to do. Summer only gonna have to know it in head, that all."

I just stared at her.

"That Many Heart, he be doin' this stuff for long time. Summer think she gonna die or somethin'?"

I shrugged.

"Blah! That gonna do it all right. That kinda attitude gonna fail Summer for sure!"

"No-Eyes," I softly began, "how do I gain confidence and faith in doing this sort of thing? I'm not saying I *won't* do it. I'm not saying that at all, but I need that strong confidence and faith to feel comfortable with it."

"What be most important, Summer?"

"One's spirit and its advancement."

"What be most important work in whole world?"

"Helping people's spirits to advance."

"What so! Now you gonna be doin' most important work! Now Summer gonna feel some strong feelings 'bout that. No-Eyes not be speakin 'bout Summer helpin' somebody buy new car. No-Eyes not be talkin 'bout no material stuff here. No-Eyes be talkin' 'bout sending lost spirits back *home!*"

Yes. Yes, that *was* what we were talking about. The magnitude of it had finally sunk in my thick skull. Yes, if I could assist just one lost soul, wouldn't that be a beautiful event? And the more I thought about it the more comfortable I felt.

"What Summer think?"

A sheepish grin crept up my face. "I think I actually *want* to do this. . .at least try."

"Blah! That be no good! Summer need to not think 'bout that 'try' stuff. Summer gonna need firm decision and belief in success!"

"Yes," I smiled. "I *do* want to do this and I *will* help them back."

The wise one closed her eyes and rested back into the chair. We were done. . .or so I thought. When she next spoke it was from a very weary body. She leaned forward.

"So now that Summer see that she already grew up with many spirit stuff, she be plenty comfortable with new job, huh."

I grinned at her. "Let's just say that it won't feel so foreign now. I certainly wouldn't go as far as to say that I'd be plenty comfortable."

She threw her palms up. "Maybe it gonna feel strange at beginning, but Summer gonna get hang of stuff real quick—Summer *have* to. Summer not been so bad when she convinced future woman to leave house of deaths! Remember that time when you be in Future an' send wayward spirit of woman back?"

I though back on that. "Yes, but that was all done psychically—in the spirit. This is totally different—it'll be actual."

"What so! Same methods apply. It not be so different."

Silence.

"Now what be the matter?"

"How do we find these places where these wayward spirits are? What I mean is, people generally don't go about admitting to seeing ghostly manifestations, you know. And I hardly think I'll go knocking on doors asking if anyone's seen a ghost lately."

My smart mouth tickled the old one's fancy. She snickered instead of reprimanding me. An impish sparkle glinted behind her elfin eyes. "No-Eyes gonna take care of that part. No-Eyes gonna tell all 'bout some places—then Summer an' Bill gonna go find rest."

"Are they very far away?" I asked, privately worrying about the semi-fragile condition of our old truck.

"Nope. Summer an' Bill take many little trips 'round mountains anyways, might as well go places where you can help."

My brows furrowed down as I tilted my head at her. "Places like where, No-Eyes?" I asked suspiciously.

She nonchalantly rolled her eyes about the room. "Ohhh. . .just little stuff. Places like where some little one be heard cryin' out on that Thunder Mountain. Summer an' Bill go over to town of Sweetwater an' talk that nice lady into stoppin' her waitin' for somebody who never gonna show up.

Down on Ute Pass you gonna find out why that Ute shaman still be makin' himself be felt to local peoples."

Well, that didn't sound all that bad. . .it certainly didn't sound scary or dangerous. Then the old one leaned far forward. Her brow rose.

"Then you both go over to Miner's Creek an' make that axe man go home. Phantom Canyon got funny stuff goin' on with that psychic fire." She chuckled over that one. "Maybe you gonna even discover who them hell demons *really* be."

My spine tingled.

"Then Summer an' Bill gonna go visit near that St. Elmo ghost town an' talk to that determined nightstalker. . .there be some crazy madness down in Bogan Flats too. Don't know yet, but maybe you even gonna find out what bad force be hangin' 'round in Grizzly Canyon. That place be full of real bad medicine. Whew! That be real bad stuff!"

Scalp crawling.

Then an impish twinkle sparked within the visionary's obsidian pools. "An' you gonna go meet that Indian couple who been stayin' 'round west of Hagerman Pass." Then the aged hands flipped back and forth. "That be just little bit of where Summer an' Bill gonna go."

I was aghast. "*Little* bit! *Nightstalkers*! *Axe* man? Bad *forces*? How *can* you expect us to *do* this?"

She merely shrugged her narrow shoulders. "Blah! It only *sound scary*. It gonna be *fine*, maybe be *fun* even."

At that last comment, I gave up completely. "Sure, we'll have barrels of fun."

Her nose wrinkled. "What this barrels of fun mean?"

"Nothing, No-Eyes, nothing. I was just being a smart mouth again."

The onyx eyes narrowed as the visionary bent low to me. The voice was low and full of high wisdom.

"Watch for the owl, Summer. Owlman know things. . .he know special sacred spirit things. He be great spirit world messenger. Summer gonna know some great *somethin'* when she next see Owlman." The dark eyes closed on the cryptic subject. "Watch for the *owl*."

And so it was that, during the long night hours and far into the morning, the wise one worked hard at instructing me in the complex Dreamwalker methods of dealing with wayward spirits from the plane of physical reality. Different techniques were used according to the varying circumstances. One single method couldn't possibly fit all encounter situations. She was patient and adeptly thorough. I strained my senses and mental faculties to the limits in an attempt to adequately grasp and gain a fragment of her wisdom. Tomorrow would again be spent in reviewing and practicing the difficult mechanics.

When we finally broke for rest, I lay on the old woman's lumpy couch; she preferred the floor. She quickly fell into the innocent slumber of babes while I remained wide awake, fearful of my dreamscapes being visited by terrifying encounters with mad nightstalkers, bad forces and the dreaded axe man of Miner's Creek.

I lay awake looking about the room filled with writhing shadows cast by the snapping fire. . .shadows that grotesquely contorted and gesticulated threateningly around me. . .shadows that boldly reminded me that within the dark recesses of the deep, lonely woods and behind the creaking doors of decrepit hollow buildings, there were those who lurked in the spectral shadows. . .there were phantoms afoot.

The Encounters

In the Dark
of Black
Wolf Canyon

Though the skeptical criticism of men would encircle me—their clouded minds filled with the ignorance of scathing ridicule, I remain undaunted, for I dwell within my Spirit that is filled with the heady essence of Sage, Cedar and Sweetgrass, and with a head held high do I walk into the light that illuminates my new trail.

The weekend following my harrowing spirit lesson was the worst in my life. The Saturday following the intensive instruction was the one that broke my heart. My sweet visionary had left me. . .she left the physical side of life. . .and my heart was on the ground.

It was only after hours spent in loving reminiscent memories that the real reason for the old one's tears struck a hard and cold chord in my heart. That last weekend tears had coursed down the creviced trail of her cheeks were because she knew we'd never see one another ever again. . .at least in the physical. . .at least never being able to warmly touch or hug again.

I didn't experience anger or resentment, but rather a great emptiness filled my being—and my days. A vital part of me was now missing. It was so like her to have handled the parting the way she did, no tearful displays of high emotion, just business as usual. Then, out of the blue. . .gone.

So while my heart was filled with the pain of her goneness, I plunged myself into the only thing that kept her beside me; I began the writing of her beautiful story. I threw my mind and my heart into long hours of furious writing in the wee hours of the morning, oil lamp burning low, the thoughts and vivid memories coming faster than the pen could record them.

I finished the first installment of the promised books in less than two weeks. I had quickly tried to recapture and record the magnificent life and profound wisdom of this century's most enlightened and memorable individual. And, as she so wisely foresaw, the result was a literary nightmare; it was a real mess. I just had too many events to record. . .it ended up being two books instead of one. But as she also predicted, after I sent them off to Donning, the publishing company that Brian Many Heart suggested, the president, Robert Friedman, recognized the golden thread of beauty that glinted through the pages of my literary jumble. He worked to consolidate the two books, deleted the unimportant material and brought the pure gold through to the surface. He retained my title for the second book. His magic alchemy was called *Spirit Song*. And by June of 1984, I had kept my promise to the old one. . .I had obtained a publishing contract for her story, but, more than that, I realized I had not only created a mere book. . .I had been a messenger for the visionary's deep wisdom and impeccable vision. . .her simplicity and philosophy left a beautiful legacy for all those who wished to cherish it. Little did I know then, while writing my heart out during those wee hours of the morning while tears flowed with the remembering, just how far-reaching her life would be. . .how many hearts and spirits my sweet teacher and friend would touch.

After the initial book of the series was finished, I found myself at a complete loss for meaningful activity. My days were always invaded by visual flashbacks of our times together. A technicolor film replayed continually over the screen of my mind's eye, and the consciousness grasped the frames to freeze the action and revel in their sweetness. Sometimes her former words would shout out at me, sometimes they came as a whisper, soft as butterfly breath in my ear. A barked reprimand or a soft moment of endearment brought new mistiness to my eyes.

Although my family made valiant efforts by lovingly rallying around me, their own tears frequently streaming, and Rainbow would occasionally attempt to give her own offering of canine solace by licking at my salty tears, it remained a long trail for me to tread. . .it was a steep uphill climb back to being functional in the everyday world I was left with.

One sunny morning, while Bill and I were still in bed, he put his arm around me and snuggled close. "Want to get away today?"

I just grumbled sleepily.

He kissed my neck. "I think it's time we get away—take a little trip somewhere."

Subliminally I remembered that it was Saturday and normally I'd have already been long gone on my own routine trip. . .out to the cabin. I didn't dare give the fragmentary idea conscious energy. I wriggled my body into the warmness of my partner and closed my eyes.

Another feather-like kiss landed gently on my neck. "What do you say?"

"Mmmm? About what?" I drowsily asked.

"About that little trip."

My mind was still semi-numb from steep. "To where?" I mumbled, not really prepared to get out of the cozy, secure womb of the bed, much less open my eyes. I pulled his arm tighter about my chest and sighed heavily.

He turned me over to face him. "I'm serious. We'll just take off for the day and spend some time in the mountains. Look at it as a therapeutic treatment for the senses. We'll see if that ole Nature still has its magic to heal."

"The soul?"

He looked down into my questioning eyes and grinned. "That's what I'm talking about—the soul and heart. I have the feeling that Nature is just the heart-mender you need right now."

"I tried that, remember? I did go up into the mountains and all I did was rock back and forth and chant through the sobs."

His brow rose. "It emptied you, didn't it? Didn't the mountains take all that initial pain away and leave you exhausted and empty inside?"

"Yes," I whispered.

"Well, now I think it's going to fill in that emptiness."

I gazed up into his pools of steel blue. "You've filled the emptiness."

"Not completely; nobody could and I understand that, but now's the time to reacquaint yourself with Nature again and let it do its healing. The wound in your heart isn't completely closed, honey. We have to close that before the real healing can begin. I know that it's still bleeding."

"Yes, still bleeding," I murmured.

"So. . .what do you say?"

"You never answered me. Where are we off to?"

"Wherever. . .you. . .want," came the answer, voiced between a volley of soft kisses.

It tickled and I grinned. "That tickles!"

"See there? Already you're smiling. Now where are we headed?"

"There's nowhere special I want to go."

"Then that only leaves one thing left to do."

I flashed him a suspicious look. "What's that?"

"We'll just let the spirit lead us."

I frowned. "Oh great. That could really get us in a lot of trouble."

"Maybe trouble's what you need. You want trouble? I'll give you trouble!" And before his last word was voiced, his fingers began climbing up my ribs. He tickled unmercifully and I giggled and struggled until I was out of breath.

Hearing the commotion, Rainbow charged headlong into the room and pretended to attack the two on the bed. It was a mass of confusion. The more Bill growled and tickled, the more I screamed. The more we played, the more Rainbow barked and tried to nip. Then the girls joined in the ruckus and the bed was full of joyful family love. It was an incredibly beautiful way to begin a day, and suddenly I realized that I wanted very much to take that trip. Suddenly I desperately wanted to get back into the arms of Nature once again, and, more than anything, I wanted to take my loving mate with me.

The mad silliness on the bed calmed. We dressed while the girls fixed their favorite breakfast. . .pancakes sinfully smothered in warm blueberry sauce. I gave the usual instructions and their parents were out the door and on the road before another hour had passed.

I noticed that the driver made his turns without any signs of hesitation and I looked up at him.

"Either your spirit's giving definite orders or you know exactly where we're headed." I peered around at him. He had a rather sheepish grin pasted on his face. I glared. "Uhuhhh," I sang. "So where are we really going?"

He let out a laugh. " *You're* the one who's making me do all the silly grinning. You and your untrusting suspicions. I said we'd let the spirit drive us around today and that's what I meant. What do you want me to do, sit in the driveway until it decides? Gotta start someplace. Besides," he added, "this direction gives it the most open options."

I continued to eye him for a couple more seconds before settling in closer to him. "Okay spirits. . .lead on."

As we leisurely drove, I began taking in the pristine personality of the late spring day. It had been a while since I'd allowed myself to enjoy the beauty of the mountains. The air was clear and the colorful wildflowers nodded along the roadside as we passed. Cattle languidly grazed in bright green pastures. Birds glided through the bright blue sky and sunshine sparkled everything it touched. I put my sunglasses on.

"You're being awful quiet," I said to the silent driver.

"Just contemplating."

"Oh? On what are you so deeply contemplating?"

"On where the spirit leads when it's given its head."

"Guess we'll soon find out, won't we."

He turned and smiled wide. "Guess so."

A few silent moments passed between us before I voiced my private thoughts. "What's it feel like letting the spirit lead?"

"Strange. Consciously, it's a little weird being the driver and not knowing what the destination is, but I suppose wherever we end up is going to be our intended destination for today."

"Kind of weird, all right."

He eyed me. "You've experienced 'weird' before."

"Yeah. You'd think I'd be used to it by now."

"Well," he soothed, "this is a little different kind of weird. This one's definitely got a surprise ending for us. Who knows? Maybe we'll end up in California?"

With that I rolled my eyes. "Any more bright ideas like that and you can just keep them to yourself. We're supposed to be experiencing nature today, not taking a major vacation," I said as he pulled off the road and cut the engine in front of Jan's restaurant in Lake George.

"Let's eat. I don't know about you, but I'm famished."

I heard my stomach agree with a gurgle. "Me too."

Inside the roadside cafe, the sound of satisfied customers greeted us. The little place was packed and patrons were deep in their conversations. The radio blared country music, the cook belted out his singalong tune, and the waitresses laughed. I looked to my companion and smiled as our twin thoughts met between us. Yes, life goes on and it's a good life at that.

He led me to the only available booth and we slid into the thickly padded seats. Jan had recently hung Indian mandalas and paintings around the place and I felt very much at home. The ethnic decor had no negative effects on my tender sensitivities. Instead, it made me feel darn good inside.

After we placed our order, Terry, the U.P.S. man, came in and sat at the counter. He noticed us and began talking over the crowd. Soon another friend of ours came in and sat with us for a few minutes before joining Terry. The general conversation of the room was typical of the mountain ranching community we were in. Talk of the numbers of spring calving, the difficult ones and the sad losses. Talk of new equipment and how much it had set this one or that one back. It looked like a good year. And yes, wasn't that May blizzard a real killer.

At the mention of the recent spring blizzard, Bill reached over to hold my hand. In an effort to distract my thoughts, he spoke. "So! Why don't you scry into that teacup of yours and predict where we're going."

I chuckled and shook my head. "Boy, for an enlightened person, you sure miss the boat sometimes."

He playfully frowned a hurtful look. "Now what'd I say?"

"Prognosticating's done with tea *leaves*, not a tea bag."

He grinned. "Sorry, nobody ever said I was supposed to know everything."

Hot plates were placed before us and were piled high with steaming breakfast delights. Jan never scrimped on portions and her hash browns were always mouth-watering and laced with sweet onions. I proceeded to smother them with butter.

"When you ever gonna learn," came the quick comment from across the table.

"Probably never," I smiled. "Real butter is one of my frailties. I love it." I didn't buy the stuff for home because it was too expensive, but when we were out, I relished it like pure gold.

Bill shook his head while scraping two pats off onto his own mound of potatoes. I didn't bother commenting.

"This was some idea, huh honey?" he said between sumptuous mouthfuls.

I nodded, noticing how he was savoring the sweet butter.

"Personally," he added, "I think this is going to be very interesting. Sort of a mystery trip if you know what I mean."

I dipped the golden wheat toast into the sunny egg yolks. "Sort of makes you wonder what our spirits actually have in mind."

"Yeah, that's what I mean." He shook his head for emphasis. "I have absolutely no idea where we're going."

"Shhh, don't say that so loud. People will think we've finally lost it."

His lowered eyes furtively scanned the roomful of people we knew. Although this was not our routine eatery in Woodland Park—it was a ways west of there—we still knew quite a few patrons through Bill's service work.

My mischievous companion leaned far forward over the table and winked. "Wait 'til they read your book," he whispered.

I sighed. "I don't want to think about what folks'll think about your wife's secret life—her *other* side."

"Ehhh, not to worry, not to worry."

"Easy for you to say, Mr. Congenial; *you're* not the author."

A brow rose. "Neither are you, really. From my first-hand point of view, it seems that No-Eyes was the real author. I mean, if you look at the reality of it, most of the philosophy came right from her mind, not yours. You're simply the messenger, right?"

I thought on that. "Yeah, that's a good way to put it. I like that."

He smiled. "I'm glad you like that."

I smiled back, bravely pushing aside the sudden jab of pain that speared my heart at the mention of my mentor's name.

"Finished?" he asked in a chipper tone.

"Yep!"

"Well, let's get this Mystery Trip moving then."

Outside, the mountain air filled my lungs with renewed vigor as it served to purge my mind of the toxins of hurtful memories. I breathed deeply of the healing essence before climbing back into the pickup.

While the driver pulled back onto the road, I realized that I wouldn't ever be completely without frequent thoughts of my old friend. I knew in my heart that she'd always be with me in spirit, but the conscious goneness of her would also be a very strong part of me. That cold realization forced me to reevaluate my current situation and to view it as a permanent fact of life. I'd have to gracefully deal with that and, as we headed west this bright morning, I firmly decided that I could deal with it, for memories were all I had left. They wouldn't hurt—they'd warm the heart and heal it. It was all up to me.

Forty-five minutes passed, but it felt more like a mere twenty. I had immersed myself in the Being of Nature so completely that I hadn't bothered to take notice of the time, and Bill had respectfully allowed me to have the extended sacred time alone. For the first time in many days, I was beginning to feel alive again. As I rode along beside my silent companion, I took in all I saw—I literally absorbed it like a dry nature-starved sponge. Both sides of the two-lane road were heavily blanketed with thick wildflowers. From horizon to peaked horizon, the nodding faces of multicolored blossoms greeted my happy heart.

The truck veered off to the roadside, slowed and stopped.

I looked to the driver.

"I can't stand it anymore," he said. "Let's get out an' take some time to smell the flowers."

My eyes lit up and I hugged him. Quickly we got out and raced hand in hand into the fragrant meadow. I twirled and spun around and around, face upturned to the Eye of Ra; I threw out my arms and felt as free as a bird. I slowed and stopped. Bill had been watching me, thoroughly pleased with the satisfying effects of his idea. I held out my hand. He took it and pulled me down into Mother Nature's sweet patchwork quilt.

Together we lay back onto the scented pillows of velvety petals. Anyone passing by along the road would not be able to see us; we were totally hidden by the swaying field of flowers. I gazed up into the brilliance of my magnificent Colorado sky. A deep sigh escaped.

"I could lose myself in those blue depths," I whispered.

My best friend made no comment.

I again exhaled deeply.

"What's all the sighing for?"

"Relief."

"Already?"

"No, not from the grief. I feel a great relief that I haven't lost it after all."

"Lost what?"

"My union. My bond with Nature."

Bill leaned up on one elbow and stared down at me. "You were afraid you didn't have that any more?"

"Mmmm."

"That's ridiculous! That kind of thing isn't acquired like some material possession—it's inherently ingrained in the soul itself! I can't believe you felt like that."

"Are you upset because I never said anything before this?"

"No. Well. . .yes. I don't know."

"It was a very private fear," I said, trying to explain my lack of communication about it. "For so many days I felt so empty, so out of touch. It was like nothing in nature could ever uplift my spirit again."

"I know," he soothed, smoothing back my hair. "But nature doesn't cease giving just because you're temporarily numb. It remains alive. It's constant and retains its power."

I looked down past him into the forest of flower stems. "Yes, I know that. Nature is full of power—it never wanes. . .only people's appreciation of it does that."

My mate reached down between us and pulled up a flower.

"Don't do that!" I cried.

He grinned in spite of my objection.

"Ohhh, now look what you've done! You've killed it!"

"Not to worry, hon. It died for a noble cause," he said as he entwined it in my hair.

Our eyes met.

"Wish we'd thought to bring the camera along," he mused.

"Nahhh," I groaned, "I'd just break it."

"That's not funny. It wasn't even cute. When are you going to stop thinking you're ugly?"

"Doesn't matter," I grinned back, "you don't have the camera anyway."

"Hey. Would I have married an ugly woman?"

"You were only nineteen. . .you didn't know any better!" And with that, I tensed my muscles for what I knew would follow on the heels of my comment.

"Why you little minx!" he spouted, turning on me with all the tickling tricks he could devise.

I giggled and screamed for the second time that morning. And after I became visibly weak and breathless, we stopped. . .we froze. Eyes locked in seriousness. Love rose up to dominate the golden moment and we kissed. Long did we embrace upon Nature's essence-filled comforter.

When we broke away, my companion's gunmetal eyes had melted into warm devotion and deep caring. "I love you so much."

I took his hand and caressed it. "I love you too, honey. And I'm sorry I've caused you so much trouble lately. It couldn't have been easy living with me being so numb of heart."

"It was hard, but that's what I'm here for. . .that's what we're both here for—each other. The hard times only seem to bring us closer. You an' me—a pair, a matched set, the right an' left wings that allow us to fly as one. Don't be sorry. . .don't ever be. You've had every right to feel the way you have. The pain you felt was a real tribute to a lost legend."

I repeated his last words. "A lost legend."

"Yes. Wasn't she a legend? Someone far ahead of the times? A living master? Hasn't she left a beautiful legacy?"

I looked deep into his eyes. "That was just beautiful."

"And so are you."

Again we kissed. He rested down into the wildflowers of the mountain meadow, spread his arm over my chest and closed his eyes. Together we slumbered until the rays of Apollo were directly over us.

"Honey?"

"Mmmm," I mumbled, nestling my head deeper into his shoulder.

"Honey, it's getting late."

I opened my eyes, then squinted from the brightness. "Late for what?"

"For our destination."

Oh yeah, that Mystery Trip that I no longer cared about. "Maybe this was our spirits' destination. It feels pretty good to me."

"No, c'mon, we need to keep going."

"Who said?" I asked, trying to pull him back beside me.

"They said."

"They?"

"Oh for heaven's sake, will you stop leading me around in one of those infernal circle dances. We've got things to do, places to go, towns to see, woods to explore!"

My brow rose. "Oh, we're doing all that in one day, huh?"

"Who knows? How do I know? Maybe we'll be led to Jesse James' buried loot or something."

"Or maybe the golden coins in some leprechaun's big pot."

"Now you're getting cornier than I am. C'mon, get up."

Once back on the road, we continued past more wide stretches of meadows that looked more like ocean waves as the gentle breeze wafted the multicolored blossoms to and fro in a unison Dance of the Flowers. The gracefulness of the movement reminded me of the schools of clown fish that weave and dart in unison beneath the azure depths of the Great Barrier Reef. It made my heart shine to watch the silent, lithesome ballet of the Wind's experienced choreography.

Before long, we found ourselves turning up and down unfamiliar roads. We were definitely climbing now, and the scenery that presented itself dramatically altered. The narrow dirt road was completely shadowed by towering lodgepole pines and spruces. A new scent permeated the atmosphere. Gone were the delicate perfumes of the wildflowers; heavy in the air were various incense aromas of fresh evergreens that drifted boldly through our opened windows. I filled my lungs with the sharpness of them.

"You're going to get stinking drunk," said my perceptive driver.

"Ohhh! But isn't it just intoxicating?"

He sniffed the freshness of the crisp High Country breeze. "At least there's no woodsmoke."

I playfully whacked his arm. "That was terrible! Besides," I added a bit defensively, "it's only spring."

"Thank God for that. If it was fall, you'd probably be flitting around in these deep woods like some kind of sprite."

"Can't wait," I grinned.

Like the visionary, Bill frequently took great pleasure in teasing me about my love of woodsmoke scent in autumn. But that was all right—facts were facts—and I too wasn't lacking in little things to razz him about in return. But now I allowed his comments to pass without going in for the lunge and the even score of a touché.

"Will you took at that!"

I peered out the windshield.

Before us, on the right side of the road, set back into the timberline, was an old wooden building. A weathered sign hung above the covered porch and I could hardly decipher the faded lettering.

"Black Wolf Mercantile. Looks pretty deserted, doesn't it."

But Bill wasn't looking at the old building; he was studying the gas pumps out front. "Ever see such relics?" he softly exclaimed.

I squinted through the wavering shadows to get a better look. "No, can't say that I've ever seen anything like them." I gave them another once over. "Where's the pump? How do they work? Are they broken?"

He shrugged as he glanced down at one of his gauges.

I saw his concern. "Oh great, please don't say we need gas."

"We need gas."

"I just told you not to say that."

"Sorry. Think there's any fuel in those babies? Any *good* fuel?"

I paused to psychically search for his answer. "Pull over, buddy; surprisingly enough, those little contraptions are all set to go."

"You sure? About that 'good' gas, I mean."

"Does a bear sleep in the woods?"

"Okay. . .here goes nothin'."

And as he nosed the truck over beside one of the ancient, paint-peeled relics, an old man sauntered down the creaky grey steps.

"These any good?" the doubting driver inquired.

The gentleman winked. "You betcha, son. Gravity, you know. Cain't hardly beat 'em." And the old man soon had the younger one engrossed in the miraculous workings of "good ol' dependable machinery."

I didn't know what the heck the man was talking about and it didn't appear to me that it was something I needed to know either. I glanced up into the sky-high pine boughs, then cast a speculation back at the building. I wondered if the mercantile contained any more bygone memorabilia within its time-tested walls.

I eyed the two men. They were preoccupied. And, unnoticed, I slipped out. Maybe, just maybe, I too could discover some marvelous antique of my own.

Once inside, I was pleased to be confronted by an authentic Norman Rockwell painting. Surely the scene before me represented a living model for him. Three sourdoughs—beards, suspenders, pipes and all—sat in bentwood chairs around a cold potbelly. The stovepipe went straight up through the roof. Rows of dry goods and shelves of foodstuffs crowded the small spaces and closed in the walls. An ancient register dominated the small counter. Between two of the men, a furry mutt peacefully snoozed, paws twitching with dreams of meaty bones and the thrill of a rabbit chase.

I smiled at the group that'd become coldly silent after I entered.

"Nice place you have here," I said. "Mind if I just browse a little?"

An Abe Lincoln type waved me on in. "Help yerself, ma'am."

And I did.

The over-the-counter drug section was full to bursting with the usual variety of offerings, but, one shelf down, there were age-old remedies that I'd thought had long been lost; Dr. Wisegood's Tincture, Aunt Maybell's Cure All, bottles and jars of all kinds of healing goodies, pure herbs, roots and leaves, even the old Sloan's Liniment was there. I was in my glory and I secretly wondered if the proprietor realized the gold mine he had. Then again, noticing the lack of layers of dust on the items, I imagine he had plenty of local customers coming in from the remote wooded outback areas.

My psyche suddenly pricked. I pulled my consciousness away from the odd-shaped bottles and jars, and I concentrated on the men's low conversation. A few of the muffled words tingled my spine. Then again, they were talking so softly, I couldn't really be sure.

Slowly I inched down the aisle to get into closer earshot

range. The moccasins silently carried me along the stocked rows of breakfast foods and packaged cereals.

Now things were a little more audible. I held my breath to listen harder. I had to be sure I heard what I heard. Feeling somewhat like a snoop, and hiding behind the Froot Loops and Franken Berrys, I strained my senses.

"Yup, they's goin' ta be back agin, all right," one said.

"Nope, no sirree, never fails, do it."

"Wonder when them spooks are gonna git some smarts."

"Cain't hardly tell with ghosts. . .'specially Injun ones."

My scalp crawled. What were they talking about? I wanted to know, but was also equally fearful of the revelation.

"*Shhh!*" one suddenly hushed at the others.

Bill's cowboy boots tramped like thunder on the bare wooden floorboards. "Afternoon gentlemen."

Mumbles of semi-cordial, yet guarded, greetings issued back.

My companion must've been looking around the store. "Lose the little woman?" came the comment.

"I seem to have," went the reply.

"Ohhh, I 'spect she's 'round here someplace."

"Thanks."

The thunder boomed louder as it approached. He appeared around the herbals. "Found her," he hollered back as if I'd really been misplaced.

The men snickered.

My female pride seethed. Really! As if I were someone's keys that were just found.

I eyed Bill and before he could voice another wisecrack, I snapped a finger to my lips and frantically motioned him over. "Honey," I said a bit too loud for authenticity, "did you see all the great herbal remedies?"

He frowned as I grabbed at the sleeve of his flannel shirt and yanked him close. Through a rush of hand signals; hand to my ear and pointing to the group of men with the other, he got the message and became Snoop Number Two.

As the men quietly took up the subject where they had left off, I saw the blood drain from my companion's face. He pulled me closer to the end of the aisle. Now the partners-in-crime stealthily listened behind the boxes of Lucky Charms and Cap'n Crunch. Our suspicions were confirmed.

Bill turned and firmly grasped my shoulders. "Listen," he whispered in his excitement, "*somewhere* around here there's been *spirit* manifestations going on."

"I know," I whispered back.

The blue eyes widened with pumping adrenaline. "Don't you get it?"

"Get what?"

"Our first *encounter!*"

Ohhh my God. "You're nuts! This is not what this trip is all about! We're supposed to be letting our spirits lead us to. . ."

One of his brows raised. "To what?"

"This is insane! I'll have nothing to do with this funny business. Who says these old men aren't just flapping their jaws to make small talk? Who says they're not just yarn-spinning to make a little excitement in their lives? Who says they're even *sane?* This is just unbelievable! You're kidding, right?"

Wrong. His eyes said it all.

I sighed and turned away. I turned the *wrong* way, for my gaze rested on yet another box of silly cereal. . .*Ghost Busters.*

My mate spun me around. Unfortunately he turned me right out into the open. "You just don't want to face reality here," he accused.

"Oh yeah? Well what is reality here anyway?"

"It's the fact that. . ."

Suddenly we both realized that the little group had silenced. Suddenly we realized how exposed we were and that we were no longer softly conversing in so quiet a tone. We simultaneously shut up, locked eyes and then slowly turned our heads toward the men.

Cold stares met ours.

I smiled weakly. "Great little place you got here—very old-timey—nice an' quaint."

No response came.

Then I felt my jacket forcefully yanked forward. I pulled back, but my mate was such a gallant gentleman, he smiled wide at me, placed his arm a little too tightly around my shoulders and politely escorted me forward.

Oh hell, I thought, now what fine mess was he getting us into?

And before I could think any more about it, I heard a strange sound emit from the stranger beside me. "This here sure is a nice spot. Me an' the little woman here have been lookin' 'round for just such a place to settle."

Oh God, not the hick accent.

The men shuffled around in their chairs. "Don't say now?"

"Yep. Bet ya don't get none of them stuffy tourists up here."

"Nope," said one.

"Don't want none neither," said another.

"An' I sure don't blame ya for that. Now me an' the missus got us some real little nature lovers back home. They'd sure love it out this way, huh honey?" he said, giving my shoulder a rattle.

Seething inside with the patronizing, I managed to create something that resembled a smile.

The gas operator became the group's spokesman. "Where you folks hail from?"

"Oh up 'round the hills near Woodland Park. We got us a real nice little cabin way back in the woods."

And that was a lie. We *used* to live there.

"Don't say," voiced the spokesman. "I hear that's some mighty fine country out that way."

"Sure is, but gettin' too crowded, if you know what I mean."

The four men exchanged glances before returning their eyes to us.

The spokesman took a long, hard draw on his prized Meerschaum and stood. A weathered hand extended out to Bill.

"Name's Dan'l," he softened, "have a seat."

One of the sourdoughs scraped two more chairs up to the potbelly. Now we were a cozy sewing circle of six. We'd been accepted. . .we were in. The big bonus question was. . .what happens now? I could just speak up and thank them for the look-see around their nice place and tell them we had to be on our way. I could suddenly not feel so good and have to make a speedy exit. Or I could all of a sudden remember a very important appointment with the dentist. Anything but remain sitting there expected to be the cute but silent "little woman" while the men did all the important discussing. Anything but get involved with their story. Anything but be led into the spinning tale of ghosts. And, most of all, I was prepared to do anything to avoid our first spirit encounter. If this thing was real, it had just come up too damned fast. . .I wasn't ready. My heart fell into the pit of my stomach just thinking about it.

I'm not usually so easily drawn into dramatic scenes such as the one I presently found myself in. I meekly sat on one of the offered chairs and remained mute like a good "little woman" should. I think my mind was temporarily shut down from overload. I think I was in the state of semi-shock. Voices rambled about me while my mind thawed by degrees.

"So, Daniel," I heard my companion say, "we'd sure be awfully interested in hearing that ghost story of yours."

My gaze cleared as I focused on the spokesman.

Sourdough Number Three leaned far forward to get my attention. I looked into the hazel eyes that rounded wide as an owl's.

"And what about the little woman here? *She* wanna hear?"

Was the old man actually trying to scare me? It certainly appeared that way to me. Well! I thought, *this* little woman was no meek lamb afraid of her own shadow! Suddenly all my energies ignited and sparked to full attention. I felt a queer twinkle beam behind my eyes and my chin jutted up slightly.

"Oh yes! I'd very much like to hear this story."

Sourdough Number Three inched forward again. I noticed he was nearly off his chair. The eyes flared at me. "This ain't no *story*, missy. This here is God's own *truth!*"

I wasn't ruffled by his intended spookiness. "I'm sure it is, Mr. . . ."

"Call me George, ma'am, just George."

"I'm sure it is, George. Most *are* real."

George's bushy brows rose and he jerked back like he'd been hit by some invisible force. He furtively eyed his three cronies. From the way they all shuffled their feet and fidgeted in their seats, I knew they were all sharing the same revealing thought. Just what kind of little woman was this anyway?

I was pleased with myself for the reaction I'd gotten. Unfortunately, my smug gaze then settled on Bill's eyes. Oh-oh. Somebody was not very pleased with me right now. I had not stayed in character and if looks could kill. . .I'd be dead, buried and turned to ashes by now. I flashed him a demure smile. "Right, honey?"

He couldn't believe his ears. *"What*, dear?"

"I said isn't that right that most tales of ghosts are really based on truth."

The four mesmerized men looked from me back to Bill. They reminded me of a crowd watching a tennis match.

"Yes," he stammered, "yes, they usually are."

I turned my attention to Daniel. "Could we hear it?"

Momentarily, the older man was at a loss for words. His gaze checked into those of his friends whose expressions displayed a unified front—confusion. Then they shrugged.

The spokesman decided the issue for them. "Guess it ain't gonna hurt none seeing's you folks is mountain an' all."

I smiled to alleviate the gentlemen's obvious fears. "We stay with our own," I said. "This won't be the first ghost story we've heard."

Daniel still wasn't thoroughly pleased with this decision. "Only a few folks 'round here knows 'bout this."

"I understand, Daniel. You don't want it getting around either."

All four heads slowly moved from side to side. "No, ma'am. That sure would be the end of our peaceful little community here. I know it don't look like much from the road out there," he said, inclining his head toward the door, "but there's a might number of cabins 'round out in these woods an' they're there 'cause folks like it that way. They likes the quiet an' solitude."

My smile widened with genuine concern. "I know what you're saying, Daniel. You and the cabin folks don't want curiosity seekers trampling through your peacefulness. I can appreciate that, really I can. You can trust us...we're mountain too, remember?"

A sheepish grin uplifted Daniel's kind face.

I sat back. It was a signal for Bill to take it from here.

After a bit of ice-breaking talk, we found ourselves completely absorbed with Daniel's colorful yarn. The other three frequently interjected their descriptive two cents' worth and finally the deed was done—the strangers had heard the tale of how Black Wolf Canyon was haunted.

After the final word was voiced, the men were visibly anxious to hear our opinion. I really think they were all afraid the two strangers would think they were nuts, especially the way the man and the little lady looked at one another during the silent moments that followed on the heels of the story.

In those brief telling moments, my heart thundered like the pounding hooves of a thousand buffalo. In those brief telling moments, I knew this was our spirits' destination, and when my eyes latched onto Bill's, I heard the thunder of his own heart. We were right where we were supposed to be and, whether we liked it or not, the die had been cast by unseen hands.

We thanked the men for their trust. They were relieved. Then Bill moved in to bet on the longshot.

"Would you folks object if we took a look at the spot?"

"Well...," Daniel hesitated, searching the surprised expressions of the others, "I suppose not. Don't suppose there'd be any harm in just lookin'.

Bill and I both knew he had more than a simple look-see in mind. Figuratively speaking, he slapped his money on the table.

"Think we could stay the night there?"

The silence was a living thing.

"We'd just like to see for ourselves, is all."

Sourdough Number Four eyed Daniel. "He don't b'lieve, is why."

"That so?" the spokesman asked.

"No, not at all. Of course we believe the story; that's why we need to spend the night down there."

"Spooks is spooks," George stated. "Seen one ya seen 'em all."

I cleared my throat.

Eyes shifted in my direction.

"Gentlemen," I began as gently as I knew how, "we believe your story and want to spend the night down there because we want to talk to them."

Eyes widened into orbs the size of dinner plates. Great breaths were loudly inhaled. George was the first to rediscover his voice.

"I ain't never heard of nobody wantin' to talk to no *ghosts!*"

"Me neither," agreed Number Four.

"Why you wanna do some fool thing like that for?" Daniel asked.

"So we can help them. . .at least try to," I replied.

George cocked his head to squint at me. "You one o' them ghostbuster folks I heard 'bout from the kids 'round here?"

That definitely brought on a grin. "No, we're not ghost-busters, George. We just want to help, that's all."

"How you do that?"

I looked to Bill for an answer. When he gave a shrug, I returned my attention to the older man. I didn't have a definite answer either and I didn't pretend that I had.

"I don't know."

Four pair of eyes shifted back and forth. "Then. . .how you gonna help?"

"I don't know that yet either."

Frowns appeared around the sewing circle.

"Look," I began again, "I'm not making myself clear at all here. What I mean to say is that each haunting case is different. No two are ever exactly the same, and until we can actually see what's going on and find out what's causing it, we can't know which method to use to help it go away."

The group considered my concept. A couple men scratched their heads over it. Daniel thoughtfully stroked his beard.

"There's more 'an *one* way ta do this thing you say?"

I nodded. And with all my might I hoped the man wouldn't ask me how I had come by these methods. Lady Luck was with me.

Daniel just sighed and shook his head.

Number Two spoke up then. "Learn somethin' new ever'day. Yes sirree, learn somethin' new ever'day, just ain't no stoppin' it."

Bill and I smiled.

We left the Black Wolf Mercantile with a fresh thermos of black coffee and a simple sketch of directions to the infamous canyon. We left four sourdoughs standing in the shade of the worn wooden porch. We left with a promise to return with our own yarn about how it all turned out. . .after all, we owed them one. We waved goodbye and pulled away.

After a few prolonged moments of silence had elapsed, Bill turned to look at my ears.

I frowned at him but made no comment. What the hell was he looking at anyway?

He grinned and again gave the road his full attention.

I looked up into the rear view mirror at myself. Did I lose an earring? Was there dirt on my ears?

Suddenly he spoke. "What're you looking at?"

"What were *you* looking at?" I snapped back.

"Oh nothing. Just thought for a minute there I saw steam coming out of your ears."

I seethed. "Nothin' wrong with *your* eyes, Bud. You *bet* I'm hot! I don't care where we are or what the reasons are, don't you ever call me the *Little Woman* again! I'm not *The Missus*, a *Missy* or your *Tootsie Pie* either!"

The driver made the major error of grinning.

"It's not funny, dammit! I hate that kind of patronizing."

"Will you cool it. I only said that back there because it was the kind of back mountain talk those guys were comfortable with. . .you know. . .that down-homey feeling."

My eyes were deadly cold when I looked at him. The voice was dripping with icicles. "Find *another* way to get 'down-homey.'"

"It got us in, didn't it?"

"Find another way to get us in next time."

"Jesus," he groaned, "and you think *I* give the Evil Eye?" Then the grin returned. "Hey, you practice that look in the mirror or something?"

"No. . .I always look that way. It's completely natural."

"That's what I thought."

And then it was my turn to grin.

We were back on track again.

Although we were perfect for each other, we weren't without our little go 'rounds. That sort of open communication—freely expressed and spontaneous—was just the cement that sealed the rightness of the long relationship. The off-the-cuff sarcasm balanced the spur-of-the-moment expressions of love. . .always there was the balance that continued to maintain our enduring bond and commitment to one another.

Now the driver was intent on observing landmarks.

I snuggled in closer beside him. "Honey?"

"Mmmm."

"Who would've ever thought that when we started out this morning that we'd be headed for our first encounter?"

"You kidding? Look who did the leading?"

"Well I know, but we had no idea it'd turn out to be this."

"No, that's for sure."

I became pensive while he inspected the scenery.

"You nervous?" he asked.

Silence.

"Hon?"

"Bill. . .I'm not ready yet."

He squeezed my knee. "Yes you are, you just don't want to admit it."

"No. . .I'm serious."

"You just *think* you're serious. You *think* you're not ready because you think you're scared."

"No. That's not right."

"Which one?"

"All of the above, especially the last. I *know* I'm scared."

"Don't you think that's to be expected? I'm pretty nervous too. I mean, how many times does one experience their first spirit encounter?"

I sighed. "Do we have to do this?"

He just looked down at me.

"Yeah, I was afraid you'd say that."

The navigator rechecked the sketch and made a right turn onto a rutted dirt road. It was scattered with embedded rocks and stones.

"You sure this is right?" I asked.

"Uh-huh."

"Then why are we going *up*?"

"What's the matter, you scared of that dropoff over on your side?"

I craned my neck to peer out the window. "It is quite a drop."

"I know," he said, "you're wondering why we're going up if the canyon is down."

"Not really." I knew by now that mountain roads most always go up first before they go down into one of those canyons. "I guess I'm still hoping this isn't the way."

We bounced about for a few more miles of twisting shelf road.

"Honey?"

"What?" he said, trying to maneuver the squeaking truck.

"Do you think No-Eyes was involved in this trip?"

"Never really crossed my mind, but it's certainly a good possibility."

"You think so?"

"Sure I do. She was probably in cahoots with our own spirits. It was probably all planned out and arranged. Besides," he considered, "it'd stand to reason that she'd want you to get your feet wet as soon as possible while the lessons were still fresh in your mind."

I thought on that.

"Well?" he asked. "Doesn't that sound logical—like something she'd do?"

"Yeah. It sounds exactly like something she'd do."

We cleared a sharp curve and stopped.

"There it is," the navigator announced, "Black Wolf Canyon."

I looked down at the canyon. "It's so wide. How'll we ever find the right spot? I mean that place is *miles* long!"

"Nice try, honey, real nice try. C'mon, we got some scouting ahead of us."

And, as the truck descended, so did my last remaining hopes of successful evasion. Destiny beckoned.

Reaching the bottomland, the sounds of the meandering stream sent up a repeating chorus of encouragement. We pulled over near the watercourse and got out. Broad cottonwoods crowded along the edges of the sparkling mountain waters.

"It all appears so peaceful," I commented, "so normal."

My hand was squeezed. "Remember what No-Eyes said?"

"She said a lot."

"I mean about appearances."

"Yeah, that appearances are deceiving."

"That's right. It would seem that this is a prime example."

I gazed up and down the stream. "Where do you figure they show up?"

Bill pulled the folded piece of paper from his breast pocket, studied it a minute, then looked around. He pointed to my left. "Should be right beneath that damaged cottonwood."

I stared at the big trunk that'd been hit by lightning. Its scar struck a chord of pain in me. "Want to check it out?"

He smiled. "Might as well. Now's as good a time as any."

We strolled through the soft meadow grass to the target. Immediately we felt our psyches tingle their first warning bleeps. And without another word spoken between us, we walked the distance until the sensations eased.

"This is the end," I informed. "This is where they disappear into."

Bill agreed then turned to look back at the tree. "If they really do manifest beneath the tree, that doesn't give us a hell of a lot of time. Given the fact that they're moving, we'll have some fancy footwork to do."

Butterflies swarmed in my stomach. "I have a gut feeling about this," I whispered.

"What?"

"It's very nervous."

He laughed and pulled me to him. "It'll be all right, honey, you'll see."

I circled my arms around him. "I'm just so scared."

"I know, I know, but I'll be right with you every step of the way. We'll be together."

At that precious moment, the warmness of him that radiated through his shirt felt like security. I wanted to lose myself in it and never be found. I just wanted to melt into it and disappear.

Gently I was eased away. My chin was lifted. "You okay?"

I nodded. "I'm okay."

My forehead was kissed. "You always were quite a trooper."

We clasped hands then and retraced our steps. The vibrational field again altered until we cleared the cottonwood again. There were clear sensations of release that indicated the edge of the vortex. It felt like being released from the pull of a magnet.

"That's it then," Bill concluded.

"Yep! That's it!" I chirped a bit too eagerly.

Again our eyes met. "You're trying to be so brave, babe."

I felt tears begin to sting but forced them back. "Nothing left but that."

His arm went about my waist. "Let's get something to eat."

That thought definitely didn't agree with my stomach, but I knew it was necessary. It was well past lunchtime and we wouldn't be eating any dinner. Together we walked back to the truck.

The pickup itself had been fitted with a large topper we'd bought from friends. Bill and I had masterfully joined minds to create our first and only piece of carpentry work—the entire back end and door for the semi-camper. Inside, a raised bed, just cozy enough for two, allowed us a measure of comfort if we ever had to spend a night in it. Thick blue carpeting covered the floor, and curtains, hung over the louvered windows, afforded us privacy. There was plenty of storage beneath the bed, leaving half the floor space open. We were always well stocked. Driving through the high country of Colorado could present unexpected hazards, especially during winter, and one had to always be prepared for the worst scenario.

The space beneath the bed was filled with extra blankets, Bill's shotgun, a battery-operated camping lantern, first aid supplies, a propane cookstove that could double as an emergency heater, axes, and a large box full of vehicle supplies such as tire chains, windshield washer solvent, antifreeze, flares, quarts of oil and transmission fluid, cans of Inflate-a-Flat, and a host of handy tools. On the wall hooks hung bright orange rain ponchos and extra-heavy winter jackets. And, unimposing, yet a great convenience, the Porta Potty was tucked away in one corner.

Now, in the afternoon light of Black Wolf Canyon, seeing the long vehicle parked so near the singing stream gave me a sense of security. I swung the door open and hauled myself in. Sunlight flooded over the carpet. Bill entered and perched up on the bed.

"What sumptuous delights have we got in the cooler?"

I flashed him a dubious look. "Same gourmet spread we always have—peanut butter an' jelly sandwiches and fruit."

He just grinned. "Toss one over; I'm hungry."

I popped the tabs of two cold Pepsi cans, handed one up to my partner, and scooted over to sit in the doorway. Legs dangling down over the back bumper, I sipped from the pop and gazed up the sides of the canyon.

"Thinking about tonight?" came the gentle question.

I shook my head.

"Mmmm. I would've thought that'd be heavy on your mind."

Again my head went from side to side.

"You going to tell me or do we play Sixty Questions?"

"What's the matter, you don't like that game?" I teased.

"Let's just say we don't have time for it."

My face lifted into the warm rays. "I was just thinking about how peaceful it is here. It's so full of solitude and serenity."

"Only during the day, remember."

"Aside from that," I said, panning the long expanse of the valley. "It doesn't have all the pines that I like to see, but those cottonwoods give a lot of shade. I guess they complement the rest of the scenery."

"No two areas of Colorado are quite the same. Elevations vary a lot. Plains and mountains, marshes and sand dunes, high mesas and deep canyons, they all make it so different."

"Guess so," I mused.

"What's really on your mind?"

I looked back at him. Somewhere near, up the mountainside, sibling squirrels were playing tag. Among the broad cottonwoods, birdsong twilled.

"Nature here is very normal," I replied.

And, looking down beyond me, he smiled while inclining his head. His voice was low. "It would appear very normal. Don't look now, but you seem to have a beggar approaching."

I grinned and slowly turned my head. A wee prairie dog was perched on its small hind legs. Little forepaws held up to the tiny chest, wee heart furiously drumming beneath the fragile rib cage, it stared with pleading eyes in hopes of softening my own heart for a crumb or two. My heart needed no softening when it came to the four-leggeds.

I spoke softly to it and slipped off the floor ledge. Soon tiny hands were upon mine, soft pads and pinpricks worked nervously over my hand-held morsels. When the eats were gone— so was my little fair-weather friend. I watched him scamper away and disappear behind a scattering of rocks.

Bill's voice was full of humor. "Now he's going to bring his whole family back here."

A trio of Stellar blue jays landed nearby. "Doesn't matter," I said, pointing to the newcomers, "the neighborhood's already got the message." I crawled back into the camper and put away the food. "Now what?"

Bill lifted up a corner of a curtain and glanced up into the sky. "Well? We don't exactly have a textbook on this subject, but I'd say it's time we got that required rest in."

I eyed him. "We're really going to do it, aren't we."

He smiled. "Close the door, honey."

I closed and locked the door, scrambled up on the bed and snuggled beneath the quilt. Warm arms encircled me. And soon I knew my mate was deep in slumber. How could he sleep? I wondered. Wasn't he nervous? A little scared of what was ahead?

While I listened to his soft breathing, I thought about the story we had heard earlier. Thirty spirits lost. Thirty women and children on an eternal journey of searching for something that's not even there. Thirty! Good God, I thought, why'd there have to be so many? Why couldn't our first encounter be only with *one*? Then the trail of playback scenes and fragments of the discussion speared my consciousness. What Daniel had said was probably right. We'd only have to deal with the leader because the rest followed her. I wasn't sure that comforted me much. I wasn't sure that helped at all. What if something major went awry? What if the leader became upset or angry? Could she control the others? Make them use all their powerful energies against us?

Bill twitched and groaned. He turned over and again became lost in the obliterating depths of sleep.

I sighed. I had to control the fear that was taking hold. Didn't the visionary have faith in me—in our tandem abilities? Had she ever been wrong? Just once? No! I closed my eyes. Oh No-Eyes, where are you now? Help me to have the same confidence you had in me. Give me courage. Make me be strong. No-Eyes, wherever you are, please give me the right wisdom for this.

I don't know when I finally fell asleep, but sleep I did, for a blaring sound shot both pair of eyes open and brought us fully awake. Bill looked out the window and turned back, a silly grin crept up his face.

"What is it?" I asked, straightening my dishevelled clothes.

"Those 'good ole boys' are here. Let's go see what they want."

"The ole guys from the mercantile?"

"The same."

We hurriedly shoved our feet into our boots and opened the back door. A crisp breath of early evening air blew in. And just as we tumbled out, an unpainted International bumped and squeaked its way to our site. The men's rickety vehicle pulled up beside our rickety pickup as if to say "how do, Pal." When the engine was cut, it coughed, gave a trembling shudder and sighed.

Bill rapped on the hood as we came up to the driver who hung an arm out the window.

"Come to see the show?"

Daniel's eyes twinkled. "Just be in the way, son. We all got ta wonderin' if you two found the place okay." He looked about. "See that ya did all right."

"Thanks to your fine directions," Bill praised.

The man behind the wheel seriously studied me. "Look son," he began, "I don't mean ta pry none, but we just wanted you an' the little woman there ta know that ya don't have ta do this here thing on a'count of us."

Bill patted the man's arm. "We appreciate that, Daniel, but we don't do it for people at all—we do it for them."

"Well. . .I knows that too, but we just got ta thinkin' 'bout it an' decided to tell ya that we wouldn't blame ya none if ya changed your mind."

"Appreciate the thought, we really do, but we'll stay the night an' see what's what."

Daniel closed his eyes and nodded his understanding. "You folks need anything?"

"Thanks, we're all set."

Pipe smoke swirled from the open window. "You all right, Missy?"

I smiled. "Yes, thank you."

"Okay then. Guess you don't need no old fogie in yer way. I'll be headin' back now." The engine sputtered to life. "Don't ferget ta stop an' see us in the mornin'."

"We'll do that," Bill assured.

And we watched the reliable contraption ramble back up the road. We watched until it was out of sight and the sound of it was gone. The sudden silence was loud in our ears.

I glanced about. "We're all alone now."

"For a while, babe. . .just for a while."

Evenings in deep canyons are short-lived. Shadows quickly come and go as they're swallowed up by nightfall. The air soon chills. And darkness becomes pregnant with creature sounds and calls.

Back in the camper, I switched on the lantern light to LOW. The yellow glow helped to soften the edge of my anxiety. I pulled on another sweater. Bill snapped up an additional down vest. We talked of the encounter for a long, long while. We discussed the facts as we knew them, we shared our inner feelings, and we prayed for a successful conclusion. Finally I felt the pressure of time.

"We need to prepare now," I solemnly announced.

And without another spoken word passing between us, Bill turned out the light and settled down on the carpet. I reclined on the bed and closed my eyes. Strong visualizations began. Powerful energy reinforcing electrified the room. Spirits joined. Silence prevailed.

Then. . .our eyes shot open. A vibrational shift had pricked at our psyches. Bill whipped around to the window.

"It's begun," was all he said.

At his words, an icy finger traced down my spine. When I peered out, vague forms were appearing beneath the scarred cottonwood.

"Right where we figured," I whispered.

In a flurry of activity, we donned our outerwear. Bill zipped his jacket up over the vest and I nervously fumbled with a jean jacket, then pulled down the serape over it. Yanking on gloves, I silently hurried out the door behind Bill.

Once outside, we took a golden moment to embrace. This singular action was not generated by our deep love, but was an essential aspect of the total procedure. The high psychic energy produced by deep love serves to bond the pair and spiritually empower them. We separated and softly voiced our love before stealthily making our way toward the entry point of the vortex.

It was not hard to feel the altered atmosphere. The darkness was a living thing. It nearly congealed in its thick blackness. The moon was a second away from clearing the ridge line. Its silvery light would help. . .how much I couldn't tell yet.

We were a tree away from the target one. Silently we watched as thirty forms manifested. One by one they formed in behind the apparition in front of them. One by one they followed after their leader. Not a sound was heard. The thing was as eerie as eerie gets.

As soon as the last spectral form appeared, Bill tapped my arm. "Let's go."

I hesitated.

"Now's not the time to get cold feet. C'mon. We don't have much time here. Once that leader reaches the end of the vibrational field, they'll all follow her out. . .we won't have anyone left to help. Are you just going to stand back here and watch them come and go? Are you just going to watch?"

"That's not a bad idea. Maybe we should just observe a few

of these manifestations so we can get used to seeing them. This isn't one of your more common everyday sights, you know. Then after we're more comfortable, we'll be better prepared to approach them."

"Nice try. C'mon."

We moved ahead. And, with Bill on my left, I inched up behind the last spirit of the column. I literally brought up the rear and, strangely enough, had the urge to touch the form in front of me. She was an aged Indian woman. Hunched and hidden beneath a tattered blanket, she shuffled forward on rag-wrapped moccasins.

My hand began to rise up in front of me. It momentarily hung in the air as if it were hesitating with the wiseness of the mind's intent.

Bill watched in anxious curiosity.

Slowly I inched it forward until it connected—sort of. The tips of my fingers perceived substance, yet it was undefinable. The new sensation that the sensory nerves experienced and sent back to the brain elicited no responsive readout computations. The fingertip probes connected with something like a fine gel. Nothing within the scope of three-dimensional solidity registered. A fragmented concept occurred to me. . .divergent forms of two incompatible vibrationary rates were now connecting, or more accurately, were occupying the same space and time. They were joining existences to meld into an integrated mass. Deep curiosity obliterated my former nervousness as I anxiously pressed to discover more.

I withdrew my hand and moved up beside the woman. I studied her with increased interest. The entity was very aged. She cowered beneath the blanket covering her head. I peered around and bent down to see her better. No recognition of my presence was indicated.

I advanced up the line and observed the general overall formation. Turning to my partner who remained close by my side, I whispered, "They died during the winter. See how they're all leaning forward as if into the wind?"

He nodded while I continued. "It was snowing too because they're all trying to protect themselves."

I was overcome by heightened fascination. I sidled up beside a young mother cradling a tiny infant in her arms. The woman's head turned ever so slightly. Did she perceive my presence? Then, when the face was directly even with mine, my heart plunged. The complexion was horribly pocked. The large dark eyes stared at me. . .no, *through* me. And suddenly

I had to quell the twinge of fear that stabbed at my mind when I saw the woman's fixed, catatonic look. Slowly she faced forward again and resumed the mindless shuffling. The eeriness of that vacant stare was hard to shake. It was so listless, so pathetically akin to a state of comatose, it was frightening.

Silently we inched up the line. I stopped by another elderly form and peeked around at her. My scalp crawled. It was just like looking down at a time-etched face hidden at the bottom of a newly-opened sarcophagus. Creviced skin, leathery and sunken. Parched and cracked lips. Ebony eyes, empty. Autistic awareness. I recoiled and backed into Bill.

With a swirling blend of contrasting emotions, I whispered to him. "This is like watching zombies! Look at them shuffle along. It's just like they're nothing more than mindless automatons."

"I *know*, but get to the one in *front*."

We gave a cursory once-over to those we passed. They were all identical. It was just like we two were accompanying a bunch of zombies out for their evening stroll. It unnerved me. I hadn't been prepared for this type of bizarre behavior. No-Eyes' manual hadn't covered this possibility and I worried.

Bill urged me forward. He was becoming visibly impatient with the dawdling. Time was becoming of the essence.

As we approached the leader, I noticed that she was quite tall. Slender of build, her head was held high. She was clearly a proud woman and still retained most of her youthful beauty. By the manner of her carriage, she exuded strength and determination. That in itself didn't bolster my meager courage any. I just stared at her.

Bill pushed me. "Will you get *on* with it? Look how *close* they're getting!"

The urgency in his voice was contagious. I snapped my head forward and gauged the distance—it wasn't a lot. I approached the leader.

"Miss?" I said stupidly.

The measured meter of her stride changed. It paused ever so slightly before going on.

I ignorantly attempted to tap her shoulder. "Miss?" I called again, noticing how my hand had no effect.

The head rotated around to face me, but the large almond eyes were not clearly focused. Again she resumed her mission of leading the forlorn band of lost souls into the Land of the Lost.

Bill grabbed me and I spun around. He was frantic. "What

the hell's *wrong* with you? For *Chrissakes,* that's not somebody on the *street!"* He shook me. "Bring it *up,* dammit!"

My eyes were wide as saucers as I stared into his flaming orbs so filled with desperation. What the hell *was* wrong with me? Had my mind frozen up with stage fright? Had I suddenly forgotten everything so soon? And I was forcefully hit with the realization that, through my own incompetence, I was failing. I was failing ourselves, No-Eyes, and all the souls now shuffling beside me. What pained me the most was not the thought of failing the thirty souls, but the thought of letting down my mentor. With the shocking jolt that that thought brought to my heart, I was electrified into action.

My eyes narrowed at Bill and my lips pressed together with renewed determination. Power coursed through every atom of my being. The new me made him smile wide.

I quickly motioned for him to move ahead of the column to block the exit portal and I twirled around and ran to stand between him and the approaching woman.

Now I was directly in her path. *"Stop!"* I shouted at her.

She halted in mid-step and raised her head. The eyes cleared by degrees.

"Get out of my way," she said calmly.

I shook my head. "NO! *You* get out of *my* way!"

The woman glanced from side to side for alternate routes around me—there weren't any. She needed to go straight and I was posing a problem. Behind me a short distance, Bill stood his ground before the portal. It was all too clear the lady didn't especially like what she saw and I hoped it wasn't going to get ugly.

I stood firmly planted to the spot and watched the expression on her face harden as a slow burn raged deep within her. Its blazing fire ignited her eyes. Her voice was low, very low, yet full of a commanding power. The flaming black stones that were her eyes seared through my soul.

"Get. . .out. . .of. . .my. . .way."

I had to maintain the upper hand. Somehow that was no problem and I didn't dare take the time to question it; there'd be time to analyze the performance later. Now, all that was vitally important was for me to display more power than her—at least to make her *believe* I was more powerful.

My arms shot out. They were rigid with power. "NO! You don't *belong* here!"

The intense eyes flared up with anger. She was gathering her forces.

"You don't *belong* here!" I raged at her.

A flicker of a shadow crossed the eyes to cool them. I didn't dare give her time to speak. . .not yet.

"You walk the *wrong* trail! You journey the wrong *way!*"

The head cocked. The pair of embers grew cold. They appeared to soften as did the sound of her next words.

"This is our trail. We walk this trail to home. It will take us to our men who await our return."

Oh God, she was so confused.

Movement behind the leader distracted my attention and caused me to glance beyond her. A measure of awareness had nudged the band into a semi-conscious state. The women were beginning to break formation and were shuffling forward. Curious heads bobbed up and down and craned sideways to see why they had halted. I didn't want to be crowded and tried to ignore the thought as I gave the leader my full attention.

"I am called Summer Rain," I began. "I have been sent to help you find home."

A frown creased the smooth forehead. "Who sends Summer Rain to do this thing for us?"

"The Great Spirit sends me."

I wasn't sure I had said the right thing, but the gathering crowd, upon hearing my response, sucked in their breath in unison and shrank back in fear. I hadn't wanted their fear; I wanted their trust.

"This is true," I continued quickly. "The Great Spirit sends me to show you the trailhead that will lead you to your men, your fathers, brothers and grandfathers."

The leader had been intently studying my serape while I spoke. A small hand extended to touch the woven fabric. It connected—sort of. When the delicate fingers passed through the material, the hand was withdrawn with the speed of one reacting to a burn. The crowd gasped. A rumble of murmurs rolled through the frightened throng.

The leader tilted her head. "What manner of woman is Summer Rain? What manner of blanket is this that I cannot touch?"

Now that her mission was distracted by her recognition of our physical differences, I felt more at ease.

"What are you called?" I asked.

"I am called Cloud Woman."

"Can we sit and talk, Cloud Woman? We will speak of what manner of woman Summer Rain is and why she is here."

Cloud Woman sat.

The band followed suit. So did I.

But before I could begin in earnest, the leader surprised me by smiling wide. Eyes bright with wisdom, she again reached to touch the magic serape, then my moccasin beads. And, same as before, the delineating vibrational rates that distinguished Cloud Woman from Summer Rain made themselves evident by passing through each other. The leader's white teeth showed behind the knowing smile that illuminated her face.

"Now I know what manner of woman Summer Rain is."

Relief came to me on blessed wings. This one was easy to convince. My work was almost over with her realization.

"Summer Rain comes from the Land of Spirits to show us the way home," came the cheery statement from behind eyes twinkling with shining happiness.

Relief hadn't come on blessed wings after all. It didn't even alight, but quickly flew the coop as the rug was pulled out from under me. I realized it was a logical conclusion on her part but a few little items of it weren't quite right.

"No, Cloud Woman, *you* and your *people* here are from the Land of the Spirits."

She sweetly smiled at the confused Summer Rain who had things so mixed up in her head.

"Tell me, Summer Rain, if we are from the Land of Spirits, where are our beloved families who have gone there many moons ago?"

Again good logic. And I was at a loss for a way to explain why it wasn't logic.

The leader had great sympathy for poor Summer Rain.

"Summer Rain, I will tell you of my band and why what you say cannot be so."

I sighed heavily. I'd listen and maybe buy some time while I thought this craziness out.

"Summer Rain," she began, "many moons ago, our camp had little food. We were cold too. Some kind soldiers gave us many blankets soon before our men went off hunting. People left behind at the camp, mostly women and children, became very sick. When the bad sickness left, we became well again. But our men never returned. Now that we are well, we travel to find them again. We travel to join camps."

My stomach nearly retched with the stabbing reality of her story. It churned and my heart ached with a powerful pain to know that these gentle women and children had died of the smallpox-riddled blankets the very "kind" soldiers had passed out to them. Little did she know that the white government was not showing kindness in an effort to help the women and children by warming them, but was rather showing hate in an effort to eradicate them by killing them off like flies. The women's men never returned because they too had been given the beautiful Army blankets.

My eyes misted over. Now it would serve no meaningful purpose to enlighten the leader of history's sins of genocide. There was no reason to go into the terrible truth—the black crimes of ignorance that happened so many wintercounts ago. Even if it could make her see the light of the matter, I didn't want to add to the deep sorrows she already carried within her tender heart.

"Summer Rain," Cloud Woman whispered, disturbing my heavy thoughts, "you of the Spirit Land know much magic. Have you come to use your powers to show us the way?"

More intelligent logic, but only half of it was right. This was getting difficult to handle with simple words that would only make the matter murky. Then an idea came to me. If magic was expected. . .magic she'd get.

I searched the ground and picked up a pebble. I looked into Cloud Woman's eyes, then offered the stone to her.

She reacted with the natural reflex to reach out. She took it. It dropped.

I quietly plucked up a weed, a wildflower and some wildgrass.

Again I held it out to her. And again the woman reacted by taking them. Again they fell to the earth.

I stared at her and plucked more blades of grass and deposited them into the fabric covering my lap. They didn't fall through. Cloud Woman observed me as, one more time, I pulled up weeds and placed them in her lap. They disappeared. The murmurs of the stunned crowd intensified. Mothers shielded their babies.

The leader looked back and forth between the two laps.

"Summer Rain has much magic."

No, this would not do. She was in denial now. She had to exit that constrainment.

For the last time, I pulled up a handful of grass and held it up between us. "Cloud Woman," I addressed softly, "this is grass—*my* grass from *my* land. Look. See how I hold it in my hand? See how my *lap* holds it?" I said, placing the clump on the serape. "I do not make this grass, these pebbles, these wildflowers and weeds into things of the spirit. I do not make magic here. They are *real!*" I anxiously waited for her reply.

A long silence hung heavy in the night before she spoke. The voice was as heavy as the silence was.

"Summer Rain speaks true. Cloud Woman and her people are of the Land of Spirits. Cloud Woman and her people do not belong here. Cloud Woman and here people are dead. . .we are lost. . .forever. Our trail is lost. So. We will never return to our men."

Her sorrow deeply affected me. I wanted to hold her but couldn't.

"Cloud Woman?"

"Yes?"

"I bring magic that only you have the power to use."

She tilted her head, eyes widened at the wonder of my words. "Me?"

"Yes, you, because you are the leader here."

The woman peered down at my waist.

"No, Cloud Woman, a medicine bundle cannot hold this great power. . .nothing can."

A frown disturbed the delicate brows. "Magic," she whispered.

"Yes. Magic words filled with power. You must tell your people to say the sacred *words.* "

"What will the sacred *words* do?"

"Take you home. They will show you the trailhead that leads to home."

"And our men?"

"Your men too. They will be waiting." Then I stood.

Cloud Woman followed suit. We faced the group as they rose to their feet.

I spoke to the small band. "I am called Summer Rain. I come from the Great Spirit. Summer Rain comes with much magic in the form of sacred words. The power words will show you the way to your men. They will take you home."

The crowd huddled and mumbled among themselves. They didn't want to listen to me because I wasn't their leader, and they never saw her pass her power to me. Seeing the confusion, I turned to Cloud Woman. She stepped forward. There was much authority in her bearing. The voice was steady and sure.

"Summer Rain speaks true. I have seen the straightness of her words. We will do what she says. I pass my power. Summer Rain carries the magic words and I do not want such sacredness on my hands. Listen to her."

All eyes turned to me. "You all *must* say the sacred words

or they will have no power. You must speak them. You must *shout* them to make them work."

Silence. Eyes wide, the group watched and listened for the sacred words of power.

I gathered my energies and shouted. "I AM DEAD!"

Silence.

I sighed. "You *must* say this." I tried again. "I AM DEAD!"

The women rocked back and forth in fear of the words.

Cloud Woman, upset with her charges, spoke. "Do you want to see your men again?"

Heads bobbed. Mumbles were heard.

"Do you *want* to see your fathers and brothers?"

Louder mumbles.

"Do you *want* to go *home?*"

Someone keened.

"We have been walking the wrong trail. We walk in the wrong land. Now with the sacred words of power we can return!"

The band was becoming alive with the excited hope their leader created as she spoke.

"Now shout out the sacred words when Summer Rain does. You *must* do this *now!*"

I stepped forward again and tried to maintain the electricity that Cloud Woman had generated through her group. I shouted the words again. "I AM DEAD!"

"I. . .am. . .dead," came the low chant.

"Louder!" the leader demanded of them.

"I am *dead!*" resounded the chorus.

It was good. Now the women had reached the energy level that was required. I didn't want them to lose it.

"I don't *belong* here!" I shouted to them.

"I don't *belong* here!" echoed back.

"I *want* to go *home!*"

"I *want* to go *home!*" they yelled amid smiles and snickers.

The excitement was building fast. I couldn't believe how high the pitch had risen. It was deeply moving to see the new hope dawning behind those eyes that had been so blank and devoid of emotion. It made my heart pound and my eyes mist with the incredible happiness I felt welling. I quickly turned to check with Bill. He was as moved as I was and motioned for me to continue the momentum. I spun back around to see more grinning faces.

I grinned back. "I *want* to go *home!*"

"I *want* to go *home!*"

"This is *not* my *land!*"
"This is *not* my *land!*"

The intensity reached a feverish pitch. It was at its zenith and it was infectious.

"I WANT TO GO HOME! I WANT TO GO HOME!" I shouted.

"I WANT TO GO HOME! I WANT TO GO HOME!" echoed back.

"I DON'T BELONG HERE! I DON'T BELONG HERE!"

"I DON'T BELONG HERE! I don't. . .belong. . .he. . ." The women's voices trailed off into a smoldering murmuring.

I frowned at the sudden change. I tried to revive it. "I WANT TO GO HOME!" I shouted.

Silence. The crowd was gathering and shuffling forward. Necks craned around me to look behind. Eyes flared in shock at some terrifying sight. Jaws dropped as mouths gaped. Then. . .smiles broadened. Deafening squeals issued forth. And a great riot of clicking tongues began amongst the piercing keening. Women, old and young, began running toward me.

I spun around.

Behind Bill, a glow had manifested. Forms were appearing. They were beckoning with outstretched arms. And as I watched in spine-tingling awe, thirty women and children raced keening and crying into the awaiting arms of their husbands and fathers. Moved beyond all reason with the intense drama unfolding before me, I let the tears course freely and, without being conscious of my reaction, I released my own shrill keening.

Silence. Darkness. It was finished. Black Wolf Canyon was clear.

Deep within a type of transcendence, I stood within the residual magic of the moment. Exhausted, I didn't even give a thought to moving. I just wanted to remain with the warm feeling I was left with. I was drained, yet fulfilled all at once.

A strong arm gently encircled my waist. I looked up and felt so much love.

We strolled over to the stream's edge and watched the starlight dance upon its rushing waters. A voice as soft as butterfly breath came on whispered wings.

"You did it, honey. You really did it. . .I love you."

Birdsong, joyous and spirited, roused the two snuggled so warmly beneath the camper quilt. Stream voices, giggling and carefree, brought contented smiles to our faces. Gentle kisses smothered my neck. When I turned, the steel-blue eyes were soft as a fawn's.

"You did it, Mary. Last night you showed thirty lost souls the way home. You really did it."

I kissed him back. "No I didn't, honey. . .we did it."

Before the pickup had rolled to a complete stop, three men huddled together on the wooden porch. Daniel was already beside the driver's window. Bill quickly held up our empty thermos to him.

"Mornin', Daniel. S'pose we could get this filled?"

The man was taken aback by the first words out of Bill's mouth. He had been expecting some special kind of "news."

"Why sure. . .we got plenty inside."

Bill and Daniel went into the mercantile and returned with the thermos full of good black brew. When my partner climbed back in and started up the engine, Daniel figured we weren't going to talk about our night. But the wry little man had to have his own say about it. Arms folded on the vehicle's window frame, he closed in face to face with Bill.

"Now. . .the way I sees it, you folks don't wanna brag none 'bout watcha done down there last night an' that's just fine by me. You bein' mountain an' all that's right understandable. But me now, I gotta get somethin' off my chest." A sparkle winked in his eye. "I couldn't help m'self. No sirree, it was just too temptin'. I done drove down there last night an' watched the whole thing. Yes sirree, dangdest thing I ev'r saw too. Yep, ol' Daniel done seen it all."

"You did, did you," Bill grinned.

"Yep! An' if you an' that fine little woman of yours ever gets up this way again someday, why. . .you just might hear of some tale 'bout how two young whippersnappers come through here one time an' sent them ghosts apackin'!"

"Yeah, maybe we'll hear about that one someday, Daniel, maybe we will."

The old sourdough winked, patted Bill's shoulder and wished us a safe journey home. As we passed the mercantile, three more men waved us a friendly farewell, their faces grinning from ear-to-ear, anxious to gather 'round the ol' potbelly for the telling and retelling of a brand new ghost story. . .one that had an amazin' endin'. . .one that really was God's own truth.

A Sound of Crying on Thunder Mountain

Driving home from that first encounter in Black Wolf Canyon, our spirits were soaring as high as they could fly without leaving their bounded confinements. We were full of a new type of high exhilaration—one that came naturally from helping another in need. And we had helped thirty such souls. We had helped thirty souls find their way home. We weren't prideful or puffed up with inflated egos at our grand success; we were more in awestruck wonder at the entire scenario— how our spirits had orchestrated our ultimate connection with destiny. And we were left with the beautiful residual feelings that remain after one has participated in carrying out their spirit's purpose. We were so very happy. Feelings of our deep love for one another radiated from our cores like rays from a mid-summer sun.

We were light-hearted as we journeyed back home. We laughed about the "little woman" episode and how irritated it had gotten me. Now it seemed so foolish and inconsequential. Looking back on events with the light of hindsight always did diminish things like that and this seemed even more minimized.

We talked about the sourdoughs we'd met and, yes, didn't they seem to have the idyllic mountain spot. Their lives were so uncomplicated by society's pressures and demands. They had the perfect blend of solitude, nature and like-minded neighbors.

We spoke of different aspects of the manifestation and the various factors of the encounter itself. We analyzed and intellectualized over it, especially the part when I'd seemed to have drawn a blank in procedure. Although I now laughed over how I had initially made such a ridiculous attempt to get the leader's attention, the matter was gravely serious and I knew that. We chalked it up to stage fright and I expressed my hope that I'd never experience the dreadful phenomenon again. We both commented on the total surprise of seeing the other spirits manifest within the portal—that was a probability I hadn't been briefed on and we wondered how many more unfamiliar aspects we were going to be presented with in the future. At least, we concluded, it was certainly going to keep our work interesting and we foresaw much valuable learning coming up.

Lastly, we chuckled over Daniel's uncontrollable curiosity. We wondered just how much he actually understood seeing that all the encounter conversations took place on another level and he couldn't hear the spirits as we did. Yet I suppose the sequence of events he'd viewed had made it all clear enough. We envisioned the four men as they revelled in the colorful yarn of their new ghost tale. It was a happy thought to finalize a story that had a happy ending.

Most of all, I could now think of my sweet No-Eyes without grief clutching my heart. Now she seemed more touchable to me—now I realized just how close she really was. And that definitely made me feel good—so good.

When we got home, we didn't tell the girls about our unusual trip. We told them we had a good time and how happy I was that Dad had come up with the idea. They were concerned if my sorrow was still as bad. And they were ecstatic to know it wasn't because when mom hurt—they hurt. That's the way a strong family bond works. Each member possessed total empathy for the other, but, when it worked for happiness, it was a beautiful feeling shared.

During the ensuing week, Bill and I could hardly keep reins on the heightened excitement that pulsed within our yearning spirits. We had tasted but a drop from the bottomless well that contained our new work, and our spirits were thirsting for more—and soon. Both Brian Many Heart and No-Eyes had tried to convince the skeptical student of the work's contagion factor. . .I didn't believe it could happen, at least certainly not with me. . .but now. . .I believe. I believe! It *was* true. They *had* been right. *Nothing* is more spiritually important than helping lost souls find their way home.

So during the evenings, long after we were certain the girls were asleep, we'd speak of our new work. We plotted and planned as the excitement grew. I took out my notes that I'd made from the visionary's lessons and we'd review the cases she informed me about. Bill pulled out the state map and the raised-elevation plastic one so our course could be outlined with logic. We not only had to judge the possible difficulties of each encounter case, we also had to figure in the affecting travel factors of the mountains, such as snowmelt, elevation, accessibility, distance, weather, etc. Certain locales could only be ventured through during the mid-summer months due to late pass openings and then early fall snowfall which closed them again for the season. Our work was cut out for us.

With the kerosene lamp burning low on the kitchen table, I quickly scanned No-Eyes' list.

"At least none of these have *thirty* to deal with," I breathed in relief.

Bill agreed with my sentiments. "That was really getting our feet wet. No-Eyes never did like pussyfooting around when there was a job to do."

I eyed him sarcastically. "Tell me about it." Then my attention returned to the notebook, then I craned my neck to see the map.

"Show me where Thunder Mountain is. I never heard of it."

"I have," he said, searching near the top. "I think it's up north near the Medicine Bow Range by Wyoming." His finger stabbed at the worn paper. "Here it is."

I studied the location.

"Which one is that?" he asked.

"The kid. I figured that after doing thirty, we'd go back to something a little more our speed. Think we can handle a crying kid?"

He grinned. "Can't exactly say you haven't had any experience in that department." He nodded. "We'll do that one next. When do you think?"

I glanced up at the wall calendar. "Saturday?"

"This coming Saturday?"

I nodded.

A frown furrowed his brow.

"What's the matter, don't you think we're ready?"

"That's not my question. Didn't that one have some sort of weather factor attached to it?"

I thought it had, but double checked anyway. "Yeah, the kid's only heard on stormy nights."

His straight teeth gleamed in the light of the oil lamp. "According to the weatherman there's a front moving through.

Can't do any better than that." He folded up the map. "Let's hope it holds."

I sighed in playfulness. "Sure hope I don't have to do my Rain Dance—all that chanting and stomping around gets so tiring."

"Save your energy; you're going to need it." And he blew out the flame.

When we awoke Saturday morning, a pearly grey cloak covered Father Sky. It shrouded our bedroom and cast a dreariness about the panelled walls. I had opened my eyes only to quickly shut them again. Turning over to my slumbering mate, I snuggled tightly into his warmness and entwined my legs around his.

"What do you think you're doing?" came the very awake voice.

"Shhh. You're supposed to be asleep," I whispered.

"Oh really? Isn't there a special little something on your mind this morning?"

"Uh-huh."

"Well?"

"Shhh! I don't want the girls to wake up yet." My foot played with his.

"Oh-ohhh. Why do I get the feeling you're not thinking what I thought you were thinking?"

I nuzzled his neck. "I don't know. What did you think I was thinking?"

"Thunder Mountain? The *kid?*"

I sprang up. "Oh my God! I forgot all about it! I can't believe I actually forgot it!"

He laughed and pulled me back down. "Believe it. So tell me. . .what were you thinking about? I think I'd like to hear about that."

I grinned. "Yeah, I bet you would, but we've got work to do."

He let a low groan escape. "Happened again, didn't it?"

"What happened again?"

He winked. "Another *kid* interrupting business."

Playfully I slapped at his arm. "*You* can't complain, Romeo. C'mon, we've got some traveling to do."

We quickly dressed and informed our girls that we'd be gone again and that Robin would keep an eye on them. They naturally assumed we were going on another one of our frequent "land hunting" trips. They didn't come right out and ask; nor did we volunteer otherwise. In a manner of speaking, these new journeys were a combination of two purposes. Most of the regions we'd be traveling through were new to us and not only were we going into these areas to assist spirits, we were also presented with the golden opportunity to discover land that felt harmonious with our own spirits. Although Brian Many Heart had revealed the National Forest our sacred land was located in, we still had the free will to choose another. Our ultimate destination was completely up to us. When the determining factor of time made the move possible, we could literally go wherever we felt we belonged.

After making sure the girls understood their instructions and Robin had safely arrived, we were on the road to our second encounter.

We headed north.

The sky hung low and its ceiling was roiling with gently tumbling clouds. Along the roadside, the woods held their breath in high anticipation of the approaching storm. Wee four-leggeds skittered nervously about in the tense atmosphere. Nature awaited that which was in the wind.

I happened to glance down at the pickup's gauges.

"Better slow down," I cautioned.

The driver instinctively checked the side mirror for a State Trooper. Then he looked down at the dials.

"What do you mean? I'm only doing. . .damn!" he cussed, striking the steering wheel in frustration. "Now what?" The speedometer needle had fallen to zero. It had died.

Bill eased onto the shoulder and let the engine idle. He looked at me in exasperation. "We just got this out of the garage with a new transmission. I'm not going another mile until I know if we'll be all right." His grey eyes bored through mine. "Let me talk to him."

This request wasn't a request at all; it was an order.

I sighed and looked away into the dense woodlands. After a moment or two I turned back. "He's not around right now."

"How convenient, how friggin' convenient," he sneered in disgust. "Then *get* me someone who knows about engine mechanics, preferably *this* engine. Get me an answer or we're turning back right now."

"Honey. . ." I tried.

"I want an *answer*. Is this old engine going to make it without falling apart or what?"

Silence.

Waiting.

"We're okay. It'll be fine."

"You sure about that?"

"Yes."

Grumbling beneath his breath, he shoved the gear in place and pulled back onto the road. Checking the speedometer again, he complained. "This is so damned ridiculous trying to push this thing around these mountains."

And it was ridiculous. Half the time when we'd climb a particularly steep Pass we'd sit inside and silently say, "C'mon Betsy, I know you can, I know you can." And under the hood, the old woman of an engine would be huffing, "I know I can, I know I can."

My hand gently rested on Bill's arm. "Hon? Let's go back."

Eyes left the road a second. "You having doubts about your source?"

"Oh no! But I know you're not totally comfortable with it today. Why don't we just turn around and reschedule this one?"

He adamantly shook his head. "No deal. They said we'd be all right and I go with that. You said you were sure. Besides, the weather's cooperating today. Who knows when that factor will be right again?" He paused a moment. "You were sure of your answer."

"I'm sure."

"Then we go on."

The situation was frequently frustrating. Figuratively speaking, it was tough keeping the vehicle going with Band-Aids and quarts of Geritol. Yet, when the chips were all down, if we were meant to make a particular journey, things stayed glued together for it.

We drove for a long while in silence.

Finally my companion rubbed my knee and spoke. "You hungry?"

"Starving. I though we were going right to Godmother's after we left the house."

"I wanted to cover some ground first. There's a little town up ahead. I'll cruise through while you check it out."

"Sounds good to me."

As was our routine procedure when passing through new towns, he'd drive through it while I checked out the choice of eateries. He really didn't care all that much where we stopped as long as it was clean. I was the particular one.

We cleared the town limits. "Well? See anything you liked?"

I smiled wide. "Back on our right. A little cafe called Annie's Place."

"Annie's Place it is then," he said, wheeling us around.

Annie's turned out to be the traditional mom an' pop restaurant. Crisp blue and white checked curtains were tied neatly back from the windows. A profusion of living greenery hung in abundance about the place. Wide booths were upholstered in naugahyde the color of deep ocean blue. Dark pine table tops glistened beneath many coats of clear varnish. Milk glass bud vases holding fabric blue columbines centered each table.

We picked a booth and settled in. Bill had a silly grin on his face and I asked him what it was for.

"This place was made for you."

"Yeah," I smiled back, "it's real cozy."

The waitress ambled over to us. She was a rotund yet spry little lady. Her hair was the color of fresh-fallen snow. And I wondered if her name was Mrs. Claus. It wasn't.

"Good morning, folks," she greeted in a chipper tone while placing the menus before us. "I'm Annie an' I own this place. If you don't see what you want on the menu there, just ask an' we'll see if we got it."

We thanked her and attended to the menus.

The woman didn't leave.

We both gave our attention back to her.

"You two on a honeymoon?"

I snickered. Bill laughed.

"We've been married nineteen years," he informed.

The woman's pupils dilated with surprise. "You don't say! My goodness! You don't hear of young folks staying together that long anymore." Her gaze went from one to the other. "Well, you certainly look younger than you are, I guess." She hesitated a moment by placing the end of her pencil to her cheek. "Tell you what. You pick out what you want on that menu an' it's on the house. It'll be Annie's special treat."

We protested the kind offer but Annie wouldn't hear of it.

"Now this is my place an' Annie gets what Annie wants. Hear me?"

We eyed each other and graciously gave in to our hostess.

She beamed with pleasure. "Good!" Then, "You two aren't from around here, are you?"

We shook our heads.

"We're from Woodland Park," I informed.

"I know where that is. . .nice spot. What brings you way up here on a dreary day like this?"

Bill took that one. "We've been doing a little weekend jaunting around the state. This time we headed north."

The woman nodded knowingly. "It's always nice to get away from the kids once in a while, isn't it?"

"How'd you know we had kids?" I asked.

The bright sky-blue eyes twinkled. The voice lowered. "Ohhh, Annie has ways of knowing things about folks who come in here. I seen plenty of people come an' go. After a while you just get real handy at reading them, that's all. Now," she said, tapping the menu with her pencil, "you decide what you want an' it's on me. I won't keep you any longer." She waited for our decisions.

When Annie brought the steaming food, she bent down low to speak to us. Ample breasts nearly touching the table and ring-bedecked fingers splayed on the surface, she whispered, "You two enjoy your breakfast and when you're done, Annie's gonna tell what else she knows about you." And she disappeared into the kitchen to join Mr. Claus.

As we ate, we kept the cryptic statement well in mind and refrained from talking about ourselves in any way or our intended mission. Annie frequently passed our booth while taking care of her other patrons, and we were cautious not to unintentionally reveal any little tidbits she could pick up on. We occupied our time by immersing ourselves in the local paper. Bits and pieces of local customers' conversations could be heard. Both clearly attested to the usual small town goings-on. Rumors of town government corruption or conflict of interest with city council members. Mayor recalls. Tax complaints. Grumblings about construction expansion. It was the same in most all the mountain towns we'd been through.

Finally Annie returned. "I see you're finished."

"Yes," I said, "give my compliments to the cook—everything was delicious."

Bill reinforced my sentiments.

The woman beamed. "Wanna hear it now?"

"Sure," I said, sliding over in the seat to make room for her.

Annie squeezed all of herself in.

"Now," she began softly, looking first at me, "You got a lotta Indian in you."

I furtively eyed Bill. That fact certainly didn't take a psychic to perceive, I thought. But Annie had only begun.

"Now I don't say that just because you got that feather in that long hair of yours or 'cause you're wearing a conch belt an' them beaded moccasins of yours." The head shook. "Nope.

That's not why I say that at all. Anybody can dress like that. That stuff's just on the outside an' Annie don't pay no mind to the external dressings. Annie looks elsewhere. See. . .it's all in the way you walked in here. . .the carriage and the style."

I must have frowned.

"Oh yes!" she emphasized. "Everybody's got their own special walk an' l can tell more than people think by observing that."

I grinned at her. "So? Go on. How did I walk?"

"See! You don't even realize how you walk, do you?"

"I guess not," I said, smiling in amusement at the jovial woman beside me.

"Ohhh, but others can see the difference. You know people walk their own way too, but you never realize you got one also. Anyway, you walked in here like you're used to really *feeling* what you set your feet on. There was real grace to it."

I looked to Bill in question—for verification.

He pursed his lips and nodded. "She's right. You do walk like that."

"I do?"

Annie slapped my arm and chuckled. "See? You didn't even know it. And I'll tell you what," she whispered, "you two get real fey at reading each other."

Now it was Bill's turn to frown. "Don't tell me you got that from how we walk."

"I told you, I just got real good at reading folks. Now you," she said, pointing a pudgy finger at Bill, "you are the anchoring aspect here. You balance the impulsiveness of your wife. Now by 'impulsiveness' I mean her tendency to overdo at times. You're the protector and regulator. You both have analytical minds and don't hold to illogical thought from others. Most of the time you're on the same wavelength and know what the other's thinking or going to say."

My eyes sparkled. "That's incredible. How'd you know all that?"

"And you're happily married too. You're more like good friends. I know all that 'cause I read folks, remember?"

She "reads" a lot more than that, I thought.

"You're quite an extraordinary lady," Bill complimented.

Annie simply waved her hand at him. "Nonsense. Anybody can do that sort of thing."

And that, I knew wasn't true at all. Only an experienced sensitive could've picked up on all she had.

"Well, it's certainly been interesting," I said, reaching for my jacket.

The lady took the cue and squeezed back out. "You folks have a nice trip, you hear?"

"We will," I said.

Mrs. Claus wrinkled her nose. "Nasty weather, though. But then again, some folks *prefer* this rain."

That last statement didn't slip by us. We again thanked Annie for her generosity and told her to give our praises to the cook. As we left, I tried to make conscious note of the way I walked.

Bill nudged me forward. "Whatever you're doing I wish you wouldn't. . .you're waddling like a duck!"

I sighed and walked out the door.

After we cleared the town, we discussed our unusual meal at Annie's Place. It was clearly evident that the woman was a sensitive.

"Did you happen to notice her jewelry?" I asked.

"It wasn't exactly hard to miss. The ankh pendant and moon crescent earrings were rather obvious. Know what?"

"What?"

"Our Mrs. Claus is an astrologer. I bet she's worked up hundreds of charts. That's how come she's so precise. Even her choice of terms pointed to that."

"Yeah. Words like 'tendency' and 'aspects' aren't exactly choices your average person makes use of."

"Huh, she sure was some fine little lady."

Silence.

"Now what're you thinking?"

"You tell me."

"You're wondering if she knew where we were going."

I smiled. "And why should I be wondering that?"

"Because of what she said about some folks preferring the rain."

I didn't have to tell him he was right. "Well? Think she knew?"

"Only if she was aware of the kid's story."

"Somebody like her would've heard of something like that. Sensitives are always aware of those unusual things."

"Then she knew."

Silence.

I slouched down in the seat. In the sky, low dark clouds hung above us like great clumps of grapes. The wind kicked up and hard drops of rain began splattering on the windshield.

Bill started the heater up and the warmth and the hum of it was soothing. The wipers beat out a mesmerizing chant. I glanced out the side window.

"How come it's so flat around here?"

"Thunder Mountain is a ways off yet."

My eyes drooped.

"Why don't you snooze a while," he suggested. "There's nothing to see through this rain anyway."

"No, I'll keep you company," I said, trying to ignore the drowsiness the heater caused.

The driver pulled my head down to his lap. "Why fight it? You'll be asleep sitting up in two minutes anyway."

And I didn't fight it. I let the hypnotic hum and the blanketing warmth lull me off to Never-Never Land. I fell asleep to the monotonous thrump-thrump of the wipers.

When I awoke, the wipers were silent. The sun was still hidden beneath the whitewashed day. I groaned as I straightened up and looked about. The driver greeted me.

"Hi, Sleepyhead. You stiff?"

"Just getting old. Where are we anyway?"

"Getting there. We've just begun to climb. You've got your trees back again."

We were ascending into a different zone and the roadsides were now heavily wooded. Thick forests spread out on either side of us.

"This is real nice," I said, peering around.

"I've got to stop pretty soon an' stretch," he complained while arching his tight back.

"Want to pull over and I'll give you a rubdown? You could stretch out on the bed and I could massage it for you."

"No, there's some kind of town right up ahead. It's nothing more than a speck on the map, but I thought we'd get out for coffee and a roll or something. . .maybe walk around a little. I just need to get out of this lopsided seat for a while."

The "town" turned out to be all of seven buildings in the middle of the woods. The single eatery was nothing more than a tiny diner, but beat-up pickups crowded the parking area in front. It was obviously a popular place. At four in the afternoon, the busyness of it was somewhat unexpected.

We entered the greasy spoon and were immediately met by cold stares. The noisy buzz of conversation halted. The place was packed in like sardines. Not a booth was available, nor were there two side by side stools open at the long counter. Something else bothered me. . .the patrons were all men.

I felt my escort's arm tighten protectively about my waist.

A burly man at the counter glared at us, stood and slid his plate over.

"You folks can sit here," he mumbled. "We all kinda take this place over 'bout this time of day."

We thanked the man and proceeded to wedge ourselves onto the narrowly-spaced perches.

Conversations around us hummed again. Soon they had ascended into a virtual din. We were soon forgotten.

A wiry waitress made her appearance and slapped two dog-eared menus before us.

"I'm a mite busy, folks, but I'll try an' get to ya in a sec." Then she vanished from our sights as she attended to a booth behind us.

Bill rolled his eyes.

The waitress had been a classic example of the typical scatterbrain. Short, bleached hair fuzzed in semi-curls around her face. Fake eyelashes, reminding me of Daddy-longlegs, rimmed the big green eyes, and what made the finishing character touch complete was the bright pink lips that moved nonstop as the bubble gum went crack and snap. I knew my distinguished mate was not entirely amused.

When the flighty woman returned, my knee casually nudged Bill's. He placed the order with finesse and we waited. . .and waited.

"So!" came the unexpected voice that shrilled in Bill's ear like the sound of a child's first violin lesson.

My partner started and turned from our private conversation.

The woman, elbows on the counter, was nearly nose to nose with him.

"So!" she repeated. "Where're you guys from?" Snap, snap. "Whatcha doin' here?" Crack, crack. "Name's Kari. What's yours?" Crack-snap. "Ya stayin' here?"

I increased the pressure of my knee to his while he replied to the rude woman.

"Woodland Park, passing through, Bill and no."

Kari's head recoiled back and the eyelashes stuck to her upper lid in surprise.

"Huh? Whadya say?"

"I answered your questions, Kari," he said with more composure than I expected.

"Oh! Oh yeah." Chomp, chomp. Crack-pop.

Then the bell dinged and she sped away for our order.

While we ate, our appetites diminished by leaps and bounds—not because the food was all that inedible, but because Bill was becoming increasingly angered and I was becoming increasingly upset with his anger. Behind us, the crowd of burly lumberjacks were cracking off-color jokes in a bawdy manner.

My partner was doing a slow burn. Finally he slowly swiveled himself around to glare at them and I was fearful he'd bitten off more than he could chew. These weren't some mild-mannered accountants; they were big hunks of solid muscle.

I tapped my mate's shoulder. "Honey?" I said aloud.

He didn't stir a hair.

"Honey?"

The stool slowly pivoted around. The man's face was livid. I whispered. "It's okay! This is their place."

"Well you'd think they'd at least have a little respect for a *lady* being present!" His tone rose. "You think they'd have some *manners!*"

The crowd silenced.

My scalp crawled.

Bill rotated himself again to glare at them.

They glared back.

I swallowed hard.

Then the men decided to return to their jokes—only quieter. I sighed a great breath of relief.

Bill's fuse was ready to explode. He turned back around to the counter and was again face to face with Kari.

"So!" Snap-snap-crack!

I stepped on Bill's boot in a warning signal for him to maintain his composure.

"How'd ya like the rolls? Ain't they somethin'? Ever taste anything like 'em in your life?" Chomp-pop.

"Fine, yes, no."

The waitress giggled. "Mister, you are so funny!"

Quickly I jumped in to get the woman out of Bill's flushed face.

"Kari?"

The waitress looked at me as though she'd just discovered I was there. "Yeah?"

"How long have you been here?"

The woman was thrown off guard by the question. She spun to look for someone behind her then turned back with fingers spread out on her bodice.

"Who, me?"

I smiled and nodded.

Kari was visibly flattered that someone had asked something about her private life. A chewed-up finger nail pressed to the chin. Eyes rolled up to the ceiling as if her answer was written there.

"Ohhh, let's see now. if you count the months I spent with that no good. . ." She flushed and flapped her hand at me. "Well," she giggled, "I s'pose that don't count 'cause now I live down the road aways with somebody else." She hemhawed a bit more. "But if you count the months I worked as a. . ."

I didn't especially want to know what else she had worked as. "Kari," I cut off, "I just wanted to know how long you worked here at the diner."

"Oh yeah." The woman then proceeded to count on her fingertips while making the high mathematical computation. When our eyes met again, hers were sparkling. "I been at this place for almost sixteen months now."

Long enough, I thought. Then I crooked my finger for her to lean closer.

Kari, anticipating a dark secret, bent low over the counter.

My voice was purposely kept low. "Have you ever heard a story about a little kid heard crying in the woods around here?"

I hadn't realized that I'd just opened a smelly can of worms. Kari reacted with absolute fear. She froze and looked as shocked as if I'd just set a ticking explosive between us. The eyes rounded. Mouth gaped open. A pink wad fell onto the counter. Without ungluing her eyes from mine, her hand, robot-like, picked up the goo and replaced it back into her mouth. Eyes shifted suspiciously to either side of me as they checked out and locked on those of the silent crowd at my back.

Finally the woman's mouth defrosted. "No, ma'am! I ain't *never* heard of *no* tale like *that* before!"

She was lying.

I nearly winced in pain as a heavy cowboy boot rocked hard over the soft toe of my moccasin.

"Well," I said, forcing cheeriness, "I guess I heard wrong then."

Kari's head bobbed. "Guess ya did." Snap-pop.

A chilling blast of icy air had settled within the little diner. Kari had scuttled off into the kitchen and the customers were eerily silent. A bearded face leered out at us from behind the clouded window of the kitchen door.

In a snap, the waitress was back. Our check was slapped down on the counter.

"That'll be three twenty-seven an' have a nice day."

We certainly knew when we weren't wanted around any more. Bill placed a five dollar bill beneath his cup and told the woman to keep the change. I noticed the cook was still peering at us. He looked as though he wanted nothing more than to knock our big busy-body noses down to size.

As we were leaving, Bill held the door for me and loudly suggested that his gullible wife not be so eager to listen to rumors anymore, and we had better get going because we had a long way to go yet today. For some reason that I couldn't quite put my finger on, the cab of ol' Betsy sure gave me a warm sense of security.

The engine started up and the wipers swished away the drizzle that had begun. The driver eased out onto the deserted mountain road. In the diner window, heads bobbed to take note of our direction.

I shivered.

"You cold?" Bill asked, sliding the heat lever to HIGH.

"Yes, a little bit from the weather and a *lot* from that diner."

He shook his head. "It's been a long time since we've felt that kind of cold. You see the face on that cook?"

I rolled my eyes. "Jesus, how could I not! He had those crazy eyes we come across once in a while."

Thunder rumbled in the distance.

"Well," he soothed, rubbing my leg, "we're out of there now so you can relax."

I exhaled a long breath of relief. "Do we have to come back through here?"

"Nah, we can take another way home—it's a little out of our way but so what?"

Snuggling over beside him, I now wondered about the purpose of our trip.

"Honey?"

"Mmmm."

"We didn't get any information in there. How are we going to know where to look for the kid?"

"Good question. Guess we'll just have to work on that one. In the meantime, we'll have to do some fancy footwork."

I had secretly been hoping that the trip would be cancelled after striking out at the diner. Without specific information on where the apparition manifested, our mission was nearly impossible. Now his last comment led me to think otherwise.

"What's that supposed to mean?"

"We need to do some backtracking on this one."

"Explain."

"You saw those people back there. There's no way they'd admit to the story. There's also no way they want anybody fooling around with it either."

"What exactly are you saying with all this?"

"I'm saying that they don't want their small ghost disturbed."

"*Their* ghost?"

"Sure."

"Nobody *owns* a ghost—a spirit."

A brow arched. "You want to go back and tell that to them?"

"No thanks." I thought about what he had said and then mentally reviewed the entire incident.

"That's crazy. . .no, that's sick. Why would they care about what we did?"

"Can't you guess?"

"I'm afraid to."

"Obviously they like having him around—you know, local color and all that junk."

"Oh God, I think I smell trouble."

"That's why we'll go out of our way to throw them off our track. We'll drive out a long way and then double back after dark."

I didn't care for the smell of this wonderful plan. "Let's just keep right on driving until we hit home."

His mouth dropped. "What? You suddenly getting cold feet?" Chicken sounds squawked in my ear.

"That's not funny. I'm just not at all thrilled with the vision of meeting up with any of those lumberjacks out here after dark. Spirits are one thing, but lugs with mentalities like that are another."

He grinned. "The equalizer's riding along in the back."

That wasn't exactly comforting either. "Oh great. Now we're going to play Make My Day! No thanks, Pale Rider, no thanks."

He tried to smooth it over. "It's going to be okay. I was just kidding about the gun."

Silence.

"Babe?"

"How far do you figure we'll need to go?"

"Depends. I'll know when it's time to turn around."

"I hope so."

The heater was warm; the hum of it mixing with the metered

wiper sounds began to lull me again. I closed my eyes. Soon my head jerked. I slid down in the seat and drifted off.

I was walking in a strange nightwood. The creature sounds frightened me. Underbrush rustled and overhead branches wavered. Furtively did I place each footfall. I didn't want to be heard. I knew not why, only that a dark presence was felt. It gave me gooseflesh. I only knew that I had to hide because it was tracking me. No untoward sound signaled my senses, but my psyche had perceived its close presence. I turned. Two bulbous eyes glowed yellow out of the night's Stygian blackness. They were floating. . .advancing. I crouched low in the brush. They silently passed me by and were gone. When I stood, they were back, retracing their path to me. Closer. . .they were getting closer. My mouth opened in a scream—no sound emitted.

"*Honey!*" Bill hollered while shaking me.

My eyes flew open and I jerked upright. I felt disoriented.

"You all right?"

I glanced about the darkness and nodded.

"Must've been some bad dream. You were twitching and moaning so much I thought I'd better wake you. What were you dreaming about?"

"Eyes. Great yellow eyes. They were following me through this pitch black forest and I couldn't seem to hide from them. Well, I did manage to hide, but then they knew and returned." I rubbed at my eyes. "Weird thing about them was they were just floating and sort of bobbing all by themselves."

"Interesting."

When I looked to the driver, his expression scared me. "What do you think it meant?"

"I don't have to think—I know. Your 'eyes' are still with you."

What did he mean by that?

He inclined his head to the passenger side mirror. "See for yourself."

I frowned at him in curiosity then leaned over the seat to peer into the mirror. I sucked in my breath.

"That's them! That's *them!*"

"Well, 'them' have been with us practically all the way."

At first I didn't make the connection. Then, as the cobwebs cleared from my drowsy state, it hit with full force.

"Since we left the diner?"

"You got it."

I couldn't believe that. "But that doesn't mean we're being followed!"

"Doesn't it? Maybe it means we're being cordially escorted off the mountain then."

"Or maybe it means we're not the only vehicle taking this road—it *is* the only one through Thunder Mountain, you know."

"I know that, but while you were off in the Land of Nod, I tested that vehicle. If I let up on the gas to give it room to pass—it slowed. If I punched it up to sixty—it stayed with me. Honey, that guy wants to stay right where he is. . .following us."

"Ohhh God. Now what?" I worried, staring into the eyes of the mirror.

"Like I said before, we go out of our way then backtrack after. . ."

"STOP!" I screamed.

The truck swerved with the sudden outburst.

"JESUS! Don't ever do that again! We almost went off the road!"

That hadn't bothered me because I was now preoccupied with a far greater concern.

"Did you *feel* that? Did you *feel* that back there?"

"Yes I felt it, but little good it's doing. That four-wheel isn't about to let us stop."

It was very black out. Although it had stopped raining, the storm clouds still obliterated the sky light. The high pines that swayed along the roadside all looked the same—there were not outstanding landmarks to distinguish the spot and guide us by. My spirits fell when I realized there'd be no backtracking this night. There'd be no encounter. There'd be no one helping the little crying spirit this night.

The blinding glare from the floating eyes reflected in the mirror. I squinted and moved closer to the driver. Maybe it was just as well, I thought. Things hadn't started out on the right foot from the beginning. I should have read more into the broken speedometer than I did. But we weren't warned to turn back at that point—we were simply told that the vehicle would be all right. Was that a contradiction? Then and there I decided it'd be best if we just went home. And that conviction felt very good because there was no way I was going to take a chance on bumping into angry lumberjacks waiting to ambush us in those deep woods. With the comforting thought of leaving all those terrors behind, I smiled to myself.

"What's the smug grin for?"

I rested my head on his shoulder. "Oh I was just thinking how nice it'll be to get home."

"Yeah. I'm looking forward to leaving all this behind too. Funny," he mused, "No-Eyes told you about this one and we've had nothing but hassles with it."

"So what about it?"

Silence. He was deeply pensive.

"Hon? What about it?"

He shrugged. "Nothing, I guess."

"Maybe the timing was off."

"Maybe," he said, sounding unconvinced. . .more like he'd left much of his thoughts unsaid.

We drove for a while in silence, each thinking thoughts about the day and how it would end—endings that ultimately were comprised of completely different scenarios.

The truck slowed and eased over into a rest stop clearing.

"Why are we stopping?"

"Gotta stretch."

I stiffly climbed out and glanced back up the road. It was deserted.

"They've been gone for quite a while," Bill informed.

"Whew! That was some weird experience. Now they're probably waiting back there for us just to be sure." I chuckled with the visual thought of it.

"I doubt it," came the unexpected comment as we picked our way over to the picnic table.

I watched in the bad lighting as my companion did some stretching exercises.

"Why'd you say that?"

"Because they're not the type. Quite frankly, I think they'd wet their pants to be face-to-face with their ghost."

"You think they're scared? You're kidding!"

"No I'm not. Just because they like the idea of it doesn't mean they relish *seeing* it. I bet you every last one of them is home right now watching television and drinking beer."

"And they're not waiting for us?"

"Nope. I told you, they're not the type. Big muscles and mean looks are exterior dressing. Remember what Annie said about that?"

"Yeah, but. . ."

"No buts about it. I'd be willing to bet they wouldn't go anywhere near those woods on a rainy night."

Moonlight washed over us.

"It's not raining," I said, gazing up into the sudden cloud break.

Sighing a finality to the activity, Bill sauntered over to the table and lay on its uneven boards. He watched the patterns of shifting clouds beneath the silver orb.

"Look," he pointed to the sky, "thunderheads. Storm's not over yet."

In the milky light, rising shadows were outlined. It looked like volcano plumes of ash.

My mate mumbled.

"Say what?"

"I said the gods are with us."

A chill shuddered through me. Suddenly I didn't feel all that comfy as before.

"Explain," I ordered.

"What's to explain? By the way those babies up there are spreading, we'll be able to go back soon."

I couldn't believe my ears. My stomach began churning with the dreadful possibility that he didn't mean what I hoped he'd meant.

"Back *home*, right?"

"No Babe. . .back *there*."

"I thought we were going *home!* I thought because of all the hassles we were *leaving* this one."

His head shot up to see me better. The disappointed tone of my voice surprised him.

"I never said that. Where'd you get that idea?"

"Well I. . .those *men*. . .the eyes, the headlights."

He sat up and wrapped his arm around my shoulders. "I don't know how it happened, but somewhere along the line we got off the same wavelength. When did we talk about not doing this one? Did I miss something or give you the wrong impression?"

"Remember when I smiled and you asked me what the grin was for?"

"Yeah."

"And then I said because it'd be nice to get home. But then you *agreed*. You said that you were looking forward to leaving all this behind too!"

"Oh Honey," he soothed, squeezing my shoulder. "I meant *after* we're done."

I jerked my shoulder away. "Well dammit! You didn't *say* that."

"I'm sorry. I didn't know what you were thinking."

Silence. He was right and I was terribly wrong. I had been guilty of the same thing I was accusing him of. I had changed the plan and forgotten to voice that one-sided decision. Not only that, but I was also guilty of the unaware act of assuming. I had not sought verification for the assumption that was in error. How could I have been so utterly stupid? I leaned back into his chest.

"I'm sorry. It's all my fault. I guess I'm the one who's guilty of not saying what was meant. We played word games and we didn't even know we were doing it."

He kissed me. "Are you scared?"

"Yes."

"Of those men?"

I shrugged my shoulders with uncertainty. "I don't know. What you said about them not being the type made sense. I think that whole diner incident unnerved me."

"Probably more than both of us realized."

A long silence passed between us.

"Babe?"

"Mmmm."

"I'll take you home if this is really bothering you."

"You will?"

He smiled. "You know I'd never force you to do something you're scared to do."

"Yeah. . .I know."

"So what'll it be. . .the kid or home?"

"I don't know," I whispered dejectedly. "I know it sounds silly and I'm probably being fickle about it, but I can't decide. Half of me is scared stiff to go back, and the thought of home sounds so warm and safe. Then half of me tugs the other way—the thought of home sounds so chicken while the kid seems right. I guess I'm very confused right now."

He attempted to clarify the confusion. "What part of you wants to go home?" he softly inquired.

"I do. . .me."

"And?"

"And what part of me wants to go ahead with it? My spirit does. I can feel how badly it wants to do that."

He prompted further. "So. . .which wins? Which do you feel is dominant?"

I sheepishly grinned. "The *me* is very strong too."

"That's not what I asked," he emphasized with a gently raised brow.

The powerful Mind versus Spirit tug of war pulled at my

heart. What did my *heart* want? And that didn't even consider debate. The heart gave judgment and proclaimed the victor.

"We go," I whispered.

He whispered back. "Go where, Honey?"

My eyes solidly locked on his. "Go back."

The moon vanished. Raindrops sprinkled down from a roiling night sky. And a 1973 pickup swung around on the slick mountain road.

The sprinkles multiplied. Sheets of silver rain blew back and forth before the twin headlight beams. The wipers strained to keep a clear tunnel view. The only sounds heard were the constant thrump-thrump of them and the shushing of the radials through the wetness of the road. We had each given the other some much-needed space to think.

Bill was the first to break the prolonged quietude.

"Having doubts?"

"The time for those has passed. I've made my decision."

"You sure?"

"Yes."

"Just checking."

I looked at him and smiled. "Thanks, I appreciate that."

A few more solemn moments passed before the driver spoke.

"We need to discuss it."

"I know," I said, working my way into the delicate issue. "Why do you think he's crying?"

"How about because he's all alone."

"That's what I was thinking. I also think the actual convincing isn't going to be hard either."

A curious expression crossed his face. "What made you deduce that?"

"He's just a kid, isn't he? I've certainly got lots of experience along those lines."

He laughed freely. "That's gotta be the most hilarious thing you've ever said."

I hadn't thought I'd said anything so hilariously funny. I bristled defensively. "What the hell's so funny?"

"You want to know what's so funny? I'll tell you what's so funny. Ready for this?"

I huffed my reply.

He chuckled again. "This is really incredible. Here we have an entity in total command of it's psychic energies—powerful ones, I might add—and here you calmly sit completely convinced you're going to control it into submission just because it's in the *form* of a child. You think you're going to *mother* it!" His head shook from side to side with the incongruity of it. "You can't even *think* of treating a child spirit like a real kid! Can *our* kids use their minds to move things? To *direct* them?"

"Not yet," I slyly slipped in.

"Granted, Aimee's close, but we're talking about *massive* powers here, not developing ones or the *potential* of them. This is real!"

"Okay, okay, so I don't mother it. I still think it'll take some type of child psychology though."

"That's more like it. It'll all depend on the reason it's bound here. Once we determine that we can go from there."

The headlights reflected off the tall pines that wavered along the roadside like sentinels guarding the child's domain. It gave me a creepy feeling and I feared the sensation came not from nature itself, but rather emitted from the psychic signals of the encounter. My former decision to go back wavered. I was still awfully new at this and wasn't beyond having trepidations.

"I don't see how we're going to find that spot again," I sighed, hoping we wouldn't.

My mate eyed me. "It wasn't raining before either. Wonder if that'll change the vibration now."

"Probably. We probably won't feel it again."

"I don't think we will either."

"And there weren't any outstanding trees or boulders."

"Not that I noticed," he agreed.

"That's a shame," I lied.

"Yep."

The sound of that one word came out in a humorous tone instead of a disappointed one. The man's mouth was compressed in an effort to smother some joke.

"Want to share the funny?"

"Nothing's funny but your nice try at wheedling out of this thing."

"I'm not trying to wheedle out of anything! There's no way for us to find the spot again. Is that my fault?"

"No," he replied behind the suppressed grin that threatened to break loose.

"Therefore, with this rain pouring down, we're not able to pick up on anything either. Right?"

"Right."

"So there you have it. That's the finality of the whole. . ."

The vehicle pulled onto the soggy shoulder. Through the

pelting water, our lights illuminated a numbered post...a mile marker.

"So there you have it," repeated the driver. "If you hadn't been so engrossed in looking in that side mirror at those 'eyes' of yours before, you would've seen the marker pointing the way. Sorry to ruin your evening, but...we're here."

My cold eyes shifted to his. My voice was icy. "You tricked me."

He shut off the headlights and wipers. And resting back against the seat, he lit a cigarette. "No I didn't, Babe, you tricked yourself."

I didn't respond. Instead I watched the rivulets of water that coursed down the windshield. Beyond the glass, the deep woods were nearly as dark as caves. There was little light and I worried about that. It would serve no purpose to voice my new concern. Digging down in my purse, I pulled out the extra set of keys and tossed them over to the driver.

"Better get the raincoats, we're going to need them."

Ducking out into the downpour, he quickly retrieved our equipment from the camper. We donned the ponchos and checked the lantern. With the engine still running for warmth, we spent a long time silently preparing ourselves. Individually, we had to raise our energy levels, strengthen our spiritual power and work to reinforce our protection. Mentally we had to be armed with the weapons of determination, faith and trust. It was a sequential process of powerful visualizations that established the foundation for the higher levels we'd have to build on when the time came.

When I opened my eyes, Bill was still working. While I waited for him, I noticed the rain had let up a little. It was still steady, but wasn't quite as drenching as before. Studying the unfamiliar woods, I tried to get a fix on our starting point. Certain fragments of information speared through my mind. Feelings washed over me.

"Babe?" came the gentle voice beside me. "You ready?"

I indicated that I was. "He's pretty far in," I informed. "He's crying because he feels abandoned. That's what I felt just now—a great pain of abandonment. He's waiting for somebody special to come and help him but we're not them. We may have a big problem here...he's going to fight it."

"Why would he fight our help if that's what he wants?"

"He is not within Trust."

"Did you get any kind of fix on his power capabilities? Does he even know he has any?"

124

My look was cold. "He knows. It's strong. And he uses it."

"Did you get anything else?"

"Just that there've been others who've tried before us."

"And?"

"They failed."

Bill's arms reached out and pulled me into them. We embraced so completely we were lost within the rosy aura of our love. That singular bond would ultimately be the strength—the power—that reinforced everything we would do from here on in.

"Which way?" Bill asked, switching off the engine.

I pointed to our right.

He winked. "Ready?"

I pulled the hood over my head. "Ready."

"Remember," he stressed, "whatever happens, we stay *together*.

That had been one of No-Eyes' cardinal rules. I nodded. "Let's go."

And armed with firm determination, we left the warm and dry cab to pick our way into the cold and wet forest. Holding hands for balance support through the slippery underbrush, our advance was hampered by the strangeness of the area. The pelting rain, although somewhat diminished by the high density of pines, remained a difficult obstacle we had to contend with. Between the rain sounds and the rolling thunder that frequently cracked above us, we had to holler to communicate. The light of the high-beam lantern made valiant efforts to force its illumination through the silver surround that obscured our visibility.

Bill halted to check for vibration aberrations. He spread out his hands then pointed in another direction. We veered off to the left and continued deeper into the depths of Thunder Mountain.

Our progress was painfully slow, but we were encouraged to bravely forge ahead because now the strength of the vibrations intensified with each advancing footfall.

A fallen lodgepole loomed before us to block our path. It rested at an angle on a high boulder and we crouched on hands and knees to crawl beneath it. Now our pant legs were soaked through. When we again stood against the rain, my radar was bleeping at a faster rate and I guided my companion through a stand of old aspens. Ahead of us, the golden beam was lost in the yawning blackness of a ravine. A new sound joined that of the teeming storm. A river coursed down below. Its rushing rain-engorged waters roared in our ears.

We knowingly looked at one another. There was no reason for words to pass between us, for we knew our objective was located on the other side of the raging watercourse. We needed better bearings. To charge pell-mell down the slope could prove to be a very fatal mistake. Rocks loosened by the rain were precarious and unstable.

Bill advanced a couple of steps to shine the light around. He was methodically plotting the best course of descent. Finally he had it mapped out and eased me over to the soft precipice.

"I'm going first," he hollered through the din of the roaring water and storm. Lightning flashed in his face and thunder pealed. "You follow right behind. Try to stay in my footsteps as much as you can."

It was steeper than it had first appeared. And as we descended, I realized that this was not an adventure I would've gone for in the best of weather. I was actually thankful for the darkness and poor visibility, for my ignorance of the dangerous slope served to shroud my potential fear. The handholds—what there were of them—were slippery with soggy lichen. We slipped too many times and proceeded on our bottoms the rest of the way.

Pausing beside the river to catch our breath, we gazed back up the side of the ravine. our trail stood out in stark muddy relief. The lantern beam scanned our path of descent. Disturbed debris threatened to dislodge.

"That's unstable now," Bill warned. "I wouldn't trust it."

I looked up at the mountainside and imagined the entire thing sliding down on us like an avalanche of rocks.

We hurriedly gave our full attention to the river now. We stood beside a tall ponderosa pine and watched as the beam of light weaved back and forth along the bank. Rocks, slimy with thick moss, littered the waters. It was difficult in the bad lighting to tell how deep it was. Bushy willows spread along the mushy ground.

When the sound came, it was barely audible, but it was perceptible enough to give me goosebumps. Without thinking, I grabbed at Bill's poncho and yanked him behind the pine trunk. Milliseconds later, a landslide swept and rumbled past the sheltering tree. Loose stones, rotted logs, bushes, and boulders tumbled into the river while we huddled behind the saving wall. It was over within the flick of a squirrel's tail.

Bill moved his arm around to shine the light. The beam

illuminated our old descent trail—it was gone. All trace of our recent passing had been totally obliterated. Our eyes met to give verification to the sinking feeling we both experienced. Had the child caused the slide to deter us or, more unthinkable, to get rid of us? Had the slide been purposely created to cover our tracks? So we couldn't ever be found?

These were not paranoid thoughts here. We were firmly instructed to think the worst of all situations when dealing with spirits. Their great energies and illogical minds made them potential enemies of the most dangerous kind. It was not paranoid to think the spirit had tried to do us in. We were the enemy.

Scattered movements continued up the ravine as settling occurred. We couldn't chance remaining where we were. If one of the larger boulders broke loose, the pine would tumble like a fragile matchstick and we'd be crushed beneath it.

Cautiously we inched out from our cover and worked our way along the treacherous bank. Newly-fallen debris made the going difficult. We stumbled over to a more stable section and again surveyed a course across the raging waters that would give us the least resistance. It was a hard choice.

Bill pointed. "What do you think?" he bellowed, panning the beam across.

I nodded then anxiously glanced back up behind me.

He was as apprehensive as I was about the possibility of another attempt on our lives. With great wariness, he stepped down into the swirling, cold river. With each step the beam illuminated the waters. Then it went back to me as I took a testing step in response. It was impossible to hold hands while attempting this hazardous crossing. If one lost their balance he'd pull the other down. What we were doing was pure folly. Mountain streams and rivers were dangerous enough in clear, calm weather, but to traverse them during a full-fledged thunderstorm in the dark of night when they're angrily churning and swelling was an act of utter folly. It was the work of fools.

Bill had now managed to clear the halfway point and stood frozen in place while I teetered and advanced through the current by pacing myself with the speed of a snail. We were going to beat this kid with his bag of magic tricks. We were doing okay and I looked up through the rain at my anxiously awaiting partner. I was now halfway. A smile of courage tipped the corner of my lips.

Then, from out of nowhere, the current dashed a log into

me. My legs folded like a floppy rag doll and I went down—completely submerged. I screamed and instinctively thrashed in a futile attempt to get a stronghold on the slippery rocks. I calmed then. Placing each foot securely between streambed rocks, I rose.

Bill was at my side. "You *okay?*" he bellowed.

I nodded. But eyes flared wide in surprise as my skin crawled. They were fixed on something behind Bill. . .they were fixed on a small figure standing at the opposite bank. A twisted smile marred the childlike features.

"Oh. . .my. . .God," I moaned.

Bill's eyes widened and he spun around, saw the child, perceived its power then quickly turned back to me. He noticed that the moisture coursing down my face was more than rainwater—they were tears of frustration.

"We're *going* to beat him!" he shouted at me. "We're going to *win!*"

I blinked away the wetness that'd obscured my vision. I was shivering uncontrollably.

"I'm so cold," I chattered.

In the middle of the rushing river, he embraced me. He kissed me and whispered in my ear. His hands came up to hold my face before his. And his eyes said it all.

I squeezed my eyes tight and desperately worked. I worked to reinforce my end of the tandem power and I worked to strengthen my protection. When I again opened my eyes, the spasmodic shivering had eased to an occasional tremble. I was ready to go on. We both turned to eye the ten-year-old.

The child was shocked to see the two in the water turn to him. He saw the flaming determination that fired in their eyes. He back-pedaled a few steps as the pair made their stumbling way toward the bank. He watched in utter amazement as they crawled up onto the grass and paused to catch their breath. Why were they ignoring him? They should be shaking in fear. Something wasn't quite right and he didn't like it—no, he didn't like it at all. Especially now that the two rose and stood tall together. Especially now as they faced him head on without a hint of fear. He'd have to see if he could change that. Yes, he would definitely change that.

The child's arms shot out before him like spears. The power in his aura flared and spiked.

"Go *back!*" he shouted with hate burning from his eyes.

Silence.

"Go *back!*"

Silence.

The hate-filled eyes glanced above the pair standing beneath the white pine, then the sights returned to the target. He glared hard at them then smiled cruelly.

Like a rifle crack the thick branch above us broke. But instead of fleeing, we darted forward to avoid the plummeting limb. It crashed to the ground with a sickening thud.

The child's menacing grin vanished.

We were closer; we had narrowed the gap between us.

The rain eased into a sprinkle. Quietly I thanked God for that blessing. The thunder rolled over the sky a distance away.

The child looked skyward. He did this more than once before devoting his attention to us. His short arms shot out again like lances. They were stiff with pulsing energy. Fingers splayed at the ends of his small hands.

"DIE!" he hollered at us.

"NO!" we bellowed back as one. Our arms had instinctively shot out before us just as the child's had. I didn't know about Bill, but my arms felt as rigid as newly-forged andirons. Fingers, stiff and trembling with energy, aimed at the child.

Together the trio beneath the wavering pines stood frozen in time. Small arms quivered with pure power while the mind generated its force. Four long arms quivered back while the two minds maintained the counterforce. The eye contact was electrifying.

While I worked to sustain the optimum energy level, something subliminally speared through my consciousness. The child was not as strong as he could be. Did he doubt his power? He was nervous about something. His eyes kept darting up to the sky. Why?

"*Die!*" he bellowed, suddenly breaking the stillness.

"*No!*" I bellowed back. "You almost killed us with that landslide. You tried to kill *me* with the river log! NO! We *won't* die!"

Eyes went to the night sky. "*Leave* me!"

That was definitely a backing-down order. Now he just wanted us to go away. Was that because he knew he no longer had the power to kill if he wished? Did that mean his power had drained? Was he actually helpless and reverting to orders instead of threats? All these options raced through my mind as I wondered about what his source of power was. My question was soon answered.

Distant thunder rumbled. Evergreens dripped down around us. Moonlight spread over the forest floor.

A small head jerked up to see the silver orb that had inched along the treetops.

"Nohhh!" he screamed up at it. "Go *away!*"

We lowered our arms. We wouldn't be needing the extra energy anymore. The storm had passed and had taken the spirit's power source with it. Now we looked upon a defeated child. He had crumbled in a heap and sobbed curses while striking a balled fist at the ground. It was a pitiful sight to see such anger and frustration in one so young.

I stepped forward.

His head shot up. "Stay away!"

"We're here to help you," I softly replied.

Sarcasm dripped from his mouth. "Go earn your badge somewhere else."

I smiled. "Do you know who you are?"

"Dumb question, Lady," he sneered, sitting back on his heels and grinning smugly.

He was fortifying himself with a defensive hardness. I'd have to crack through that to reach the softness I knew lived inside.

Undaunted by the childish ruse, I sat across from him and crossed my legs.

He spied my Indian earrings and chuckled. "We gonna have a big pow-wow now?"

"Maybe," I grinned.

"Go away. I don't want you here. You're just do-gooders like all the rest."

"Oh?" I sparked. "What rest?"

"Them dumb dead guys, that's what rest."

"Dead guys tried to help you? Why?"

"'Cause they was *stupid,* that's why." He spat the words out in disgust. "They came here a long time ago an' tried to take me away with them." He chuckled again. "Boy, they must've thought they was so great, but I showed 'em real good."

"You didn't want to go?"

"Would *you,* Lady?" His brow rose with his cleverness.

It was a clever trick. That one was real good.

"Only when it's my time to go. . .I'd go then."

He frowned.

"Look, son," Bill interjected.

The spirit glared over at him. "I ain't your son. I ain't *nobody's* son."

And that gave us our entry into the boy's desolation of abandonment. Silence permeated the woods while I garnered the required information. Bill remained mute while psychical-ly passing me additional energy.

"Davey," I said.

"Hey! How'd you know my name? Only them dead guys knew that." He looked me up and down. "You ain't dead."

"It doesn't matter how I know your name."

He sighed.

"What matters," I explained, "is what's going on here."

"Nothin's going on here but you creeps nosing in my shit," he barked, still playing at being the tough little man.

Bill jumped in then. "Seems to me you got it all backward. Seems to me, using your own words, *you*, little Buddy, are nosing into *our* shit.This happens to be *our* dimension, in which *you* do not belong."

"Oh yeah?"

"Sorry, but that's the way it is."

"Davey," I said, gently squeezing into the discussion, "what's most important here is the truth. It's really important that we be honest with each other and it's most important that you also be honest with yourself."

"Oh yeah? Who made *you* my mother? Well I'm *sick* of dead guys tellin' me what to do an' now I'm sick of you too. I'm doin' just *fine* where I am. I don't need *nobody!*"

My brow rose. "Who said you did?"

"Well. . ."

"Davey, *do* you need somebody?"

"I don't need nobody!"

"Davey? *Are* you lonely?"

Silence.

"Davey?"

"YES! Yes, I'm lonely! I'm all by myself here!" He broke down and cried.

"You miss your folks. I know that you do."

"They didn't come an' look for me. Why didn't they come instead of them dead guys? I didn't wanna go with them, I wanted to go with my ma an' pa."

"Listen to me, Davey. I'm going to tell you something very important. Will you listen? Just for a bit?"

Silence. He wasn't about to admit he wanted to listen, yet didn't object to me speaking.

"Davey, when you got lost that day so long ago, your folks were very, very worried. It tore them apart not knowing if you were safe or not. They got people to come out in force to look for you. All day and night they searched these woods. For weeks it went on. Until finally they believed the worst and had to stop. Your folks never got over their great loss, Davey. You were the light of their lives. One day, because they were so filled with their grief, they decided they couldn't go on living without you. Do you know what they did?"

No reaction came. Davey remained mute.

"They decided to join you. They did that so you'd all be together as a family again."

I could tell the boy was shaken by what he'd heard, but he maintained his stubbornness.

"That's a lie! That's a damn LIE!"

"No it's not, Davey."

"Is *too!*" he spewed in my face. "If they're dead then where are they? Huh, Lady? Where *are* they?"

The perfect question. And I had the perfect answer to match.

"When they became total spirit and reached their destination, they couldn't find you. They searched and searched for their son but he wasn't anywhere around. So still your folks are very sad because you're not together yet. They're still lonely and miss you very much. Davey," I whispered, "they're not *here* because you're in the wrong place."

"Then they can *come* here. Them dead guys did."

This was a very stubborn child.

"Your folks can't do that. Only certain spirits are permitted to travel between dimensions for reasons like that. Only those who have the job of helping can go from there to here and back. Maybe your folks sent those other dead guys here to get you back to them."

He was thinking about that one. And while I had him thinking and before he could come up with another smart reply, I kept the momentum going. Now I was finding out that it wasn't easy dealing with a hard-nosed smart-mouth.

"Davey, you don't *have* to be lonely—not ever again. You can make your folks so happy by going back." My eyes sparkled then. "Why, you can even *hug* each other again!"

His head raised with the last idea. He sneered. "Boy! You must think I'm some dumb kid. Dead guys don't hug—they can't! Look Lady, in case you haven't noticed lately," he smirked, slicing his hand through me, "dead guys can't *touch* nothin'!"

I smiled. At least he had some facts straight in his head. "Oh, but that's only because we're so different. Doesn't air pass through houses?"

He was thinking.

"How could we breathe if it didn't?" I paused. "Davey, one time, just one time, I hugged a spirit. I was able to do this because a very special lady showed me how. But I do know it's done and it is more beautiful than anything you've ever imagined." I was suddenly filled with deep emotion from the sweet memory of that singular experience.

The boy noticed. "No lie?"

"No lie, Davey."

Silence.

"Would you like to make your folks happy again. . .make *you* happy again?"

"Well. . .yeah!" he squeaked, jumping to his feet.

Bill and I stood.

"Would you like to stop being all alone here?"

"Yeah!"

"You need to go back, Davey." I informed.

"Yeah! I need to go back first, huh?"

I nodded as he looked into our eyes.

"I *wanna* go back an' see my folks. Why, I can see their faces *now!* Can't you just see their faces when they *see* me? I can *surprise* them! Oh BOY! An' we can *really* hug?"

"You can hug all you want," I said behind a beaming smile.

He excitedly paced around. "This is *great! Really* great!" Then the idea really hit home. The child's eyes brightened with the sudden realization. "*I'm* going *home!*" he proudly boasted, "I'm *really* going *home!* I'm gonna see. . .my. . .ma an'. . ."

And Davey went home. He simply wasn't there any more.

A breeze sighed through the trees. Bill spread out his hands to gauge the vibrations.

"It's clear, Babe. Thunder Mountain's clear."

A shiver trembled through me but I felt nothing but warmth.

Bill placed his arm around me. "You're soaking wet."

I didn't care. I was still in the euphoric state left from what we had just witnessed.

"C'mon, honey, you've got to get out of those clothes."

I gazed over at him and smiled. "All he had to do was *want* it. It was so simple. All he needed was the desire, and he could've done that all by himself."

"Not quite," Bill said, "he needed someone to *show* him he had the desire."

Water still dripped here and there from the evergreens. Moonlight still shone down out of a clear mountain sky. Only one thing was different about the woods—a sound of crying would never be heard again.

Our journey back was uneventful. The river was calmer now that the storm had passed. And the ravine was not difficult to climb because of the moonlight illuminating our course. Once we gained entry to the camper, Bill's first priority was to light the propane heater. Warmth soon dissipated the chilling dampness and we helped each other tug off the soaked clothing. Once dry and snuggled in securely beneath the quilt, slumber soon guided us into a soothing sleep.

Pine cones toppled onto the metal roof. Birds twilled their sunrise song. Tiny four-leggeds scurried about for their first meal of the day. Underbrush rustled and kaibab squirrels chattered. We had received our official wake-up call and were ready to be back on the road.

Sitting in the cab, Bill looked at me. "Do I go the long way?"

My eyes twinkled with mischief. "I'm starved. Let's take the high road."

"You sure? Those lumberjacks may be around."

"So?" It wasn't that I no longer cared about meeting up with them again, I just figured they'd had their breakfasts long ago and would be busy buzzing trees in the woods by now.

"Okay. Let's get something to eat then."

And the pickup nosed out onto the road that would take us back the way we had come.

The driver gave me a peculiar took. "You sure you want to go in that diner?"

"I said I did."

A suppressed grin came over his face. "You happen to look in a mirror this morning?"

I sucked in my breath and shot my hands to my face. "Do I look awful?" I cried, yanking the rear-view mirror askew to check out the terrible face.

He laughed. "You look great. . .for a grown up Shirley Temple, that is."

"Ohhh," I moaned. "I hate this hair," I said in exasperation while trying to comb down the corkscrew ringlets with my fingers. "Good thing I don't live where it's humid; then I really would look like Shirley Temple." I sat back in the seat. "Oh well, guess you're going to have to be seen with me like this."

"Babe, I'd be proud to be seen with you anywhere. . .no matter what you looked like."

Some men always knew the right things to say.

The diner came into view then. We parked out front and strode in.

"Morning, Kari," Bill greeted.

The woman turned with a smile that dropped onto the floor. She managed a half smile.

We took a booth. We had our choice. My former idea was indeed verified—all the men were gone. Our order was placed and we ate with gusto. We were very hungry after our exhausting night. All the while we were in the booth, Kari snuck curious glances at us. When we were finished and strolled over to the counter to pay, Kari finally found her lost courage.

She beamed and leaned over the register.

"Hey you guys," she whispered cryptically while checking out the empty kitchen window. "I gotta tell ya something." Crack, pop went the bubble gum.

We leaned closer.

"Ya know that story you asked about yesterday?" Snap. Snap.

"The one with the kid?"

We nodded.

"Well. . .it's true!"

Bill slipped the change into his wallet. "Thanks for everything, Kari, but we gotta get going."

Her head pulled back on her neck. "But don'tcha wanna hear 'bout it?"

"We really haven't the time right now. Don't work too hard," he said.

And we left.

Outside the door, Bill had an impish afterthought. He winked at me and leaned back inside.

"Oh Kari?" he called.

"Yeah?"

"I wouldn't go spreading that story around if I were you, there's really nothing to it. . .not any more."

Bill told me the pink wad fell out of her mouth when she heard that, but he was just exaggerating. . .I think.

Eternal Nightwatch in Sweetwater

Mother Nature's personality was now in its most amiable stage. She was bright-eyed, sweet and always gentle. There would be no more blustery tirades or chilling shoulders given for many months to come. Observing her new tranquility, anyone accustomed to telling time by the aspects of seasons would know that the beginning of summer had arrived. For those in the habit of having to rely on the artificial crutch of manmade measurement of their linear time—the calendar— the month was June.

In the high country of the Colorado Rockies, June is most often comparable to late April or early May of the lower elevations. Baby leaves of the rebirthing aspens have just crowned out of their birth womb-buds. Tinges of lime-colored greenery bestow a new hue to the former nakedness of their winter garb. In a week's time, the aspens would be lush in their resplendent emerald wardrobes that quivered and quaked their jade sequins like the jangling raiments of a Burmese temple dancer. Air, pure as new-fallen snow, brought myriad fragrances of blossoming wildflowers. And the high country sun, warm and constant, gilded the land with golden rays of magic, charming all the nature it touched, leaving enchantment upon the land. . .but all of this magnificent wonder was perceptible only by those who had the hearts to see it, for the true exquisiteness of nature was more keenly perceived through the appreciative eyes of the tender heart. A tree is not just a tree, but is a living, breathing entity of the Earth Mother's family. Flowers, weeds and moss—all extensions of living totality—our brothers.

So on this deliciously fragrant June evening, Bill and I found ourselves out soaking up the living essence of its magnetic beauty. We strolled down our neighborhood dirt road and inhaled deeply, drawing into our beings the emanating power of the mountain's new breath of life.

The stately evergreens were giving off the sweet aroma of their new growth. Earth, pungent with rich nutrients, was musky and fertile. A cloudless sky, clear and crisp, quietly beckoned all souls to feel and to experience the glorious magic of its hammered disc of silver that hung like a rare jewel suspended upon its velvety breast. The jewel, so radiant of being, reflected its facets in glittering rays upon the receiving land below. We walked for a long while through the etheric moonglow.

When we returned home, our hearts were beating as one and our spirits were empowered with new life. We were physically rejuvenated and mentally electrified with energy— a special kind of energy that meant only one thing. . .we were ready for another encounter.

Bill pulled out the maps and notebook while I lighted the kitchen oil lamp and poured us each a frosted glass of rosé. He opened up the folded map and spread it out on the table. I took the notebook and began scanning No-Eyes' information.

"I don't think I can handle another one like last time yet," I mused, checking over the list.

"What do you mean?"

"Getting all wet. We took a chance doing that. We should've had pneumonia."

His expression made it clear that that was never a concern.

"Our protection takes care of those things. As long as that remains strong, we're not going to see any kind of ill effects."

"Still," I maintained, "I'd like to stay away from rivers and storms for this one."

"Okay by me. No-Eyes never mentioned any specific order for these, did she?"

I shook my head. "I think I'll just take the notes and go down the list; that way we won't miss any."

He took a sip of the wine. "Shoot."

I gave the tattered pad a cursory glance then looked back to Bill.

"Honey? What about John?"

"What about him?"

"You know. Those weird things he and others have been experiencing around the ranch. That's right around here. Why don't we look into that next?"

He immediately nixed the idea. "We owe it to No-Eyes to take care of hers first. We have all the time in the world to get to that local stuff. I hardly think they'll suddenly stop on their own. They can wait."

"But he specifically asked me if we could check it out. It's kind of unnerving for them."

"I know, and we will take a look at it, I promise. But only after we do the ones on that list of yours. If we start doing one locally. . .before you know it, word gets around and. . .Bingo! We've got ten more."

"I hadn't thought of that. I guess you're right," I agreed, giving new attention to the notebook. "Where's St. Elmo?"

Without looking up the location, he shook his head.

"That's a ghost town up into the mountains south of Buena Vista. That road might still be in bad shape. We'll wait a few weeks for that one."

Returning to the list, I inquired about the next location. "Star Mountain Pass?"

He checked on that one. "It's pretty high up but it's in the banana belt. We could do that. What's the deal on it?"

"That's the axe man one."

He just stared at me. The lantern flame flickered over his face. "You're kidding, right?"

"No, why?"

"You want to go from a *kid* to an *axe* man? You really think you're ready for that?"

A suspicious grin crept up my face. "Doesn't sound like you are. What's the matter? You scared?"

"Well," he shrugged, preserving his manly self esteem, "I thought we decided to work these in order of ascending difficulty. If you want to jump right in to confront some maniacal guy dragging an axe around, that's up to you."

I thought that over. Was he calling my bluff? Who cared? It didn't take me all that long to feel my skin crawl at the thought of doing that particular one. I quickly returned to the list.

"Scared?" came the slightly teasing voice.

"Let's just say it doesn't sound like it should be next." I paused. "Yeah, that one really does give me the creeps."

"Me too," my brave but honest partner admitted.

I didn't bother commenting on his confession, but rather attended to the decision at hand.

"Bogan Flats. How about that one?"

"Never heard of it."

"Well, there's a note here that says it's by Redstone. We been there."

"Nope. No good. The Crystal River's wet, I hear. We want to stay away from rivers, remember?"

"We're going down the list, remember?" I parried. "I'm not picking and choosing; I'm taking them one by one."

"Okay. What's next?"

"Sand Creek."

"Next!"

"What do you mean, 'next'? That *is* next."

"We can do that anytime. We need to get the others out of the way first." He peered over at the list. "What else do we have?"

I gave him a curious look. We couldn't do Sand Creek any time because it was out in the plains and they got high snow drifting during winter. Frequently the roads were closed. He didn't want me anywhere near Sand Creek because he was afraid of the empathy I'd experience from the massacre that occurred there. I let it pass without comment and called out another locale.

"Phantom Canyon."

"Good grief. Do you remember that?"

I nodded "Thought we'd never get to the end. That's a long deserted stretch. Want to wait?"

"I think we should. Just out of curiosity though, what's the scoop on that one?"

Reading it first to myself, I sighed. "Well? From what No-Eyes indicated, the actual locale is way back in the woods. Some kind of fire manifests and there's also something about hell demons."

"Not literally, I take it," he frowned skeptically.

"Better not be! I just remember her commenting that maybe we'd find out who those hell demons really were. Sounds a little like there's more than one spirit involved, doesn't it?"

"Could be," he said pensively. "Maybe people see something they interpret as being hell demons but are really the wayward spirits."

"Maybe. She didn't elaborate on them."

"Well, what's left? Isn't that about it?"

"No. Sweetwater's left."

Bill checked the map index, got the coordinates and stabbed a finger on it. "Bingo! Isn't that the woman in the hotel?"

"Yes."

"We would've saved ourselves a lot of time by starting at the bottom. That one's got no water, no hell demons and no axes."

"Then you think we should take that on next?"

He raised his glass in salute. "To Sweetwater."

I lifted mine and grinned. "To Sweetwater!"

We packed our materials away and went to bed. We both felt good about our choice. Yet, after having more time to ponder it over, I was having some bothersome thoughts. The darkness of night always seemed to bring out the negatives.

"Bill? You still awake?"

"Mmmm."

"I was thinking. Do you think this one will take two days?"

"Has to. She doesn't manifest until the early morning hours."

Silence.

"Why?" he asked.

"Are we going to be able to sleep in the camper?"

He chuckled. "It'd be pretty hard to work with her from there, don't you think?"

I turned over to face him. Propping myself up on one elbow, I looked down on his moonlit face. "Don't make fun of me. I'm serious."

"I'm not making fun of you, honey, but we need to be in the hotel all night."

That bothered me—it bothered me a lot.

"Tourist season just began. Don't you think that's going to be a little expensive? A little out of our league?"

His arm came around to rub my back. "Stop worrying about the money. This is the only one that manifests in any kind of building. All the others are outside and we can use the camper for those. Look, honey," he softly said, trying to placate my concerns, "I want you to enjoy this one. Now I'm serious. Look at it as being a mini-vacation for us. A nice dinner in a nice hotel will be a real treat."

"But we can't afford it. I don't feel right about spending the money on something like that when it could go for other things."

He sighed heavily with his worrisome wife. "Honey, please? We've scrimped enough. Let's just try to get a little enjoyment from this one trip."

The sincerity in his voice was almost pleading—we never had to do that with each other.

"Okay," I gave in. "We'll make this one special."

We kissed on the deal, but when I turned back and settled onto my own pillow, I still secretly fretted. I guess the years of pinching pennies and trying to raise a family made me feel guilty whenever expenses seemed extravagant or selfish. But he was right about this particular one and I had to keep telling myself over and over that, more than anyone. . .he deserved the treat. That singular thought gave me a great deal of comfort and served to justify the plan. Then I wondered what part of the household expenses was going to be squeezed to make this trip possible. I vacillated back and forth in my head until sleep finally put a stop to it.

Buttery sunglow slanted down through the narrow slats of the wooden shutters. The bedroom was alive with Ra's royal golden aura.

Sleepily, with half-opened eyes, I watched with some amusement while a multitude of dust-motes aimlessly ambled through the warm rays. Drifters they were. Drifters hitching rides on whatever vagabond air current that happened their way.

In humor did I grin at the thoughts born of my constant observations. Dust motes—drifters. Did I always make such comparisons of inanimates? When did this habit begin? I couldn't answer that because it was something I couldn't ever recall *not* doing. All of life, even the meandering motes of dust, held me enrapt by their fascinating existence and graceful movements. What secretly amazed me was how I perceived the beauty in the simplest forms all by myself—without the assistance of any artificial mind enhancers. Maybe I was just born with a natural "high" already residing in my mind. That fanciful idea widened my grin into a silly smile that twinkled the eyes into the clarity of total wakefulness.

I rolled over to my mate. He'd been staring at the ceiling, perplexity wrinkled the sandy brows.

"That's not a very good way to wake up," I whispered. "You're frowning."

"A possible glitch just prowled across my mind."

He'd sparked my interest. "About the encounter?"

"Honey, did you realize that this is the only one that we'll be doing on private property? That means the owner will have to give us permission. We can't barge in on private property and carry on as if it's as free as a National Forest."

"Mmmm. Got any ideas?"

The pearl blue eyes suspiciously settled on mine. "We'll need to get this straightened out before we even think of leaving the house."

"You could call the Sweetwater Hotel and talk to the owner," I suggested, knowing it wasn't what he'd had in mind.

"I don't want to talk to the owner. I don't think it's wise to warn him of our intentions. I'd rather approach it differently. This isn't something that should be discussed over the phone."

"Oh. I see. . ." And I did see—very clearly. And before I rested back on my pillow, I took note of the numbers on the digital clock beside the bed.

Thirty minutes later I opened my eyes to a crocodile grin. "It's a go!" he announced, whipping the covers away. "Let's get moving."

I yanked them back over me. "Now wait just a minute, not so fast! Are you going to tell me it took a *half hour* for you to get a simple 'yes'?"

His cheeks flushed before quickly recovering. "I got answers to a few other questions I had, like—will the truck hold together, is this a good weekend for this one and are you energized enough for it?" And those were all fibs, but I wouldn't find out what they'd really discussed until later in the day.

"So!" I pushed. "What were your answers?"

"Yes to all the above."

I narrowed my eyes at him.

He crushed me to his chest and laughed. "You're the most suspicious person I've ever seen. I told you what we talked about, now come on and let's get going."

Well, I thought, if he was holding anything back, I'd find out sooner or later—I always did and he knew that.

While Bill shaved, I quickly dressed and threw a few things into our tote bag. I was busily getting out the peanut butter an' jelly makin's when he snuck up behind me and grabbed at the bread bag.

"Nope. No way."

I yanked it back. "What do you mean? I always pack us something to eat."

He was adamant. "Not this time, honey. This time we're going first class all the way."

I snickered. "In a beat-up truck?"

His shoulders slumped at my sarcasm. "Real funny. You know what I mean. This time there'll be none of those damned sandwiches."

"But we'll need to eat lunch."

"We're going out for breakfast, then I figure it'll be around three-thirty by the time we roll into Sweetwater. We probably won't even be hungry for lunch. We'll have a good dinner at the hotel."

"Then breakfast and lunch the next day. You forget about the *next* day?"

The wheat bag was being defiantly resealed. "Nope."

"Honey," I nearly pleaded, "I agreed to dinner and the hotel bill, but all this eating out is just too much."

He lifted my chin. Quicksilver eyes melted my stubbornness. "Please?" he said.

I sighed. "I hope you know what you're doing. What did you do, rob a bank or something?"

The lights in his eyes danced. "Maybe. But if I admitted it you'd be an accessory and I'd sure hate to see you in the Cripple Creek jail."

"You're terrible!"

"I have to be."

"Oh?"

"Yeah. One terrible balances the *other* terrible."

I couldn't argue with that one and we were out of the house and into our old hangout ten minutes later.

Godmother's Kitchen was full of morning tourists when we arrived. We sat in the back by the bar and ordered one of our usuals—scrambled eggs and onions with hash browns plus a side of blueberry-topped pancakes.

A friend came through the door and joined us. He worked with Bill and they shared uproariously funny tales of their many experiences out in the field. We enjoyed sharing our meals with friends. Good food and good company naturally went hand in hand. It was a pleasant beginning for the trip. We had tarried longer than we had planned and by the time our official journey began, it was going on eleven o'clock.

I suspected Bill had been right about us not having the need for those lunch sandwiches. We were both pleasantly satisfied from the filling breakfast and wouldn't be even thinking of sitting down at a table again for many hours to come.

For the first half of the drive we spoke about the other encounters we'd done and, due to their successful outcomes, wondered if we'd experience a failure, and if so, how many. We weren't so arrogant to believe all our efforts would produce the desired results, although we would've wished for that. It appeared that we would be presented with myriad personalities in this most unconventional and often bizarre work. And so it was naturally expected, for the spirits were as diverse and as distinctive in character as those touchable people we passed in the marketplace. Each one so unique, each one in possession of individualized traits, egos, personalities.

Each having different reasons for remaining within the confines of the third dimension. Consequently, each encounter would require an exact analysis and a swift plan of logical psychology that would serve to bring about a successful resolution.

Then, for a good distance we remained silent, each allowed the privacy of his own private musings. Each allowed to reap his own personal enjoyment from the ever-changing scenery.

Now we were traveling upon the black criss-crossing ribbon of highway that sliced through miles of plains, broken only by lonely cottonwood stands.

I was first to shatter the deep quietude within the cab.

"Too bad we still don't use horses like in the old days," I said out of the blue.

The driver, accustomed to my thought process, considered the statement while attempting to dig out the buried intent of it. He took a wild stab at it. "Because cars are confining."

"Yes. In more ways than one, too." Excitement grew within me as I perked up and animated my thoughts. "Just imagine riding a horse all the time. What do you envision?"

"Wet clothes."

My eyes rolled. "Come on. Be serious. What do you *feel*?"

"A sore behind."

I frowned at him. "You're visualizing negatives. Think positive!"

"You mean think romantic, not reality."

Undaunted by this logic, I parried with my own version. I smiled.

"Nature is romantic."

"You and nature think alike."

"Yes," I beamed while caught up in the network of my impulses. "Leave that boring Mr. Spock logic behind for a few minutes and envision how free one would be without metal vehicles separating one from the earth."

My partner responded and took the cue of his passenger director. He slipped into the mood of romanticism and joined me in my dreamy imaginings. He was not patronizing, but rather was preparing to honestly experience the mental exercise I was about to choreograph.

And we went into it. In depth and with great detail given to the sensual specifics, I brought all the perceiving senses to the forefront of the consciousness. The horseback ride and the feel of the stallion's powerful muscles. The wind's breath upon an upturned face and the blending of heady scents it carried. The freedom of not being confined to a road, going only where it deemed you must go. The wildness of it. The total abandonment. The feel of the earth through pounding hooves and quivering flanks.

Then I became silent when the truck hit a pothole. It had been good, the envisioning. To me it had been much more than a highly-detailed exercise in visualization. To me it had been an exercise in memory recall and the remembering had been something good.

"We'll get horses some day, honey," Bill soothed, resting his hand on my knee.

"That's not important to me anymore. Not when I can do what we just did. Sometimes I think that's just as good." I bathed in the thrilling memory of it. "I did love racing them, though. There's nothing like the feel of its power beneath you. It's like riding the wind."

Silence. Silence for a long time.

"I'm sorry," I softly apologized. "I didn't mean to be melancholy, I'm all right. I just really don't care about us getting horses anymore."

"Since when?"

"Oh I don't know. I just remember that the last time I thought about them the desire wasn't there. It's like, if it's not a necessity, we don't need it." I went deeper into it. "I think being with Many Heart changed a lot of my thinking."

"The acceptance bit?"

"Probably."

"How do you feel about that?"

"Good," I smiled with conviction. "I have no regrets about the things I no longer want. Acceptance makes that possible."

"It took a while for acceptance to overcome your stubbornness about these encounters," he added with a wry grin.

I returned it with a horrible face. "Don't remind me."

"Speaking of encounters, we should toss this one around a little. Had any thoughts on it?"

"Yes," I admitted with a silly grin.

"Oh boy, now what have you come up with?"

"Promise you won't laugh?"

He crossed his heart on it. "Boy Scout's honor."

"Well, I think our wayward lady is waiting for a lover."

He laughed. He laughed in spite of his promise and his honor.

I stiffened with indignant scorn. "Some Boy Scout."

"Oh come on, babe, I'm sorry, but there you go again with that romanticism."

Turning my attention to the scenery out the side window, I clammed up.

"Okay, Sherlock, tell Watson how you deduced your theory."

My neck slowly rotated my head in his direction.

"It was simple. If the lady was angry, there would've been evidence of psychokinetic manifestations. If she was vengeful, or if her objective was to protect her property, people would be getting hurt. If she was just mischievous, she'd be appearing to all the guests and disrupting operations. If she were grieving for a lost child or other loved one, she'd be mourning, maybe moaning or crying like Davey was. So. . .since she doesn't exhibit any of the above phenomenon, it means she's wailing for someone."

"Sounds logical enough but how do you know it's a lover she's waiting for?"

Beneath a Cheshire grin, I answered. "I'm a romantic, remember?"

"Well," he conceded, "as silly as it sounds, I think you may be right. We'll know more after talking with the owner of the place."

I spent a couple quiet moments in thought.

"When you asked about him this morning, did you happen to ask anything about the encounter?"

"Did, but didn't get any answers. Seems this is our baby."

That didn't jibe at all. "Well, how come I get information during the encounters then?"

"That's different. We're supposed to go into these cold. We're supposed to glean what we can by natural means and then use our own insights each time. 'Work as we go' kind of thing. That way the sequence of events is more natural—spontaneous."

"Still," I maintained, "the information comes from the same source.

"Does it?" he asked, implying differently. "With Davey it was *given* to you, but what about the impressions you get when you touch things? Those aren't given by anyone. Those are your own insights. The two are generated from completely different sources."

"And," I concluded, "depending on the circumstances, the specific situation determines what source serves best."

"Right."

"I sure hope we're never without a backup though. What if we're in the middle of a case and I don't get any impressions and no information is given either?"

Silence.

"Honey?"

"Then we may be in serious trouble. Do you think that'd ever happen?"

"Well, I don't always get impressions from things."

"Let's hope we *always* have that other source then."

That wasn't comforting either. "It wasn't around when you asked about the speedometer."

"*Somebody* answered."

"Yeah," I grinned, "I guess our backup has a line of understudies waiting in the wings for us."

"Let's just keep our fingers crossed that the so-called understudies know their lines."

And that was definitely not a worry, for never were we completely alone in the world. That had been proven out time and time again. The understudies were always at the ready—they *always* knew the score.

Talking about the encounter and watching the changing terrain of the landscape brought other thoughts to mind.

"I wonder what Sweetwater looks like," I said.

"I've seen a postcard of it once. It's pretty much like most of the other old-time mining towns."

"Mmmm," I pondered. "Think it's all burrowed like Cripple Creek?"

"The town itself?"

"Yeah. Remember when we were in the Cripple Creek museum and we looked at that display?"

"You mean the one under layers of glass that showed the mining levels?"

"Yes. You think Sweetwater was mined that extensively?"

"I don't think so, but then again, I'm no expert."

The plane of horizon began to be broken by scattered molehills the size of small mountains. The molehills were not earthen, but were comprised of castoff mill tailings. Soon weathered timbers stood in misshapen relief against the turquoise sky. Their leaning skeletons marked the yawning entrances to abandoned mining holes—graves now empty and devoid of the Earth Mother's rich mineral nutrients. Hill after ugly hill gave heart-wrenching testimony to the wanton abuse the Earth Mother had silently endured at the clawing hands of avaricious men of no conscience.

The horrifying vision of the glass display haunted me like a jeering specter.

"Oh God," I whispered to myself, "please just let us get in and out of here in one piece."

"Afraid the ghost's gonna get ya?" Bill teased back.

"It's not ghosts that's bothering me; it's the thought of driving over miles and miles of layered and layered tunnels that scares me. It's like driving over thin ice or trying to walk on eggs. One of these days all the empty spaces of these mines are going to be filled—with what was on *top*!"

"Not yet. Not just yet. Besides, where's your faith?"

Subconsciously my hand touched my pocket. It rested comfortably on the small bulge."

"In my pocket," I chirped with renewed confidence. "Faith is in my pocket."

His expression was full of disbelief. "You brought Many Heart's stone?"

"In my pocket," I repeated, patting it.

"What're you going to do with it?"

"Nothing. *It's* doing all the doing."

He wasn't sure what that meant and didn't ask. I don't think he wanted to know either.

"Well?" he beamed. "Here's Sweetwater!"

I turned from him and gasped. I couldn't believe my eyes. The town was nothing like my scoundrel driver had led me to believe. It was picture perfect in every respect.

"You didn't tell me it was like this!"

"I know. I wanted to surprise you. It's even nicer than the postcard," he admitted, taking a general look around.

Clapboard houses, neat as a new pin, were scattered up and down the green hillsides. Pride was the dominating aura and vibrations of friendliness emanated from the town. The residences were small but their exteriors were maintained with loving care. A multitude of colors shouted out to be seen and appreciated. Victorian gingerbread laced the buildings with contrasting trim. Yellows with browns. Dark blues with light blues. White on bright reds. Blacks on grey. Each house, resplendent in character, boasted a profuse blend of shades as they melded into the neighborhood body. So many pigments used on dwellings I'd never before seen. What imagination! What boldness to create such an eye-catching, yet pleasing atmosphere! The colors—they were all there. Indigo, cobalt, wedgewood and robin's egg blue. Jasper, jade, emerald and beryl green. Cinnamon, cocoa, russet and ginger brown.

Flaxen, gold, and butter yellow. The reds were bold and the whites were as white as a snowshoe hare in the middle of winter. Crisp. Clean. Quaint.

Not only were the houses primly painted, many of them had also been extensively remodeled with additional amenities of bay windows refit with stained glass, decks that jutted out and wrapped around to overlook the town below, trellises overflowing with thriving clematis—climbing vines of blossoms white and pink.

I was nothing less than awestruck when I turned to the driver.

"You like it?" he asked with gleaming eyes.

What an understatement!

"Do I *like* it! I *love* it! It's beautiful!"

"And that's just the outskirts. You ready for the town?"

I took a deep breath as he eased us up Main Street. My heart quivered and beat swiftly like a bird's. As I anxiously looked around, I wanted to say something intelligent, but all that came out of my mouth was "Ohhh!" I was enchanted with the quaintness, with the incredible caring I saw before me. And I didn't utter another word until Bill had reached the end of Main Street and had asked the heart-stopping question.

"You see the hotel?"

Had I seen it? I'd seen it all right. The sight of it had churned my stomach and parched my throat. The frosted etched windows, narrow and tall, had rich crimson drapes of velvet tied back on each side. The main doors, double mahogany and engraved by master carvers, threatened my meager sensibilities and shook them to the core. I was sick inside with the thought of the pickup pulling up in front of the imposing structure. What were we doing here?

"Honey?" he repeated. "Did you hear me? Did you see the Sweetwater?"

Oh God, he was going through with it. He really was. And that realization made me really feel like getting sick—literally.

"I saw it," came the cold reply.

"Well? You act like you've seen a ghost. Don't you like it?"

I probably did act like I'd seen a ghost because I felt the blood drain from my face. We weren't the Sweetwater type. . .we were mountain.

"Oh, I like it all right. I love it. . .but. . ."

"Well, let's go see what's what then." He was clearly filled with adventuresome excitement.

My hand went to his arm before he could turn us around.

"Bill? I'm scared."

He pulled over out of the traffic. The engine hummed in idle.

"What's the matter, honey?" he asked, voice heavy with deep concern. "You're going to do okay with this one."

"That's not what scares me." I glanced about the street. "There was a little motel back there. Couldn't we. . ."

Exasperated, he jammed the transmission in gear and pulled out, cruised back the way we came and parked smack dab in front of the Sweetwater Hotel. The engine sighed and silenced.

My companion gave me one final hard look.

"I *said* not to worry about the money." And he got out.

Taking a fortifying breath, I reluctantly climbed out and followed him through the ornate doors that seemed to announce, "Wealthy people—enter here!"

When the heavy doors closed behind us, all outside noises were shut out. I likened the action to the leadened lid being lowered onto a casket—mine—or the seal stone being rolled in place over a burial chamber in the Valley of the Kings. For before us, a wealth of opulence spread out like Tutankhamen's royal treasure. Glistening, gilded gold and polished ebony stared back at us in the deathly silence.

Bill's eyes sparkled with pleasure.

Mine were fixed in a catatonic stare as my head pivoted slowly from one side of the vast room to the other. Now my poor heart was not fibrillating like a bird's; it was hammering like a pile-driver gone berserk. The sound of it banged in my ears.

Bill waited in amused silence while his zombie mate absorbed it all.

The main staircase dominated the hall-sized chamber like a living thing of power. Two mezzanines spread out from the second floor landing like great wings. The wide risers of the stairs were covered with plush maroon carpeting with crimson rose designs. Sparkling ebony banisters and rails arced gracefully along the curving staircase.

Walls were rich in paper of scarlet and gold flocking. Oil lanterns flickered in brass sconces. Victorian chairs and chaise lounges, perfectly arranged in the center around gleaming antique tables, were upholstered in vermillion velvet and shiny black horsehair. The reception desk, a long mahogany monstrosity, was so highly polished you could almost use it for a mirror. Master paintings, highlighted by tiny shaded lamps from above, enhanced the walls.

It didn't take me long to soak up all the opulence and I knew that I didn't belong. I was totally out of my realm standing in the foyer of this place and I wanted nothing to do with it. No-Eyes hadn't prepared me for this and that bothered me more than a little. I wondered what Bill was thinking of the place. I knew for a fact that he'd think the decor was gaudy. But then we weren't here as interior decorating connoisseurs either. He wasn't saying anything, and I was hoping he was experiencing wise second thoughts. My thoughts leaned toward taking immediate action. Maybe we could just sort of back out the door. My feet heard the command and lifted to obey.

"Come on in, folks!" ordered a booming voice from the darker side of the catacomb. "We're open!"

My arm was firmly held and I was guided over the thick carpet. It ate the sounds of our footfalls. It would've been fine with me if it would've swallowed me too.

We approached a large man who extended his hand in a warm welcome. He was western type all the way from the turquoise stone string tie down to his tooled Dingo boots.

"Name's Cliff, Cliff Westcott. I own this here monstrosity." He chuckled then. "Well. . .don't really mean that," he laughed, "but it is different."

We introduced ourselves before the proud proprietor sighed and glanced about.

"Yeh, yeh, sunk a bundle into this little baby, I did. Imported carpet and glass. Refurbished the whole danged thing."

"It's very authentic," I complimented after finally finding my voice. Maybe we could say we had just come in to admire it. That'd be a good idea.

"Got any rooms available?" the man beside me inquired.

My stomach sank to my feet.

"Sure do!" Cliff bellowed, looking about the cavernous room.

"Ahhh, guess Julie stepped out for a minute but I can take. . ."

"Well," Bill cut in, "we can stop back to register. We've been driving all afternoon and we were going to get a bite to eat first. Any good places in town?"

The man's tanned and weathered hand came up to his chin. "Well now, you're in luck. We're just now setting up for the dinner crowd." His head bobbed to indicate the lavish dining room behind him. Smoky glass etched with roses centered the swinging doors. What I could see of this man's dining room made my heart flutter. I froze while he talked on.

"There's a couple a greasy spoons out on Main Street if your tastes run in that direction. An' there's a halfway decent cafe up the other way too."

Mouth-watering smells wafted by our hungry mouths. Cliff's kitchen was cookin'.

I delicately yanked on Bill's arm.

"Well," he said, "I hate to turn down a good restaurant. We'll try the Sweetwater."

"Good choice," the man declared with pride, "good choice. You won't be disappointed. We serve everything from Maine lobster to Chateaubriand."

Oh Lord, I thought as we were proudly escorted through the dining doors and into the massive room. Maybe we'd have a chance to sneak out after we were seated. Yes, we certainly could do that. People did it all the time. . .I saw them do it.

It would appear to me now that all my escape routes were thwarted. My last exit plan had been cut off at the pass, for when we were seated, Cliff pulled out one of the heavily-carved high back chairs and joined us. Didn't he have some important business to attend to? Behind me, a massive grandfather clock ticked loudly in my ear. Ordinarily I loved those soothing mechanisms, but for some menacing reason, the slow swing of the brass pendulum agonizingly reminded me of sweet Poe's, for I certainly felt hopelessly trapped.

I pasted a congenial smile on my face and glanced over at my companion. His was genuine. He was actually enjoying himself immensely. He knew we didn't have this kind of money, yet he really was having a grand old time. What was wrong with him? Had he finally lost it?

Cliff's voice interrupted my important thoughts and distracted my concerned attention from my crazy mate.

"So where are you folks from?"

"Woodland Park," Bill replied.

"Oh then, you're not official tourists then. You just moseying around this weekend?"

"Not exactly," came the lead-in statement.

"Oh? Business then?"

"You could say that."

Cliff waited for more to come.

It came.

"Actually, Cliff, our business is not a bona fide type of

endeavor. Our weekend business is more of a sideline—there's no money-making involved."

Our host's heavy brows knitted. "You mean something like volunteer work?"

Bill's eyes widened. "I never thought of it quite like that before, but I guess that about describes it all right."

I too liked that view of our sideline business. It was volunteer work, pure and simple.

Bill hunched forward with his elbows on the table. He was preparing to tread on thin ice.

"Actually," my mate coolly admitted, "your wandering lady brought us here."

We watched for the man's reaction.

He slid his eyes to either side of him and cleared his throat. "What wandering lady?"

"The spirit," Bill said.

The proprietor swallowed hard. "And?"

"And we'd like to help her."

"To do what exactly?"

"Go home."

"Jesus!" he exclaimed, wiping at his brow. "You one of them psychics or something?"

Bill smiled cordially. "Not really, Cliff, at least not in the context you're referring to and. . ."

"Mediums? You two mediums?"

"No."

"*Ghost* chasers?"

Now we both grinned. Poor Cliff was finding this all very confusing. I let Bill continue to handle the situation.

"Cliff, my wife spent a great deal of time with a wise Indian woman who taught her a lot of beautiful philosophy. She also taught her a way of helping out lost spirits—like your lady here. We utilize this special knowledge and technique by traveling about the state with the express purpose of assisting these wandering souls."

Silence.

Bill's knee nudged mine beneath the table. I pressed mine back against his. So far we weren't getting any clear indication of the man's attitude on the subject.

When Cliff next spoke, his words were most grave and his eyes seriously leveled with ours.

"Publicity. What about that?" he inquired with a raised brow of skepticism.

My companion and I looked at one another in question.

"I'm not clear on what you mean by that," Bill confessed. "What publicity?"

"Oh the usual stuff—television crews, newspaper reporters, that kind of thing."

Bill was outwardly shocked. "You intend to *publicize* this?"

"Hell no! Not *me!*"

"You thought we brought a television crew? Cliff, this is just my wife and I. Just the two of us. There's nobody else involved here."

Our host eyed us suspiciously. "No cameras to record the action?"

Bill shook his head. "No cameras."

"No reporters taking pictures?"

"No reporters."

"Tape machines?"

"Useless. Tape machines wouldn't even pick up our conversations. A lot of our technique takes place on another level of communication."

Cliff studied the odd couple. "Don't figure. It don't figure at all."

"What doesn't figure, Cliff?"

"You doing what you do without filming some kind of record of it."

"Why would we need a record of it?" Bill asked. "Who would we show it to—for what purpose?"

"Proof!"

"Proof for whom?" Bill sighed. "Look, Cliff, we don't advertise what we do because we don't want any publicity or people getting in the way. What we do is very private. It's just between us and the spirit itself. There're no cameras, tape machines, or anything else."

"What about documentation? Don't you need that?"

"Again Cliff, documentation for who? For what purpose? To *prove* we were here? What for? This isn't anyone else's business. It's a private affair. Purely volunteer work."

"Why? Why do it if you don't get any recognition for it?"

And that was the bottom line. That was the singular reason nobody understood our secretiveness—our desire for complete anonymity.

"We're not looking for recognition, Cliff. No recognition, no publicity and no pats on the back."

"Why bother with it then?"

He still didn't get it.

"We bother with it because it's the right thing to do. To help a homeless or lost person is the natural humane thing to do; likewise, to help a lost spirit is the spiritually humane thing to do. That's our sole reason."

Cliff was silent while he contemplated all he had heard. Clearly it was absolutely foreign to him.

The clock behind me was loud in my ears as it ticked away the prolonged seconds.

Our host scooted his chair closer to the table and studied the napkin corner as he fiddled with it.

"You know. . .you're not the first who came in here for this reason."

My brow arched and he noticed.

"God's truth," he said. "Why, one time these folks came traipsing in here with all sorts of junk. They had camera crews and all kinds of technical equipment. They started running cable on the carpets an' it was a real mess. Well, I tell you, I'd *had* it! I kicked their butts out of here so fast their heads spun."

My fist shot up in the air. "Good for you! That was great!"

Surprised by my unrestrained outburst, Cliff stared at me while I commended his action.

"That was all *show*, Cliff. That sort of thing is all phony hype and it hurts the whole issue. Most of the time a spirit can't even be photographed. It ends up looking like a puff of smoke—a contrived facsimile. Cliff, spirits don't look like that. What you did was right."

He expanded on his experience. "Well, then there was this woman who came in here with some assistants. They were going to perform some kind of seance or something. Now I'm not talking about just anybody here—this woman was supposed to be some kind of famous medium. Anyway, there was some God-awful smell coming from their room. They were burning incense or something. And then she came downstairs in a trance and made a real racket—moaning an' mumbling— my guests were scared silly. They were real upset."

"That was a *farce*!" I angrily exploded. "That was as phony as phony gets! It was a *sham!*"

My anger held his attention.

"Yes! A complete *sham!* Cliff, seances are a joke! Incense is all show! So is fabricated moaning, mumbling and extreme animation. All that stuff is a big put on. I *know!* The *real* mediumship isn't like that at all!" Indignant as I had become, I maintained a solemnness while I leaned forward and locked eyes with his. My voice was low and controlled. "Cliff, we don't have a carpetbag stuffed with useless paraphernalia. We don't burn incense. We don't go into trances, fake or otherwise, and we don't moan and mumble. What we do is talk to the spirit. That's *all* we do."

"Talk? How is that done? Don't you need a medium for that? I don't claim to be an expert on this subject but I thought that's how it was done."

"Not the way we do it," I explained. "My teacher was very knowledgeable and very thorough in the ways of the spirits—many Indians are. She taught me several ways of bridging dimensions and altering vibrational frequencies so we can share a more common ground that allows effective communication to take place. A medium would be useless to us because we do it all ourselves."

He thought on that. "And no cameras or incense?"

I shook my head.

So did he. "I'm sorry folks, but you gotta let me get used to this."

I smiled warmly. "I understand. After what you've been put through, your reluctance is certainly understandable."

Sheepishly he looked at us. "You say you can help her home?"

We nodded in unison.

"Boy, that's gonna be strange not having our lady around anymore. I'm sure gonna miss her."

I sympathized with him, yet he had to see the situation more clearly.

"She's like a prisoner here, Cliff. She's literally caught between dimensions. Her own confusion keeps her around. She needs to be freed so she can go home where she belongs."

"Oh don't get me wrong, I understand all that, but she's become like one of us. The lady's a real gentlewoman."

I sensed a sensitive man here.

"Don't you want her to be free again?"

He hesitated. "Deep down I do—we all do, I guess. It's just going to be so lonely not seeing her around anymore."

Bill spoke up. "You'll be doing her a great favor, Cliff."

"I suppose so."

"Do we have your permission to proceed, Cliff?"

His look was long and hard as he mentally deliberated.

The clock counted off the seconds.

We held our breath.

Finally our host heaved a weighted sigh. "You two are real different, you know that? I never would've figured you for ghost helpers or whatever it is you call yourselves. What do you call yourselves, anyway?"

Bill and I looked at one another and grinned.

I turned to Cliff. "We're just people. We don't call ourselves anything special. Once you get into terms for things everything suddenly gets misunderstood and more complex than it should be. We just help lost spirits."

The man chuckled. "You ought to call your unofficial business something like Lost and Found Inc."

We smiled at that. Not because of what he'd said, but because he had come around. His next words verified that fact for us.

"All right. Since you're not interested in the notoriety or any publicity with this, I'm going to let it go at that. This isn't going to be noisy, is it?"

I tried to reassure him as best I could.

"We try to be very discreet. That's important to us. We can't second-guess or predict exactly how a spirit will react, but our methods alone are a quiet affair."

"Well. . .at least you're honest about it. Just don't want any of my other guests disturbed or frightened."

"Neither do we," I emphasized. "A woman in robe and curlers screaming her head off does little for our concentration."

Our host laughed at that. "Guess we both have reasons for keeping this under our hats." Then he rose from his chair, set it back under the table and leaned on the highback. He winked.

"Don't disappoint me now."

"We'll do our best not to," I affirmed.

"I know you will. In the meantime, you folks enjoy your meal. I suggest the Maine lobster—fresh shipment just came in this afternoon." He nodded to us and left.

As I watched him go, he paused to snare a passing waitress and whispered to her. She glanced in our direction and I hoped he wasn't already spreading it around about why we were here.

I picked up the fancy menu and diligently searched for the salads while my mouth watered for the taste of hot buttery lobster. Bill and I both loved it, but tonight would be strictly bunny food.

My comedic partner didn't help the frustrating situation. He licked his lips temptingly, "Mmmm, lobster."

I ignored him as best I could. But before I could make my

dinner choice, a svelte waitress approached our table and very ceremoniously set down a chilled carafe of wine.

"Good evening. I'm Kathleen and I'll be your waitress for the evening. Mr. Westcott sends his regrets that he's unable to join you. He suggests the Maine lobster. He says your dinner and room are on the house."

Suddenly my nervous stomach was calm. It was back where it belonged and it was very hungry.

Kathleen reached into her crisp uniform pocket and placed a key on the linen tablecloth.

"Your room is Four-Eighteen," she said in a secretive tone. "That's *her* room. You will have the entire floor to yourselves. The wine is also complimentary," she said, smiling. "Cliff thinks you'll need it. May I take your order now or shall I come back?"

We didn't even have to look at the menu—we knew exactly what we wanted.

When the waitress left, I narrowed my eyes at my dinner partner.

"You knew all along we wouldn't have to pay for all this, didn't you?"

He guiltily hung his head.

"That was a terrible thing to do to me. I've been sick with worry over how we were going to pay for all this and all the time you knew!"

"Hey, I can't shoulder all the blame. Didn't I tell you right from the beginning not to worry? Huh? But no. . .little Worrywart here goes right on fretting. Don't you think I knew we couldn't afford all this luxury?" He hesitated before dropping the bomb. "Next time I ask to talk to our Advisor, I suggest you hang around."

My mouth gaped. "*That's* what you talked about this morning. He *told* you Cliff would do this. That was sneaky the way you two connived like that."

"Oh really?" he crooned, pouring the wine. "All you had to do was to have trust. . .just trust that everything would work out. All you had to do was have faith." He raised his glass. "To faith!"

I gave in. "To faith. . .and next time I'm going to hang around."

"Would've saved yourself a lot of worry."

And that was a fact.

The dinners came, and they were sumptuous. The butter was sweet, the potatoes were done to perfection and smothered in sour cream, and the lobster was mouth-watering tender. The ticktocking that continued its perpetual rhythm behind me was no longer Poe's ominous pendulum, but rather one that emanated warm feelings of contentedness.

I must've showed some signs of my pleasure, for Bill commented on it.

"You like that clock, huh."

My eyes closed. "Mmmm, yes. Can't you just envision a little log cabin way back in the woods—so quiet—only the gentle ticking of a grandfather clock?"

"How come you like them so much?"

"Oh I don't know. I just love the contentment I feel from the sound. I really can't explain it—there aren't words for the serenity it seems to give me."

"Someday you'll have that clock, honey."

"Nahhh, it's not that important. We'll have other things to get. It's just nice sitting by one once in a while."

"You give up the clock idea like you did the horses?"

"I guess."

"Why?"

"I told you, anything that's not a necessity just lost its importance."

He wasn't sure he liked that. "I don't want you to give up everything."

My hand reached over the table to cover his. "I haven't. Some things will always be important."

Kathleen came back then to take our plates away. She'd inquired if we'd care for dessert and proceeded to enumerate some very sensual delights—all sinfully rich and tempting.

With some reluctance, we declined and thanked her for her solicitous attention.

She respectfully left us to enjoy our wine.

After a glass and a half, I was warmly mellowed out.

"Too bad Cliff sent over a whole liter," I sighed, "we'd never be able to work our way through all that."

Bill agreed. "His intentions were good."

We rested back into the heavily padded chairs and observed the incoming crowd. It was surprising to us to see the place so packed. Those that couldn't be immediately accommodated were waiting in the lounge. The overflow milled around in the main lobby. And we were feeling guilty sitting there, lingering over wine we'd never finish while people were waiting to eat. I didn't have a guilt complex, but fair was fair—we were finished with our meal and we had business to attend to.

Bill left Kathleen a generous tip and, as we stood to leave, the grandfather clock chimed a half hour. It was six-thirty. Its voice was a noble one. The clarity was crystal-clear. And quite suddenly, the reason for my love of those masterpieces also became crystal-clear. They were likened to one's soul, their wise spirits. Beneath the exterior facade of the body, the spirit lived, its heartbeat a truly eternal ticking. And when it did speak, its voice resonated with the clarity of the finest crystal.

I smiled at Bill while the single tone elongated out into the atmosphere—its vibrational sound reaching and reaching like the spreading water ripples out from a singular pebble cast upon its glassy surface. Then it folded back unto itself—its shimmering core. The immortal soul's perpetual heartbeat eclipsed through the crystalline spheres of etheric firmaments and its metered pulse was strong and alive with power. Tick-tock. Tick-tock. The spirit's heartbeat was soft and reassuring.

Hand in hand, we left the bustle of the dining room. Clearing the ornate swinging doors, we found ourselves in the midst of another crowd wave—one quietly buzzing in a myriad of separate conversations—people were milling about the lobby waiting to be seated for dinner.

Bill, knowing how crowds unnerved me, jangled the room keys.

"We got the whole floor to ourselves."

That thought sounded like heaven. Besides wanting to be away from the crowd's many incoming psychic impressions, I was anxious to set foot within the private domain of our mysterious enigmatic lady.

Moving as politely as possible, we weaved through the groups of humanity. Then, above the din of the crowd, we heard our names being called out. Looking about the massive room for the source of the sound, we zeroed in on it. Cliff's arm was above his head waving frantically for our attention. We changed direction and worked our way toward him.

"I want you to meet a few friends of mine," he said as we cleared the crowd. He patted a tall bearded gentleman on the shoulder.

"This is David Petersen, Sweetwater's resident artist."

We shook hands with the resident artist.

Our host's hand then settled on the arm of a stout man of rugged complexion.

"This is Joel Roberts. He's a rancher. Got himself a big spread a few miles north of town."

We dutifully shook hands with the rancher and I wondered what it was all about.

"And last but not least," Cliff chuckled and winked, "this is Paul Jones; he's a writer."

My neck prickled. A writer? Now my curiosity was really spiking.

"What do you write, Mr. Jones?"

His natural rosy cheeks darkened with the question. That alerted me.

"Oh a little of this an' that."

"Anything serious in the works?"

"I've been working on a novel for a long time now, but I never seem to make much headway at it."

That sounded like he was spending most of his time on other things—other writings?

"Are you a freelancer?" I asked, digging for specifics that would justify my peculiar feelings.

Now the cheeks officially blushed.

"Only with my personal writings." He knew where I was going with the line of questions and didn't particularly want to be trapped in them. "My novel dabbling's a sideline for when I have time for it. I'm a journalist by profession."

Uh-huh, there it was. "A *newspaper* reporter?"

The young man was embarrassed, yet tried to maintain his cool. "Yes," he smiled, trying to cover for the reason he was there. "I do the human interest stories."

"Ohhh, I see."

Our host thought too much had been revealed before he had the chance of gently easing things into place. He disrupted the conversation that was getting too serious between Mr. Jones and me. He faced us with a wide smile that seemed a bit forced.

"I'd sure appreciate it if you'd let me buy you two a drink."

We hesitated. We'd had our limit in that area already. However, our host's burning desire to have a more in-depth discussion regarding the matter at hand was clearly in evidence. He had been extremely generous and, although he didn't feel we owed him any return favors, we felt differently.

"All right," Bill agreed.

Relief washed over Cliff's features. His friends were equally satisfied with our response.

The five of us trailed behind the proprietor as he proudly strode into the dimly-lit lounge. All stools and booths were occupied except for the big semi-circular one in the far corner.

I imagined that one was always open, for it was reserved for the owner and his personal guests.

The lounge was cave-like—as most were—and was not without the extravagant decor that permeated the rest of the hotel. Leather booths in deep Hunter's green were offset by flickering flames within red glass candle holders that centered each table. Red and green Tiffany glass shaded oil lamps along the polished paneled walls. Various paintings of The Hunt gave the vast room an English pub feeling. Voices were low and refined. This was no western bar. There were no cowboys and no mechanical bulls to ride. High sophistication reeked from every nook and cranny, both within the atmosphere and from the patronage alike. Although I was not one to visit lounges, I liked this one very much.

We were seated and everyone gave their orders to the demurely dressed waitress costumed in the high-neck, ankle-length style of the period. The men ordered cocktails and whiskeys. We passed on the alcohol, opting for coffee instead. No one seemed to mind.

Cliff jumped right in with small talk.

"So did you sample that lobster?"

We said we had and expanded on the fare by raving about its quality.

"Quality counts," Cliff said, "but what's even more crucial to a fine eatery are the talents of a fine chef!"

We agreed.

Our host wasn't finished. "I could've ended up with a real dead place here," he explained, glancing around the place. "I could've gone under just like that!" He snapped his tanned fingers. "I've seen expensive places go under in no time flat all because they had a bad or inexperienced man in the kitchen. And I've seen real dives thrive. It all boils down to the cook. Yessir, that cook either makes or breaks a place. More than any other factor, that man is the key player. You gotta find a great cook...preferably a bona fide chef, an' then you gotta keep him happy—pay him what he's worth. He'll turn a place to gold every time!"

We voiced a few comments about what he'd said, but we both knew he hadn't invited us to his cozy little roundtable to discuss the finer points of restaurant management. I was somewhat amused with the circling trail he was taking. However, Bill and I had prerequisite research to do yet and I was antsy to get to them.

I saved the men their circling anxiety by stabbing directly into the bull's eye myself.

"I assume we're all here to discuss your lady. We're open to that."

Visible signs of deliverance came from the group, yet it was clear that there was something more to come that held them in the clenching grip of nervousness. I anticipated what it was...a child could've summed up the simple two an' two problem the men presented us with.

In all things I preferred the straightforward approach. No-Eyes had much to do with that attitude. So again I went to the heart of the matter without tiptoeing around. I addressed the journalist.

"You want to write about our encounter."

He flushed only slightly this time. He knew we were getting down to brass tacks and he strived to maintain his personal integrity.

"Yes," he said outright with forceful eye contact.

"How will you manage this? From whose viewpoint?"

"First person?"

My mate wouldn't know what that meant. I turned to him.

"Mr. Jones would like to join us tonight," I informed very matter of factly.

He displayed no facial reaction while remaining silent.

The men held their breaths in hopeful expectation.

Then Bill released a burdened sigh.

"Gentlemen, I realize you're well intended, but what you're asking here just is not possible."

Their hopes deflated as Bill spoke.

"There's more than one good reason for this and I'll be more than glad to go into them for you, but first I'd like to know how many observers the lady has appeared to in a single sighting?"

The four quickly scrutinized one another and exchanged comments. Our host spoke up.

"As far as we know only one observer at a time has seen her. Why? Is that important?"

Our brows knitted as we eyed one another. That was not good news.

"That's important," Bill underscored with a decided frown. "That's very relevant. You see, as crowded as this place gets, the odds of more than one person observing her at any one time would be excellent. In fact they should be very high. But if, as you say, she's never manifested before more than one, we may have ourselves a problem."

The situation was clear to the listeners. It was Joel who now entered the fascinating discussion.

"I see where you're headed with this," the rancher said. "It is strange that she's never seen by more than one at a time."

The men thought about that.

So did we.

"I'm wondering," I mused aloud, "if being in the presence of more than one person frightens her."

That idea seemed to amaze the men.

David nervously chuckled. "A *scared* ghost?"

It did sound grossly out of character and I attempted a simple explanation.

"David," I said, directly addressing the artist, "since spirits are the minds and personalities of bodies they inhabited, they naturally feel the same gamut of emotions that living people do. So if this lady is. . ."

"Whoa!" he cut in. "What's all this about minds and personalities?"

My simple explanation was not as simple as I had thought. I needed to break it down more and simplify it further; sometimes that only confused the issue.

"What do you think a spirit is, David?"

"A ghost?"

I smiled. "Well yes, but what's a ghost?"

"I guess some filmy sort of stuff that hangs around after folks kick the bucket."

"That 'filmy stuff' is the spirit. And the spirit is the mind. . ."

"Nahhh," he crooned in doubt, "brains don't live when people are dead."

"You're right, they don't. Brains are just the material *housings* for the mind itself—when the brains die, the mind *with* personality still exists. . .within a finer vibratory frequency called the spirit. And the spirit is immortal."

"Whew! I always thought that ghosts was ghosts! And if they're what you say, then they can think! Then it *would* be possible for a ghost to have human feelings like being scared."

"Yes."

All was quiet while the men turned the new information over in their heads.

"I knew all that," Cliff boasted. "Why anybody who's seen our little lady can tell she's got personality!"

All four heads bobbed in unified agreement, for all four had observed her at one time or another.

Now that we all agreed on the semantics, we examined them more closely.

I was thoughtful. "What is she like?"

They all began spouting her qualities at once.

"Sweet!"

"Innocent!"

"A real genteel woman!"

"Refined and shy!"

"Shy?" I said. "There's our answer then. If she's all you say she is, then my next question is, would she be *too* shy to present herself to *two* people?"

The silence was profound.

Everyone just looked at each other. No one came up with an answer. And, for us, that was bad news.

Bill was first to pierce the solemn moment.

"Those others who came here," he directed to our host, "did *they* see her?"

"You mean those loony psychics?"

Bill nodded.

"No. Never even got a glimpse of her."

"You positive about your figures?"

Again all four checked with each other. Again their responses held true. No one had doubts.

"Well then," Bill declared, "that definitely disqualifies a third party right there."

Although the men clearly saw the valid reasoning, their common reactions exemplified their great disappointment.

"I'm sorry," Bill sympathized, "but that only adds to the other reasons I mentioned earlier." He went into them. "It would be useless to have someone observing us because most often, unless that observer is himself a developed sensitive, he couldn't hear what was transpiring. . .he may not even be able to see the spirit. The techniques my wife and I use are very specialized. They were taught to us by a very knowledgeable and experienced person. It's because of these specialized methods that we have to have complete concentration—no outside distractions of any kind."

Joel's interest was heightened. All the men appeared enrapt with the subject, but it was Joel who was eager to know more.

"This is fascinating! What's involved with these techniques?"

My shoulders slumped with the question. I looked over at Bill, smiled weakly, then gave my attention to the questioner.

"If I could explain it in simple terms, I would. If I could

describe it in complexity, I would. . .believe me, I would. But I can't do either."

Paul tried to give a kindly assist. "I'm a writer," he said. "Words are my stock in trade. Maybe I can help you out."

I didn't bother explaining that I too was a writer and that that fact didn't help a damn in this instance, but that wasn't relevant to the point.

"Paul, I appreciate that, I really do, but I've already tried to adequately describe this process and I can't. I've scoured dictionaries, thesauruses, the Synonym Finder, everything that I thought could help me, but it was no use. There just are no words that fit. It's as impossible as trying to drive a car that has no engine. I'm sorry."

I sighed with the remembrance of the many times I'd tried to clearly define No-Eyes' techniques and failed. . .miserably failed.

"The closest I can come is to say that our method bridges or melds vibrational frequencies. . .it temporarily allows dimensions to be shared. The actual mechanics are far beyond my simple mind to formulate into words."

"Heavy stuff!" Paul exclaimed with a shake of his head.

Yes, it was heavy stuff. Heavy, draining and not always predictable or even feasible.

Cliff came up with a logical question.

"How do your physical bodies alter? I mean, how can they be able to get into another dimension?"

"The physical can't, Cliff. The physical form remains within the three-dimensional plane while the spirit does the bridging."

"Ohhh," he uttered, nodding as if that made it all perfectly clear.

I grinned. "I told you it was beyond reasonable explanation."

He smiled. "Stupid of me to even ask. I should've known better."

Bill didn't want the man berating himself like that.

"Don't belittle yourself, Cliff. Even the people who make this subject their business, the parapsychologists, get mixed up on their terminology and concepts. It's an obscure science that's just trying to unravel itself. The definitive boundaries are vague at best, if indeed, there are boundaries. Maybe that's the whole problem. Those who are studying this matter are trying to cubbyhole the different aspects of manifestations. . .maybe they're all variables of the one. . .altered facsimiles of each other. Personally," he admitted, "I believe they're all interrelated, sort of like the colors of the rainbow that blend together to form one manifestation."

That sounded more than plausible to the men.

While Bill had been talking, I had been thinking of our sweet lady friend. Questions were formulating, and if I could get their answers, we'd be a little ahead of the game. Taking advantage of the rare lull, I addressed no one in particular.

"How frequently does the lady vary her route through the hotel?"

The men's faces clouded.

"Why?" Paul inquired.

"Because we'll need to have some idea of the various routes. It'd help us a great deal to be aware of the different sequences."

I didn't know that I had said anything particularly amusing, for after I'd made the reply, four faces beamed above generous smiles. They were contagious and I smiled back at them.

"What'd I say, gentlemen?"

Cliff lit a cigar, puffed a second or two to get it going and then grinned.

"We understood you to be concerned about the lady's different routes through the hotel."

"Yes, that's a serious concern here."

"Not anymore," he said proudly.

"Why not?"

"'Cause our little lady's punctual. She's right on time every night. Never *known* her to be late."

Oh-oh. My eyes slowly shifted over to my partner. His had done the same and we stared at one another. My scalp tingled. Then I looked at each man in the booth.

"She appears at the *same* time every night?"

"Yes, ma'am!" Cliff said, all puffed with her promptness.

"She's *never* been late or early?"

"Nope."

Oh, say it isn't so, I thought. "How about her route? That varies, doesn't it?" Please say it does. Please.

"Not that either."

Now I was really concerned.

David didn't like the looks of my expression.

"Is there something the matter? You don't look too happy."

"Please," I implored, "this is very important. Think hard on your own observations of her. Have any of you ever observed her more than once?"

Nods bobbed all around. That was good.

"And during those different occasions, did she *ever* do anything different? Please take your time to think about this. It's very relevant. I'm looking for *anything* that can be considered a variable. Even as insignificant as a slight gesture or tilt of the head that she didn't do the time before." I held my breath while each man personally deliberated upon his own sightings.

The artist and the rancher then nodded.

The journalist and our host shook their heads.

Two for two.

My palms upturned. "What's this supposed to mean?" I asked them. "Two of you say yes and two say no. Gentlemen, a split decision doesn't help us much."

Bill had a knowing twinkle in his eye. "Maybe it's not a hung jury after all; let's hear them declare their verdicts." He pointed to David the artist.

"Does she or doesn't the lady vary her actions?"

Again he nodded as before. "Yes, she did a couple things different each time I saw her."

"Okay. How about you, Joel?"

He too nodded again. "Same goes for me—she varies."

So far so good.

Then my partner pointed over to Paul and reworded the question.

"Well? Does she repeat the same actions every time?"

The journalist's head went from side to side.

"No. There's always a little something different about her mannerisms. Maybe one time she'll touch her hair and the next it'll be the broach, but it's enough to make the variable."

My eyes widened in delightful surprise. I hadn't thought two of the men would've transposed the original question.

When it was Cliff's turn to give testimony, he had already discerned the problem.

"I see now how we got different answers, but all the same, we agree on the facts—the lady alters the action a little every time she appears."

I didn't try to hide my great relief.

"Whew! I'm so happy to hear that!"

Our host and his pals were at a loss to understand my reaction.

Cliff's curiosity got the best of him.

"What if we all agreed differently? What if the lady never altered a hair?"

"I wouldn't want to think about that," I admitted quite

frankly. "If that was really the case in point, then our trip here would've been wasted."

The men's faces were blank. They had no idea what I was talking about and I saved them the trouble of asking.

"If the lady never varied anything, and I do mean *anything*, that'd mean she wasn't *real*."

The faces were still blank. I tried again.

"There's a phenomenon called a *psychic imprint*. It's caused by the residual vibrations and energies left behind after an emotional explosion has occurred—remaining fallout so to speak."

Getting nowhere fast, I went into an example.

"Say a terrible murder was once committed in the lobby out there. Say this happened one hundred years ago. Well. . .there are instances when such explosive violence 'imprints' the atmosphere of the location with a powerful psychic recording of the event. This imprint can be observed by people and it replays itself over and over again. It'd be like watching a ghostly show that reenacts the original event—no more alive than viewing the same movie clip again and again. The guests in the hotel of this time frame would then be observing not a real ghostly murder, but the psychic instant replay of it." I paused. "By the way, the spirits seen in a psychic imprint can't hurt you—no matter how grisly or violent their actions are. They're not real."

My audience was spellbound.

"Did I explain that well enough?"

They nodded and each thawed by degrees.

Joel clicked his tongue. "Fascinating, just fascinating. And you were worried that our lady was one of those. . .ah. . ."

"Psychic imprints. Yes. If she were, there'd be no communicating at all and there'd be no getting rid of the manifestation either. She would simply replay her nightly vigil over and over again."

"What stops those imprints?" David asked, getting deeper into the interesting subject.

"In time, the energy becomes dissipated enough to lessen and it gradually fades. The scene becomes less dense, less distinct, and finally, after being no more than a haze, it's gone. But this may take many years to finalize itself into a complete resolution."

The artist had a comment.

"Would you say that what some people actually claim as a ghost encounter are really nothing more than these imprints?"

"Oh absolutely. Most people who happen upon an imprint don't usually hang around long enough to realize that it's not really happening. They have no idea they've just witnessed the illusion rather than a bona fide spirit." I smiled in amusement. "They never realized they had nothing to be scared of."

Although they thought that was humorous, they weren't at all too convinced that a psychic imprint wouldn't still be able to scare the pants off them. They were glad their manifestation was a gentle lady of refinement.

It was about then that I happened to glance down at my watch. It was getting late and we had our preliminaries to do before squeezing in some rest time before the real work began.

Bill also noticed the passage of time.

"Gentlemen, did I understand that the lady usually follows a routine pattern?"

They all concurred with that.

"Can you detail the sequence for us?"

"Sure," Cliff readily obliged, taking a fresh cocktail napkin and pulling a pen from his breast pocket. "This is the grandfather clock in the dining room." He placed an "X" on the spot "You know where that is?"

Bill and I exchanged quick warm glances. "Yes," he said.

"Okay then. She appears there promptly at three a.m. She appears to be worried and looks to the windows, then back at the clock. After a few more minutes, she turns and walks through to the lobby where she pauses at the bottom of the staircase. It's almost like she's hesitating and deciding whether to go up or not. Anyway, she glances back toward the clock once again, then climbs the stairs and takes the right wing. After reaching the fourth floor, she paces the entire length of the hall. She does this four times before entering Four-Eighteen—your room. The lady stands before the opened window, watches down Main Street for a length of time, then vanishes."

"Is that pretty much the way you three saw it too?" I asked the others.

Nods gave agreement.

Bill took the sketch our host handed him and eased us out of the booth.

"Well, gentlemen? My wife and I have preliminaries to attend to. We appreciate all your helpful information—you've been very kind. By morning, we hope to be able to tell you that your lady went home."

All four surreptitiously exchanged glances. Then they stood to shake our hands. Paul had one final question.

"Since I can't be there tonight, will you have time in the morning to tell me how it went? I'll be in the newspaper office. It's just two doors down from here."

Bill said we'd be glad to stop in before we left.

And the meeting was concluded.

Before we entered the lobby proper, I glanced back at the corner booth. The occupants were getting refills and conspiring in hushed tones. I felt they weren't exactly toasting to our success. All of them loved their genteel lady. Not a one really wanted her gone.

When we rounded the archway of the lobby, an odd sound caught my attention. I instinctively turned to it and my eyes lit up. I yanked on my escort's arm.

"Look Bill! An old-time lift!" I exclaimed, pointing to the people exiting from it.

"You actually want to ride that contraption?"

"Could we?"

"If you want," he said, grinning over my excitement. "We'll take it up but, later on, we have to take the long way down."

I eagerly pulled him into the small box and watched while he stood there.

"Aren't you going to close the gates?" I asked.

"Well, how did I know? This isn't exactly what you find in every hotel."

The ornate filigree gates closed and the lift began to rise. It was almost soundless as it carried us up through the center of the century-old building. A muted whirring was all that was heard.

I stared at the bright Oriental carpeting on the floor.

"They don't want us to succeed," I softly said.

"I know. They'll feel differently after we explain what transpired and what we found out."

I looked into the confident grey-blue eyes. "Will we succeed?"

He held my chin. "We'll do our best. We can't do better than that, babe."

The lift trembled to a stop. And the view through the gold gates made a shudder quiver through me. Bill wrapped a warm arm about me.

"You cold?"

I shook my head.

"I know," he comforted while looking down the beckoning hallway. "It's not exactly home, is it?"

Staring out at the long silent corridor, the eeriness of it was harrowing. Every fiber of my being was called to the alert.

Bill pulled the gates apart and guided me onto the soft carpeting. He closed them again and we stood upon the threshold of the spirit's private domain. The entire fourth floor was ours now. . .ours and hers. Although we'd be the only guests here, we weren't going to be alone.

Transfixed to the spot, our eyes were magnetically drawn to the opposite end. A Queen Anne chair boldly faced us. It stood out in defiant relief. Beside it, a bountiful bouquet of fresh flowers stood atop a lyre table's gleaming cherrywood surface. It struck me as being macabre. Fresh flowers on a hotel floor where no one could see or smell them? Was this the proprietor's personal tribute to his vaporous resident guest of honor?

Bill jingled the key to distract my attention from the ominous aura that wavered within the confines of the corridor. I seemed to be bewitched by it. So powerful. So magnetic. The silent preternatural surround had actually charmed me. It awaited my presence. It and I were somehow alike. We had something in common, we two.

"Hey," came an irritating voice beside me. Jangle-jingle. "The room? We came up here to find the room?"

Oil lanterns were spaced every fifteen feet or so along the walls. Their flames quietly flickered beneath fragile shades of emerald green glass. Reflections glowed softly upon the silver and jade flowered wallpaper. Mahogany wainscoting glistened. The wool Oriental carpet was plush and thick, for few feet had had the chance to matt its high nap. Here the uncanny stillness did breathe; only, presently, it intentionally held that breath. It waited. It listened.

Bill's fingers wagged before my eyes.

"Honey? You 'getting' something?"

"Shhh," I whispered, before closing my eyes.

His lips touched my ear. "You okay?"

I nodded then listened to that which listened to us. The lady's energy was very powerful. The hallway literally reeked of her frequent presence. I sniffed the air. A trace of some pungent fragrance was perceived. It was not a discernible scent, but the sweetness suggested flowers. My eyes settled upon the distant floral arrangement. No, the aroma was not emitting from that. . .it had no tangible source; it was just in the air. . .it was part of the tractable energy that pulsed and throbbed around us.

"What is it?" Bill asked, unable to hold rein on his curiosity any longer.

"She's very strong," I relayed. "She's in possession of much power. . .but there's some other underlying aspect that I can't define. That aspect is at least equal to the power she has."

My elbow was gently touched. "Let's find the room."

Mechanically, my legs began to move. Our footfalls were soundless as we advanced down the center of the carpet. The flowers on the wallpaper reminded me of a thousand pairs of eyes—shifting as we passed—watching. Behind us, the lift's well-greased mechanism whirred. It descended to the beckoning of those who were of the living. It would not be returning to the fourth floor again this night.

We softly treaded our way to the antique chair. Four-Eighteen was parallel to it. I looked back to pan the length of the corridor, and my eyes rested where we had begun our long walk. Behind the lift's closed golden gates, emptiness darkly yawned.

The infamous key was held up before me like some grand prize.

"Want to do the honors?" Bill offered.

I wiped my clammy palms down the sides of my jeans and shook my head.

The key slid in the lock.

My heart pounded.

The tumblers silently turned.

My stomach churned.

Slowly did the door swing open on silent hinges.

Someone had entered before us. The oil lamps were burning low; one on the bedside table and two on the walls. The unexpected illumination created a very eerie lived-in appearance. But what had stirred me the most was the intense in-rushing emotions I had upon being hit with that first sighting of her room.

Gentleness. Sweetness and compassion. Noble character. Refined and sensitive.

The lady's personality was overpowering. And now I knew what had eluded me previously. Although her strength was powerful, the equally balancing trait was her incredible in-grained gentleness.

Once the aspects of the spirit herself had been perceived and noted, my own feelings rushed forth like waters through an opened floodgate.

"Ohhh, Bill," I moaned. "What a room!" My voice dripped with delicious admiration.

He eased his awestruck wife into the interior of the room and closed the door. We stood in place while surveying the furnishings and decor.

The entire atmosphere possessed a living aura. The aura had color. Lavender. The glowing dark pine wainscoting rose waist-high from the rich purple carpet. The wood trim met the wallpaper, new, looking as fresh as the day it was hung, making the walls vibrant with their flowers of lilacs and lavender.

Now the former nebulous aroma that I sensed in the corridor also had definition—lavender. If my eyes had been closed, I would've sworn the room was full of vases—all holding stalks of fresh-cut lavender.

An armoire, massive, was angled in one of the corners. Dark pine, rich in grain, was masterfully decorated with intricate carvings. Brass handles and hinges were recently polished. A tall Cheval mirror, hinged with pegs, was tilted just so. An antique chaise of deep mulberry velvet dominated another corner. And occupying center stage was the object of my initial admiration. A great testor bed dominated the feminine room. Filmy yards and yards of silk hung from the wooden canopy and were daintily tied to the four posts with satin sashes. The bed, mattress high and rounded with feather quilts, was covered with a fragile draping of white lace. A dozen small pillows adorned the head of the bed in a profusion of purple shades.

Plum satins. Violet velvets. Damson silks and mauve chintz.

The bed was a rainbow of purples.

I looked up at Bill.

"Bet you really like this room," I teased, knowing his penchant for purple.

"Nahhh, too frilly."

"I was talking about the *color.*"

Then the corners of his mouth lifted. "Yeah, the color's perfect."

In his mind, it was perfect all right. If he had his way, everything in life would be purples and blues.

I crossed the room to the heavy armoire and opened the double doors. It was empty except for the penetrating lavender spice that drifted out. I stood with my hands on the doors for several sensual moments before quietly closing them again. My fingertips touched the smooth wallpaper and they traced the delicate outlines of a lilac.

Incoming impressions were vivid.

Turning, I stepped to the bed. Palm upon the lace coverlet, I closed my eyes. When I opened them again, Bill was eagerly waiting for the new information.

"She's not going to be persuaded to leave," I sadly related.

"You sure?"

"Yes. There's a great heaviness here. This room is weighted with it. The armoire gave off an extreme level of sensitivity. The wallpaper exuded sadness and," I said, sorrowfully glancing down at the intricate bed cover, "this bed is giving off a terrific force of determination."

A wry grin curled my companion's ups. "You're pretty determined yourself."

My lips didn't curl. "This is ten times stronger. She won't be convinced."

Bill crossed the room. "Honey, so what if she is determined. All we need to do is to find the right logic to whatever her problem is and then she'll see reason. We still don't know why she's bound or what she's waiting for."

Now I did grin. "She's waiting for a lover, remember?"

"You didn't tell me you got anything on that."

"I didn't. . .I just know."

He eyed me with high suspicion. "That a *romantic* mental assumption or a true *gut* feeling?"

"You want the truth or should I make something up?"

"Oh never mind," he groaned, plopping our bag on the bed.

His action immediately appalled me. "Watch what you're doing! That's real old lace!"

He released an exaggerated sigh and dramatically picked up the offending object, tiptoed across the room and carefully set it on the chaise. "Better?"

"Better," I grinned. Men just had no respect for fine workmanship.

"Maid's been here," he suddenly informed, inclining his head to the night table.

I turned to spy a Baby Ben windup clock. The alarm had even been set for two-thirty.

"Cliff thinks of everything," I quipped.

"He has to. This place is run like clockwork." The pun was unintended. The statement was pure fact.

"Well?" Bill asked, "you going to change or sleep in your birthday suit?"

I was already in the process of unbuttoning my flannel shirt.

"Semi-buff," I said. "I don't want to get too comfortable or I'll never want to get out of this luscious bed."

He stripped down to his shorts and crawled in beside me.

"Jesus!" he flared, sinking down into the billowy softness. "This thing sure wasn't meant for a man!"

I giggled at the silly sight of him trying to settle in.

"Isn't this great! Look!" I squealed, yanking out a piece of fluff from the ticking. "A feather! All the old beds had these."

He took the downy object and studied it.

"No wonder I'm so damned uncomfortable; the thing's got *arrows* stuck in it." He passed the deadly lance over to me and dropped it into my hand. "There. Arrows are your department. Now you got an official souvenir." He leaned over to blow out the lantern. Moonlight flooded through the window. The room was illuminated with a natural silvery glow.

Bill automatically stretched out his arm for me to snuggle into.

I did. But I also didn't close my eyes.

"Honey?" I whispered, staring at the glowing wallpaper.

"Mmmm?"

"I feel like we're intruding in here."

"When did that feeling come about?"

"Just now."

"A little late for you, isn't it? I got that sensation the minute we stepped into the room."

"I guess I was too involved with getting impressions to notice what I felt. Anyway, I don't think she'll mind us being here."

"What makes you say that?"

"Because she's so kind-hearted."

"Babe?"

"Yeah?"

"Go to sleep."

And I did. But not before first feeling like we were the King and Queen of Sweetwater. That royal feeling was not of my own making—it came from the room, the walls, and from the kingly bed itself.

Four hours later I was glancing about the still room. The soft moonglow had slanted its rays to illuminate the armoire. I envisioned the clothes that had once hung within it. Long gowns. Capes trimmed in fur. Dressing gowns and an array of

176

feathered hats along the top shelf. And on the bottom, rows and rows of. . .

"You awake?" asked my partner.

"Yes. I was just sort of daydreaming."

"Guess our inner alarm clocks are still working."

"Guess so."

He reached over to the nightstand and depressed the alarm button.

"What time is it?" I asked.

"Two."

"We've got a whole hour before we need to get down. . ."

"SHIT! You *feel* that?" he exploded, bolting upright.

I too scampered up into a sitting position and listened to my senses. They were going off and blaring like a dozen smoke alarms. My scalp tingled and the blood drained from my face.

Bill flung back the covers. "Hurry! Get dressed! She's *early!*"

I nervously fumbled with buttons, zippers and snaps.

"Why'd she pick *tonight* to be early?" I sputtered.

"Who knows and I don't care! We've got to pick up this place and leave it just the way we found it. *Hurry!*"

The two of us scurried about the room. If anyone would've walked in on us they surely would've thought we were ransacking it. We silently flew around the room in valiant attempt to set it aright.

"Done!" I proudly proclaimed as if just setting a new World's Record.

Bill picked up our bag and we inspected our handiwork. Satisfied, we entered the quiet corridor and gently pulled the door closed behind us.

Stealthily creeping down the stairwell like a couple of experienced cat burglars, we reached the lobby where Bill set our bag behind the counter. Tiptoeing over to the double dining room doors, we apprehensively peered over their shoulder-high rims.

My spine pricked. For there she was, standing dutifully before the grandfather clock just as she had for nearly a century. The clock eerily ticked away the prolonged seconds. The sound was loud in the ominous stillness. It was no longer comforting. It was chilling.

The lady was taller than I had envisioned, but that was the only characteristic that varied from my former visual impressions. Standing in front of the timepiece, her back was straight, her carriage dignified and refined. Fragile, yet noble. Her chestnut hair was upswept and caught in abalone combs;

wispy tendrils of soft curls shadowed the slender nape of her neck and framed the finely chiseled face. Moonlight from the windows cast a glow upon the high cheekbones when she turned to glance out. The satin gown was of rich purple, a mauve sash encircled the tiny waist and fell in graceful folds to the floor where it met the antique lace of her hem.

The lady wrung her delicate hands. She turned.

We ducked into the shadowed corner behind the doors. If the spirit remained true to her routine path, she'd be coming our way any minute. We tried to ease our nervous breathing. My clammy hand sought out Bill's. His, like mine, gave evidence to the high anxiety of the moment and they clutched each other for strength and support.

No sound prepared us for the sudden sight of the lady beside us. No rustling of skirts, no movement of the swinging doors—not even a creak—forewarned us of her advance. She was just there, in the lobby now.

We pressed ourselves into the wall, hoping the shadows were dark enough to conceal our presence.

The lady walked across the carpet, set a foot upon the first step and paused. Hand on the polished newel post, she again turned. It appeared that her green eyes had fallen directly upon us, for a slight frown wrinkled the delicately arched brows.

A cold sweat dampened my forehead.

But the lady had only been contemplating the clock. She sighed, picked up her skirts and ascended the staircase, veering off and disappearing into the darkness of the right wing.

We eased out of the shadowed corner and followed—all the while, the scent of lavender waited in the etheric wake of her trail.

Upon reaching the third floor landing, Bill halted.

"We'll have to wait here," he warned, peering up around the corner. Then he stood vigil while the lady paced the upper corridor.

"One. . .two. . .three. . .four. Now!"

I tugged on his sleeve. "What if she varies and goes five?"

"Then we'll confront her in the hall instead of the room. C'mon!"

By the time we reached the fourth floor, all that we managed to glimpse of the lady was the bottom hem of her skirts as they trailed through the door of Four-Eighteen.

I looked to my partner. "What now?"

"Look!" he exclaimed.

Her door was now opened. A cold night breeze blew down

the lonely corridor. The chilled air struck my damp forehead. A shiver trembled through me.

"It's now or never," Bill decided with finality.

I nodded and we crept down the silent hallway. We peered around the doorway.

She was standing at the opened window looking forlornly down on Main Street. Lace curtains billowed into the room and fluttered about her. She couldn't feel the cold night mountain air.

We quietly stepped inside the doorway.

We watched as the woman's head slowly pivoted and lowered. She was curiously staring at something beside her.

Oh my GOD! We forgot the alarm clock!

It was then when she perceived our presence. She spun around; shock flared across the delicate features.

"We mean no harm," Bill quickly said, trying to allay her fear. "We've come to help you."

"Yes," I underscored. "I'm Mary and this is my husband, William." To introduce him as Bill wouldn't have been in keeping with the proper names of her time. It was always important to relate as well as possible to a spirit's time-frame.

The lady's frown disappeared. The features softened.

"Please, enter."

We took a couple furtive steps forward.

The door closed silently behind us. Clear evidence of the power the woman held and the ease with which she used it.

She studied us with discerning curiosity.

"How is it you do not require an intermediary?"

She had to mean a medium.

I spoke up. "We have been shown a way that makes the use of one unnecessary."

The fragile figure angled herself to us. The head tilted. A slight smile daintily eased up the full lips.

"Please forgive my ill manners. I am Josephine Du'-Aubrois."

"Josephine," Bill repeated in contemplation, "that's quite a lovely name."

Her cheeks flushed. Then the emerald eyes widened with hope.

"You have said that you've come to help me. You have brought word of my Charles then?"

She was so sweet, so innocent. We'd definitely need kid gloves with this one.

Before we could reply to her question, she spoke again. "You have slept in my room."

"Yes," I quickly responded. "This is the room we were assigned. Mr. Westcott gave us the key. I hope you don't mind."

At the mention of the proprietor's name, Josephine smiled warmly.

"He is very kind. He is a true gentleman, is he not? He would not have shown you to this room if you were not friends. I trust his judgment, for he has my welfare in mind."

The fresh flowers outside in the corridor attested to that fact.

"Yes," I readily agreed, "he has your welfare in mind. That is why we're here."

"How splendid!" she chirped in childlike glee. "Now tell me of Charles! What manner of business has detained him? I knew he would send word, for it is not like him to be so tardy!"

This was going to be very touchy, I thought.

"Josephine," I began gently, "we came here tonight to take you to Charles."

"Ohhh, but I am to await him *here!* Tomorrow we are to be wed." Her head tilted toward the opened window. "But he is so very late this night and I cannot rest until he returns."

And there it was. The innocent Josephine had just handed the clue to us on a silver platter. Now we had the handle we needed to continue. As it turned out, I had not been smitten with a severe case of romanticism—I had adjudged the situation correctly right from the beginning—the lady *was* waiting for a lover.

I sized up the present condition. Josephine had the awareness to wonder about our lack of using an intermediary, and that would naturally mean she also knew she was dead. But her reasoning was not bearing that conclusion out. I believed she was cognizant of the facts, but I also believed she was covering those facts of reality with a psychological mechanism of her own design. Denial soothed many a troubled heart. Denial calmed many stormy waters of the mind.

I stepped forward. "Josephine?"

"Yes?" came the sugary voice.

"Your gown is very beautiful," I admired, hoping the natural reply would be for her to give a like response.

"Why thank you. Your's is. . ."

"Different?"

"Yes," she smiled amicably, "your manner of dress *is* different."

Washed-out jeans were hardly proper English riding breeches either.

"My clothes are different because we are different. We are of different times—customs and manner of style are different."

She became visibly nervous.

"But surely you jest, Mary. Everyone knows that people of different times cannot join."

I involuntarily shuddered, for the mountain air blowing in through the window had dropped the room temperature considerably.

Josephine frowned at seeing my obvious discomfort.

The sash behind her slowly and soundlessly lowered. The curtains settled.

"How thoughtless of me," she berated herself. "Now you will be warmer."

I thanked her then picked up where we had left off.

"Do you know what year this is?" I asked.

"Certainly I do. Don't you?"

"Yes," I smiled at her response, "it is nineteen hundred and eighty. . ."

Her animated reaction cut me off. The delicate hand rose up to conceal the giggle that came.

"How silly," she chirped. "This year is eighteen hundred and ninety. . ." The voice trailed off as her eyes suddenly rested upon the Baby Ben beside her. When she next turned her attention to us, her expression was one of resignation, but not for the right purpose.

"Oh, it is difficult keeping up on things lately. Inventors are always creating so many new contrivances."

"It's quite wonderful," I added, staying with her own line of thought. "Why don't you take a closer look at it. Pick it up. It's all right."

She began to go for it. Her hand extended toward the small timepiece, but then it paused.

"No," she said sweetly, "it is not mine to handle. You show it to me."

Again evidence of her strong denial.

"Well, I guess it's not so important after all," I commented, easing away from the issue. "We came to give word of Charles."

The emerald eyes sparked with renewed interest.

"Is he all right?"

"Yes, he's just fine, but he wants you to meet him elsewhere."

A deeply suspicious shadow of doubt clouded her features.

I repeated myself. "Yes, it's true. He sent us to tell you that you're to go. . ."

"No! Charles comes *here!* That is what he *said* he would do."

I sighed. "Josephine, do you know the difference between us? Do you *know?*"

The chin jutted out slightly. "I know that there are many like you and William. Your kind live below in the Sweetwater. Charles and I live up here. I know we do not mingle well. That is why Mr. Westcott keeps your kind away from this floor."

"Josephine, Charles is just like your kind. He is not like us anymore. He has gone away and awaits your company."

The woman spun to face the window. "I await Charles' company here." The tone was almost cold.

I felt a deep empathy for the woman before me.

"Josephine, what makes us so different?"

Her head tilted to me. "Our manner of dress."

Bill exasperatedly rolled his eyes. He was becoming more than mildly impatient with the extent I was willing to go to circle the point of the matter. We stepped closer to the lady.

Skirts swishing, she spun on her heels. Fear flared from her eyes. The clock on the table toppled.

Bill put up his hands. "We're friends, remember?"

The woman's knitted brows relaxed. "Yes. . .friends. But your message greatly distresses me. Charles gave explicit orders for me to stay in the Sweetwater. I dare say, he would never send a counter message with someone I have never before laid eyes on."

Bill slumped onto the edge of the bed and sighed.

I ignored his irritated expression and turned to Josephine.

"Charles sends his regrets, but wants you to know that. . ."

". . .that he's *dead!*" came the shocking words from behind me. Obviously Bill had had enough of the kid-gloves treatment and had decided it was time to take out the boxing ones.

I wheeled around to glare at him.

A brow innocently rose. Shoulders shrugged as if to imply that there was nothing left to do but to come right out with it.

Whirling back to Josephine, her angered expression made my blood curdle. My heart pounded in an effort to keep it from congealing.

Daggers shot from the woman's narrowed eyes. "That was a most cruel thing to say, William. I do not care for your unkind joke. I demand an apology this instant."

The window rattled. The clock fell to the floor.

Bill stood.

"I'm sorry, Josephine, but it's true. Charles is dead. My wife can tell you how it happened."

Oh, shit. I hadn't received that information yet. I stared into the fiery eyes that burned through me.

"Well, I. . .I'm not real sure I can do that just yet. I. . ."

Bill bought me some time by pacing the room and distracting the woman's sights. Truthfully, I'm glad they were on him instead of me, because they definitely did nothing for my searching concentration.

I tried to calm myself so the impressions would flow freely. Finally they did.

"Josephine," I began softly as the icy stare slid to settle on me, "Charles was down in the seventh level when the accident occurred."

The back of her hand flew to her mouth. She listened in a dazed shock while I explained it all.

"Some shoring timbers gave way. Eight other men were trapped with Charles. The others outside worked hard to get them dug out in time, but they just couldn't manage it. The foreman came here to tell you. Josephine, don't you remember the foreman coming to the Sweetwater?"

She was completely catatonic. A sculptured study in terror.

Did spirits psychologically create mental blocks as people did? Were spirits capable of such self-imposed defense mechanisms? Had she really locked out the truth of it? For all these years?

In slow motion, the statue moved. The mouth formed an oh. And a soul-wrenching scream emitted.

"No-o-o-o!"

The armoire doors banged open and shut. Wall pictures swung. The window sash flew up and the curtains flapped about.

"Nohhhh! My Charles! My *Charles!*"

I attempted to get near the grief-stricken woman so I could comfort her, but it was useless. Her energies wouldn't allow it. They were flying out of control in all directions. Her tears flowed like a great river. The crying was tormented and wracked my soul. We would have to wait out the initial shock wave in order to reach her again. The din of the room was deafening.

Josephine wailed and covered her eyes with her hands. Fingers nearly clawed at her face. The hands lowered, pulling the cheeks down and exposing the bottom inner eyelids. She mysteriously froze in position. It was grotesque. It was hideous the way she looked. Eyes bulged as they fixed on me.

"CHARLES! Ohhhhh my God, *CHARLES!*" she screamed.

The clamor around us eerily silenced. The window quietly slid closed. Curtains settled. And time seemed to stand still. All three of us, iced in a permanent sculpture *a la trois.* Bill stared at the two women. I stared at Josephine. Josephine, in her hideousness, stared at me.

Then I saw the eyes soften. The hands left her face. Eyes returned to normal, then actually brightened. The entire face illuminated with an expression of great happiness. A smile began lifting the corners of her mouth.

Jesus, I thought, was this insanity we were observing? The smile widened. *"Charles!"*

And, before I knew what was happening, the lady rushed forward.

I backed into the bed while she flew past me, past Bill, and into the awaiting arms of Charles.

He had quietly manifested behind us. Although he was over a century late, he had quietly made it home to Josephine after all.

Her nightwatch had ended.

"So that's about it," Bill sighed heavily, sitting on the edge of the journalist's cluttered desk.

Though he tried to show a respectable measure of sympathy, Paul's eyes bespoke his intense pleasure.

"Don't that beat all. Who'd ever expect the lover to actually come back—just who'd ever think it'd turn out that way."

Bill shrugged. "We never figured on that, that's for sure. I guess Charles just had so much love for her he couldn't bear seeing her caught like she was. Guess he thought it'd be better for her to have him there."

"Damn! Now we got us *two* ghosts. That's really something!"

Bill could read the man's excitement and didn't feel like wallowing in failure any longer.

"Well," he sighed, tossing a stray pencil down on the desk, "since Josephine couldn't be convinced there was any home better than the Sweetwater, I guess you're stuck with them."

The pencil rolled across the desk and Paul caught it as it dropped off the edge.

"Yeah, well," he softened, "if it's any consolation to you, you might be interested in knowing we're not doing the story. It'd be all right if things had worked out differently, but seeing's they're still here, Cliff'd have a fit if we spread that around." He paused with the formulation of another thought. "Hey, you guys stop in and see us next time you're out this way."

Bill said that maybe we would. Then he backtracked.

"I gather that since you're not doing the story, Cliff would be a little put out if you did."

"He'd be furious."

"He didn't appear very put out when I told him about what happened this morning."

Paul grinned wide. "No, guess he'd be a far cry from being put out about that. Guess you could actually say he's right proud of how things turned out."

"Oh?"

"Well yeah! Now the lady's not *alone* anymore. Now she's *happy!* And when *she's* happy, *we're* happy."

Bill tapped his knuckle on the man's desk.

"See you around sometime," he said before walking out the door.

He was just overjoyed how happy everyone was. . .everyone but us.

It was almost one year later when we did find ourselves back Sweetwater way again. Although we were somewhat anxious to hear about Charles and Josephine, we needed to ease into the matter in our own roundabout way. Instead of heading directly to the Sweetwater Hotel, we made our initial stop at one of the local greasy spoons.

Its interior, as the exterior, was nondescript. We sat at a table beneath the worn cafe curtains. I had parted them a bit so we could watch the town's summer activity along Main Street. The place wasn't crowded and the food was decent. But the waitress was another matter altogether.

She was one of those bothersome nonstop talkers—the kind that soothe the soul as effectively as fingernails clawing down a chalkboard. Whenever we came across one of those pesky people, Bill always said the same thing. "When God was passing out brains, she didn't get in line because she thought He said 'trains.'" So maybe it wasn't the most kindly thing to say, but it did bother us when folks didn't use common courtesy or simple manners. To endure incessant chatter while attempting to enjoy a peaceful meal was very, very irritating.

Irregardless of our polite but short responses, she still managed to find her way back to us.

"Everything okay?" she asked for the fourth time.

"Yes, everything's just fine, very good," we'd reply.

"Boy! I tell ya," she sighed, flapping her hands to hips. "It's real nice gettin' compliments around here for a change. I work my fingers to the bone an' don't get no appreciation from nobody around this place."

I felt there was more than a grain of truth to what she had said and I actually felt sorry for her. I attempted to offer her a viable alternative.

"Maybe you should look for another job," I hinted. "Have you looked into working at the Sweetwater Hotel restaurant?"

At that the girl's eyes widened.

"Oh Lord, you ever hear about that place?"

Instead of an outright denial, I just asked, "Why?"

"Ohh, the hotel had a ghost!"

"No kidding!"

The waitress liked my shocked reaction. "Yeah, no lie! And. . .seems that almost a year ago now some fool couple come through here thinking they could get rid of it. I heard they was like ghost busters or somethin'. Anyway, what they originally accomplished was to bring *another* spook in. I gotta tell ya, this town sure don't need the likes of *that* pair! No ma'am! We was real happy to see them leave town. Good riddance, I say."

I didn't feel like eating anymore. I didn't have the stomach to sit and listen to the girl talk about our failure. We got up and made random comments here and there while the girl railed on and on about the unwanted couple.

At the register, she stopped long enough to count back the change. Before she could say more, we thanked her and were out the door.

Back in the truck, Bill started up the engine. Our spirits were at an all-time low. Then he turned his head to me. He had the most astonished look I've ever seen. He was scaring me.

"What's the matter?" I blurted.

His position remained frozen. His voice was barely a whisper.

"What we *originally* accomplished?"

I didn't follow what he meant.

Suddenly he tore from the truck and raced back to the diner. He disappeared inside.

The waitress spotted him. "Hey! Ya forget somethin'?"

"Ahhh no, but what you were saying before about that

couple that came through here. . .how the town didn't need the likes of them, what. . ."

"No, no, no. You got it all backwards. What I *said* was the town don't need the likes of that *ghost* pair. They disappeared from the hotel a long time ago." She rolled her eyes to the ceiling. "Been 'bout eight months now I guess since they been gone. Good riddance to the likes of them *spooks*, huh mister?"

"Yeah," Bill agreed with a great Cheshire smile shining on his face. "Yeah, good riddance to them *spooks*."

Somehow, in some wonderful way, Charles had finally convinced his love that there was a far better place to be than at the Sweetwater. Charles had taken his sweet Josephine home.

Moon of the Nightstalker

June ambled into July and the town was electrified with excitement, for this was the fifth of July. Every year on this date Woodland Park was gifted with a real treat. The Colorado Springs Symphony journeyed up Ute Pass to give a spectacular evening performance under the stars. This sensual celebration took place on the high school football field which is located on a rise above the town. By supper time, people begin gathering on the field in front of the mobile stage. Lawn chairs and blankets are brought along with dogs, scampering children and box dinners. People milled about visiting with friends or neighbors they spotted. The atmosphere sparked with festive anticipation, for the symphony was always a delight to hear.

And the music began. Stragglers hurried to their chosen pieces of grass and settled down on their blankets. Elderly citizens rested back in their chairs. Children laughed and blocked their ears, surprised at the loudness of the audio system, and lovers cuddled closer in expectation of an entertaining evening together.

Evening slipped into night. Below the field, the lights of the town glimmered. Above, starlight shimmered and the moon, high in the clear alpine sky, shone down like a stage beacon. Up the mountainside, pines hushed and nature nourished itself with the beautiful vibrations rising on the wind from the happy crowd. This night was good medicine, for its power was felt by all living things.

As the program progressed toward its conclusion, mothers woke their smaller slumbering children to gather them close. Small babies were held tightly to breast. For the finale had begun. The annual climax was building and the 1812 Overture blasted throughout the mountains. Army soldiers stood at the ready within the cordoned-off area. On stage, the thrilling music climbed and climbed, drums rolled and cymbals clashed, then. . .BOOM! The first cannon exploded with heart-jarring percussion and the earth trembled. One after another did the soldiers detonate their cannons. BOOM! BOOM!

BOOM! The music neared its crescendo. People stood and cheered. BOOM! BOOM! BOOM! Brilliant fireworks burst overhead, illuminating the field and upturned faces.

Then. . .silence. Blue smoke drifted over the field. The program had ended. But the crowd, hearts still pounding and souls still craving for more happy, cheered their pleas for the conductor to tarry. . .he always did. And the music struck up a folk dance tune.

Hands clasped. Friend to friend, parents to children, stranger to stranger, hands joined and everyone pranced a great snaking mazurka until hearts throbbed and breath became labored. As if on cue, the dancers stopped, faced the musicians and began whistling and cheering them. The mountain folk of Woodland Park were full of deep appreciation for the symphony's journey up the pass. The conductor, always overjoyed at the crowd's enthusiasm and reception, expressed his heartfelt sentiments and wished them farewell until next year. Again the crowd whistled and cheered, the musicians began breaking down their instruments, and the people began filing out.

While we were leaving the festivities, four of our friends came up to us and we invited them back to the house. After an evening of such sensory overload, we were not in the mood to go home and go right to bed. The six of us played cards until our girls were in bed. Then we turned on the stereo and sat around in the living room. The conversation didn't take long to drift to the matter of our latest spirit work.

Carol casually inquired about our next case and I explained what we knew of it.

"I don't have a lot of background information in my notes on any of these, but this one is the nightstalker. Evidently, way back when the west still belonged to the Indians, a trapper trespassed across a sacred burial ground. The tribe retaliated by attacking him in his cabin. The trapper's Indian wife escaped. She thought he'd been killed so she never returned. Turns out he wasn't killed after all and went looking for her. He's still looking."

Carol's husband whistled low. "He think she knew about the attack?" Jon wondered.

I shrugged. "That's not in my notes, but I suppose it's a possibility."

Bill then stressed the importance of us not second guessing anything.

"We can't speculate or assume anything we don't know as

fact. That kind of thing only confuses the issue. Maybe he's just mad as hell because she took off and wasn't there to tend his wounds. There could be several reasons. All we know is that he's full of anger and he's still looking for her."

Dianne and Tony looked worried.

"What's the matter?" I asked them.

They looked at one another before facing us. Then Tony voiced their shared concern. The question was directed to me.

"Aren't you just a little nervous about this one?"

I frowned. "I'm always nervous going into these. I'm hardly an expert at this."

"Well," Dianne clarified, "Tony means the *specifics* of this one. This trapper's looking for his Indian wife."

"So," I said, still missing their point.

Her eyes rolled. "Are you dense or what? This nightstalker is stalking an *Indian* woman."

I got the point. My heart quickened for a moment then returned to normal beats.

"But he's also looking for a *specific* Indian woman."

Silence all around.

I looked at each of my friend's solemn faces, then over to Bill. Nobody said anything but me.

"Oh come on, you guys, surely you don't think this stalker's going to transfer his hate to *any* Indian woman—to *me!*"

Brows rose in unison.

"That's crazy," I said.

"Is it?" Bill asked.

What was going on here? "Yes!" I blurted.

"Think about it," he urged. "Why wouldn't that be a logical reaction for him?"

"Because I'm not his wife, that's why. I'm a complete stranger. Besides," I added confidently, "I'm no fullblood."

"You think that's going to matter?"

"Yes!"

Silence.

Although the idea seemed incredible to me, the more time they gave me to mull it over, the less confident I became.

"You guys are scaring me," I finally admitted.

But the point wasn't to scare me; it was to make me see the seriousness of the case and the possible ramifications it could have.

Jon then made it all too clear. "You're going to be the target on this one."

I swallowed hard. "Thanks a lot. I needed that."

"He's probably right, honey," Bill said. "Remember the kid? Davey? And how he drew his power from the storm's energy?"

"Yeah?" I said, not making any connection. "What's your point?"

"What if this stalker draws his from the night—maybe the moon or something. No-Eyes did refer to him as the 'nightstalker.' Maybe she was throwing out a clue."

That theory was not at all encouraging. The storm went away—the night wouldn't.

I eyed the group. "What's going on here? I mean, what's *really* going on? It sounds like you're all trying to say something without actually coming out with it. No-Eyes didn't like beating around the bush and neither do I."

They all looked innocently sheepish.

"Are you trying to convince me to leave this one alone? Is that what this is all about?"

Their eyes slid to one another. Nobody seemed to want to be the one to own up to their purpose of intent.

"Well forget it!" I snapped. "It's on the list and we're doing it." I sighed and shook my head. "No-Eyes wouldn't have listed this if she didn't think we could handle it."

Carol's shoulders slumped.

Bill tried another approach. "That's not the point. We know how much faith she had, but this one's got certain factors that can jeopardize your safety. The particulars of this one could turn out to be too personal. It's like a personal vendetta. Don't you see that?"

Obviously there'd been some heavy discussions about this one behind my back. They were presenting a unified front against me—or for me—depending on how you looked at it. And although I didn't agree, I had to admit their thoughtful concern touched me.

"I appreciate what you're all trying to do here," I said with sincerity. "You're afraid for me and don't want me hurt." I noticed hope spark in their eyes. They thought they'd won. . .they hadn't. "But honestly, I just can't bring myself to run away from the 'special' ones. If I went with your premise, that'd mean I couldn't ever attempt to help *any* Indian-related cases. What about Sand Creek then? What if *Custer's* spirit is wayward and needs assistance? Do I leave him to roam forever?"

Impish grins crept up five faces.

I smiled. "You're awful. Yeah, maybe I'd leave that one

alone." That thought definitely had the sweet ring of poetic justice to it.

"You wouldn't really leave him, would you?" Carol asked.

My brow arched. "You talk about hate for Indians? Who hated them most? Now you're aghast that I wouldn't jump right in to help a bona fide Indian hater? Seems to me you're all contradicting yourselves."

Silence.

"Am I supposed to help Custer and not some trapper?"

Deep thinking going on.

"Well?" I pushed.

Tony shook his head. "Why do you have to be so logical all the time?"

Everyone's tension broke with snickers.

"I spent two years with a Dreamwalker, remember? Everything was *based* on logic."

Jon had another thought. "But are you *ready* to handle this race factor? I think that's the real issue here."

All eyes turned to me. Bill was the only one smiling, for he knew what my response was going to be.

"In the words of an immortal legend, 'some peoples never get *anywhere* 'cause they never *think* they be ready.' In other words, how do I know unless I jump in and try?"

Nobody commented. There was nothing left to discuss. The die had been cast and, ready or not, we were going through with it.

On a Saturday morning we were on the road again. Our direction was west and the weather was beautiful. It was a magical day that I hoped would carry over into nightfall. And since our destination was less than two hours away, we'd planned on reaping as much enjoyment from the day as possible.

We stopped at the Fossil Inn in Florissant for coffee and cinnamon rolls. For once we didn't run into anyone we knew and spent the leisure time reminiscing about the symphony celebration and how much our girls seemed to love that particular summer evening. When we left the restaurant, we continued west and pulled into the roadside park of Wilkerson Pass. I loved this spot. Not only was the view of the distant Collegiate Peaks one that was frequently photographed, but I loved it also for the community of tiny four-legged people it supported.

We sat atop one of the higher boulders and waited patiently

for their appearance. It didn't take but two minutes before the scampering and darting began. Tiny paws scurried and stopped, scurried and stopped—nose whiskers twitching, testing the air and the mood of the new two-leggeds that had crossed their territory.

I giggled at their cautious antics. How tiny they were. Little black beady eyes stared hard. Tawny fur, soft as down, covered the wee bellies as the chipmunks rose on hind feet to sniff and peer around at us. Finally one inched closer to my outstretched hand. He was either the macho one of the group or the hungriest—it didn't really matter because, either way, he was going to be the first to eat.

How I loved the feel of those needle nails and soft pads on my palm. How I loved the bravery of the wee thing to approach such a monster as me. The little person, with thoughts of winter well in mind, frantically tarried at my hand long enough to pack its expanding cheek pouches with half my offering of nuts. So humorous was the sight. The little clown, now looking very much like he had the mumps, gave me a last glance before pushing off to scamper to the safety of its burrow. The others, cursing their shyness, eased forward toward the cornucopia that their brother had feasted from. Soon the sun-touched boulder was overrun with the bold and timid alike, all partaking of the free handout, all packing and stuffing their silky cheeks.

This visual experience was not only a sensory one for me, but was also a wonderfully warm sharing and union. Watching and feeling the tiny people was truly exciting, but what I loved most about it was the total act of observation which brought other facets into play. As I sat so statue-still, the mind was a receptor that translated the nibblers' thoughts and emotions. So many impressions were coming in as the tiny four-leggeds skittered, paused, stuffed and retreated. It always struck me as how incredible it was—how really easy it was—to be able to tune in to nature's different languages. From those feasting at my hand, the language and emotional impressions came fast and furious like flying embers from a sparkler. "Hurry! Hurry! Should I take one more? Must hurry! It's okay. Mmmmm, these are my favorite! Hurry! Don't push! Mmmm. Hurry!" And from those tiny heads still peering out from the security of the rock crevices, I felt a combination of great timidness and self-reproach. "Look! They're getting all the good stuff! See, it's okay. No, no, I'm afraid. You go. No, you go first. Bring some back for me. No, no, I'm too scared. We won't get anything if we don't go now. I'm scared, you go. Next time." Poor little fellas.

When the feeding was over, just as always, I threw handfuls of the feast toward the shadowed rock crannies where the shy ones hid. After we left the immediate feeding area, their high excitement could be heard for miles around. "Did you *see* that? Wow! Look at all these nuts! We didn't even have to go get it!" And the language became garbled as timid cheeks were quickly stuffed, but the emotions still came through loud and clear. . .they were very grateful. . .but not nearly as grateful as I was for the high pleasure of their company and short union we had shared together.

Leaving Wilkerson Pass, we descended down into South Park, which was a large expanse of flat land between mountain ranges. I was still floating within the sweetness of my special communion with the chipmunks when Bill squinted to peer through the windshield.

"What the hell is *that?*" he flared, voice heavy with consternation.

I leaned forward to scan the view before us. I didn't have to look very far to spot the object of his amazement. The terrain was level—all cattle-grazing land—and perched upon a wire fence post was a huge dark object. It stood out in stark relief against the deep blue sky.

"A vulture?" I suggested.

It wasn't an out-of-line guess, for we'd seen dead cattle allowed to remain along these rangelands until their bones were picked clean by scavengers and bleached by the searing sun.

The driver nixed my suggestion. "That thing doesn't have a skinny neck. Look how full it is."

He was right. As we neared the huge bird, our flesh was covered with goosebumps.

"It's an *eagle!*" I squealed. "God, Bill, it's an eagle!"

It was the first eagle we'd ever seen and its head was turned to us.

Bill was grinning with the joy of it. "Want to slow down?"

"No, it'll just fly off."

And we continued speeding toward the huge bird.

Expecting it to take to the air at any second, we whizzed past it before we knew it. Bill hit the brakes and skidded off onto the narrow shoulder. We got out. Looking back, we saw the bird still perched as before, only this time its head had turned—toward us.

A chilling wave of weirdness washed over us. It was uncanny, this bird. It hadn't flown away. Our truck had raced toward it and sped within three yards of it yet it never ruffled a feather except to turn its head to keep its eyes on us. How utterly unnatural. Our heads slowly turned to each other. Our eyes locked. His look conveyed the mirrored expression of my own.

Something was amiss.

And when we gazed back, the fence post was empty. Quickly we searched the sky. In every direction did we search.

Nothing.

There wasn't much else to do but get back into the truck and continue on. For a long while we were semi-mesmerized by the sinister experience. Finally I began panning the sky.

"Forget it," Bill said. "You won't see it again."

"What do you think it was?"

He shrugged his shoulders. "It wasn't what it seemed, that's for sure."

"Any ideas?"

"Several. And they all sound incredible."

"Try me. I've heard incredible before."

"Illusion for one."

"Illusions have causal factors. What caused the illusion?"

He took his eyes off the road just long enough to glare hard at me.

"Now you've brought in the second wave of possibilities. The causes number a score of probabilities. What's even more interesting is not *what* caused it, but *who*. Then the *third* wave enters in. . .the *why* of it in the first place."

I slouched down in the seat. "Mmmm, I see what you mean. We could speculate until doomsday and never reach the right combination."

"Exactly."

"What if it wasn't an illusion caused by anyone? What if it was a real eagle? That would represent an aberration of nature. The fact that it didn't fly off makes the occurrence abnormal. Instances of abnormal nature were foreseen by No-Eyes during the Phoenix Days. It's possible we just witnessed an example of that?"

My partner agreed wholeheartedly. "That was another one of my theories. These *are* the beginning of the Phoenix Days— that alone makes just about anything plausible."

I hesitated before voicing my next thought.

"Want to ask about it? I'll try and get an answer if you want."

He surprised me by shaking his head.

"Why not?" I inquired.

"I don't know. Maybe we need to come into our own on this one. I just don't feel right about asking for the answer—at least not right now anyway. I'd like to think on it a little more."

"Okay," I agreed, "but that sure was weird."

"There's going to be a lot of that going around pretty soon; better get used to it. I've got the feeling we're in for quite a weird show."

My brow shot up. "Show? That's an odd way to describe what's coming."

"No it's not. The way I see it, for those that are aware and are ready, for those that have done all they can do to forewarn people, there's nothing left to do but watch it all happen."

It sounded rather callous to me, but he had adequately expressed the fact of the matter. And rather than developing the conversation further, I dropped it like a hot potato. This was a gorgeous Colorado day and I wasn't about to darken it with the shadows of the future. I gazed out at the scenery that had altered from flatlands to rolling terrain.

"So much open land," I casually commented. "Miles and miles for as far as the eye can see and no houses."

"You want to see houses?"

"That wasn't my point. It still amazes me how crowded some cities are. There's so many homeless people and here there's miles and miles of nothing."

"You're getting morbid."

"No I'm not. You know what?" I asked, perking up.

"What," he grinned.

"Know what I really want to do?"

"Go live in your little cabin."

I smiled. "Well yeah, but beside that."

"Enlighten me."

"I want to help the homeless."

"That's a pretty hefty want. Some don't want help."

"I know that but there's plenty that do. And I've been thinking about something else too."

"Oh God, spare me."

My excitement was building. "I'd really like to have a foster home for Indian children. You know, care for them and give them love and self-esteem until they can be adopted."

The driver was shaking his head.

"Why don't you just legally adopt the whole world?"

"You don't like my ideas?"

"Oh I like them all right, but you're forgetting one tiny thing about all this."

"What?"

"Money."

I made a face. "Well, it's the thought that counts."

"Yeah honey, if anyone Upstairs is adding up thoughts, yours have used up all their paper. Here's one more for you. Buena Vista's just ahead. You want to stop for lunch now or check out the location first?"

"You hungry?" I asked.

"I could take it or leave it."

"Let's come back then. I'd feel better after we see the spot."

At Buena Vista we turned south and headed toward the St. Elmo turnoff. On our left, groups of rafters were making their way down the Arkansas River. It looked like fun, but it was a very warm day for wearing the bulky life jackets each had on.

"Next stop. . .St. Elmo!" the driver announced, turning right off the highway.

Ahead, the long road stretched straight toward the heavily forested mountains. I looked forward to being up in the evergreens again. The last leg of the trip had been through the more sparse piñon country, and scrub brush wasn't exactly my scenery of choice. The anticipation of deeply shadowed forests and cool streams set my spirits soaring.

The drive was captivating. After we cleared the flat stretch and began the ascent through the foothills of the mountain range, we were plunged into the emerald shadows of the verdant woodlands. The going was slow. The road twisted and climbed. The swift current of Chalk Creek rushed its clear waters alongside the road. The two were not always visible to one another, for sometimes they'd be side by side, and other times the road steeply ascended, leaving only the gushing sounds of water from far below.

We had been on better roads, but the lushness of the surround more than made up for the inconvenience. The forests were virgin and teemed with wildlife. Golden rays of sunlight speared down through the high green boughs. This was a special place.

"Bill?"

"Yeah?"

"This is a power point."

"Some of it is. I don't think our nightstalker could exist within one."

"No, neither do I." I paused to listen to the happiness of the

Water Spirit's voice. Then I decided it was time to get down to the business at hand.

"Do you think it'll be before or after St. Elmo?"

"There's nothing but a rugged four-wheel road after the town. We don't have a four-wheel. No-Eyes would've known that. It's got to be before."

The ghost town loomed before us. Cars were parked haphazardly about. Tourists were poking and milling in and out of the buildings. We pulled in and idled the engine.

"Now what?" I asked. "I never felt anything."

"Neither did I. We'll have to be more open on the way back. Want to nose around a little while we're here?"

I gazed at the town. It consisted of a few buildings and lots of curious lookers.

"No, not unless you do. I'd rather concentrate on our spot. It bothers me that we didn't sense it."

"Me too," he agreed, already maneuvering the truck around. "These ghost towns are about all the same anyway."

We had spent about ten minutes backtracking the route when the disturbing sensations began. We slowed. And they were gone.

Bill turned us around for the second time and crept back up the road. Again the feelings returned. This was it.

We made a U-turn and pulled off the road to inch in through the tree line. The engine was cut. It was an odd situation, for although the truck was camouflaged by the heavy cover of trees, we could still see passing vehicles. It didn't feel secluded enough.

"Are passing cars going to bother us tonight?" I wondered aloud.

My companion didn't think they would. "The actual location's probably in a ways."

We got out, held hands and began making our way into the dense forest. I could hear the rushing waters of the creek that ran on the opposite side of the road. As we went deeper into the woods, the sound silenced. I furtively scanned the spaces between the towering trees.

Bill noticed my mood. "Not exactly like your everyday forest, huh?"

My eyes slid to his. "It's the first one that actually scares me. Where are the birds?"

Bill raised his sights to the swaying treetops, looked back to me in a befuddled manner and just shook his head.

We'd come to a clearing. Our sensors beeped wildly as we

silently walked its wide perimeter. When we had come full circle, we stopped.

"I'm getting some confusing signals," I informed. "How about you?"

The frown indicated that he too was having some technical difficulty.

"This is the place, I'm convinced of that, but I'm not getting a clear bead on him. There's some kind of interference."

"Like a *second* impression?"

"Yes. Like overlapping vibrations."

"There's not supposed to be more than one here. What could it be? Do you think his wife's back?"

"No, it's too different."

"Let's walk it again."

When we reached our original starting point for the second time, we had more information to go on. Bill leaned up against a tree and studied the scene.

"Well?" I said, "you want to go first?"

"I'm almost afraid to say it, but I think what's clouding our impressions is a second entity—one that's. . ."

"An animal?"

He grinned. "You got that too?"

"Sorry to say it but I think our man stalks on horseback."

"Babe. . .how can that be though? Animal energy is generated from a pool of energy. How does that work if the guy's on a horse spirit?"

I grinned. "Sounds dumb, doesn't it? No-Eyes said that an animal's energy isn't always dispersed back. I think what's causing the glitch is you're forgetting that animals have minds and emotions too. Those can retain the energy form for as long as it's needed. Extenuating circumstances can apply to that concept. Even though an animal doesn't possess God spirit aspects, it still has that strong energy field to maintain a manifested etheric form."

A measure of clarity shone in his eyes. "You mean like Kevin and his dog."

"Yes. Although it died, he and his neighbors have still seen its shadowy form at different times. It's still emotionally tied to Kevin."

"But that kind of energy dissipates after a while. Why's this horse still around?"

"Because its rider is still around too."

My mate thought on that. "He's definitely got the advantage over us."

"Mmmm, we're going to have to get him off the horse. That's going to be the first thing we do."

He sighed heavily. "How come you weren't told about this added problem?"

"I guess we need to be confronted with variety. If you think about it, we're going to come up against a lot of different situations—we're going to come on them cold. The more experience we have with the various possibilities, the better prepared we'll be to handle them."

The reasoning was accepted better than the present situation was.

Bill wondered if I had received any additional impressions while we were making the second round of the perimeter.

I had. And while I voiced them, my attention was on a peculiar movement on the forest floor.

"This guy's real strong. I mean he's really strong. Also I got some audio impressions. Hoof beats. That's what made me realize our overlay impression was a horse. Later on, a coyote is going to howl."

He chuckled lightly. "A coyote? What kind of prediction is that? Wouldn't that be well expected around here anyway?"

"He's going to give just a single howl—just one. And," I added, keeping my eye on the ground, "after we're through, it's going to rain like hell."

The light chuckle exploded into a full blown laugh.

"Rain! Sorry babe," he said, looking up through the patches of clear blue sky, "the weatherman showed a high for this area all weekend. There won't be a cloud in sight 'til Tuesday. You're way off on that one."

"I heard thunder."

"If you clairaudiently heard thunder, then you picked up something that's three days away."

My eyes slid up to his. "For those who would have eyes to see, nature is very revealing."

His mouth puckered and brows arched. "Getting a little heavy, aren't you? I know all about nature's signals too."

"Do you?"

"Look, we'll make a bet then. If it rains tonight I'll treat you to a shrimp tempura dinner tomorrow. If it doesn't, you get to make me one of your apple pies."

Boy, was he going to be sorry. "You're on."

Proudly he wrapped his arm around my shoulders and together we walked back to the truck. I knew he was already relishing the mouth-watering smells of hot apples and cinnamon wafting through the house. Too bad he hadn't observed the little bug's peculiar antics like I had. If he had, there wouldn't have been a bet to place. Oh well, next to lobster, shrimp tempura ran a close second. I could taste it already.

It was nearly two in the afternoon by the time we sat down in the Depot restaurant in Buena Vista. We'd been there several times before during our land-hunting forays. I liked the Depot. It wasn't a fancy place, but it did have a certain interesting atmosphere. As its name implies, it represented a train depot. The beginning and ending serving times for breakfast, lunch and dinner were posted on a schedule display as "arrival" and "departure" times. Model train replicas were scattered about on shelves. Beautiful photographs of engines decorated the walls. Every hour a whistle hooted the time and, near the ceiling, a double track encircled the entire room. Diners could sit and watch the two trains encircle the place and pass each other. I'm not particularly fascinated with trains, but the Depot certainly was different in its atmosphere and the food was always acceptable.

We were ushered to a booth by a front window. The little trains ran directly above us. The whistle blew. It was two o'clock. And, while we ate, we quietly discussed the discovery of the horse factor and how it had been an unexpected encounter component. It was an aspect that clearly gave the nightstalker a decided advantage, and, although we knew we'd have to dismount our target, we hadn't devised any workable plan. This was one of those instances where everything would hinge directly on the play-by-play action. As things developed on their own, we'd have to systematically come up with viable game plans that fit the situation. Going cold into these encounters without any predetermined scheme was demanding. Mental faculties had to be saber sharp to facilitate split-second decisions, physical reactions needed to be honed, and the psychic sense had to be functioning at its absolute optimum capacity.

The four o'clock whistle blew. Our departure time had arrived. We left.

On the way back, we were both deeply engrossed in private thoughts as we individually mulled over the various points of our dinner conversation. I was first to break the stillness.

"We're going to whip this one," I said.

No response came.

"Honey, you hear me? We're going to win this one."

"What makes you so sure? Are you saying that because that's what you want or because it's what you really feel?"

"What's the difference?"

"Well, I just don't want you going into this one all cocky."

That brought a definite frown. "Cocky?"

"Yeah, overconfidence doesn't work with this stuff. You got to remember that this guy is full of anger and he's out for revenge. You're going to be his target and we're going to have to be really high on awareness every second."

I sighed. "You're doing a great job on my confidence. No-Eyes was adamant about the need for strong confidence. Now you sit there and tear it all down."

"No I'm not."

"Hell you're not."

"I just don't want you to lose sight of the seriousness of this one. I don't want you to overshadow it with too much self-assurance."

"I believe the word was 'cocky.'"

Silence.

I rested my hand on his leg. "I love you."

Our eyes met and he covered my hand with his. "I love you too, honey."

"I know what you're saying about being cocky and I agree, but I've got to use that confidence as a shield."

"For what? What's hiding behind the shield?"

"Fear. I'm not relishing the idea of being a target tonight and quite truthfully it scares the hell out of me and I'm very nervous about it. I'm using the attitude as a cover to present."

"But are you confident?"

"Yes."

"Good, then make it strong for him and maybe it'll do the trick."

But little did we know then that a show of confidence would not be the shield I'd need. It would ultimately turn out to be something very different and much the opposite. An exterior display of boldness and confidence would not accomplish anything this night. . .*helplessness* would accomplish everything.

By six o'clock we were ready for the prescribed rest time. Comfortably settled on the bed in the camper, I glanced over at the wall at my shoulder.

"Bill, we have to change places."

He groaned in recognition of the request. "This is not

Egypt," he mumbled, sliding over while I crawled over him to settle in his former spot.

"I'm sorry, but I can't help it. Every time I get hemmed in the inside like that I get claustrophobic. It's like the sides of a sarcophagus and I hate it."

He grumbled under his breath while trying to get comfortable. I turned on my side to face the open space of the camper that gave breathing room.

"Honey?" I whispered.

"Mmmm."

"I hope it doesn't rain before we're done tonight."

He chuckled. "It's not going to rain and you owe me a juicy pie."

I ignored the latter remark. "Well I just don't want to get all wet again. That was awful."

"Babe?"

"Yeah?"

"Go to sleep."

I closed my eyes and, although I had much to think about, the mind didn't want to be bothered with any of it. Like a downy feather falling from a spring nest, my mind drifted aimlessly through wafting currents of diaphanous illusions. I had entered another realm—one devoid of rich evergreen forests and cool mountain streams.

Canyon land, scorched and parched. Cliffs, high and sheer. Sun, searing.

Bill and I stood along the rim of the high cliff. Far below, a narrow canyon plunged the craggy walls to a dizzying depth. Beside us, a tree, skeletal in bleached white branches, supported a vulture—its feathers shiny as a killing oil slick, its eyes blood red and hungry—waited.

It was a breathless land, one dead and dying. It was a place where Death reigned as sovereign ruler. Only three hearts beat within the desolate land. Only one belonged. . .and it waited. Patiently did it wait.

Two hands moved. They sought each other. Standing upon the precipice, joined by hands and minds, our eyes locked.

And we tilted forward.

Weightless now, our bodies tumbled effortlessly as autumn leaves before the twirling wind. Down. Down. Vertigo swirled our minds with frames of the passing visions.

Cliffs. Sky.

Tumbling.

Canyon floor. Vulture on the wing.

Failing. Tumbling. Falling.

Rocky ground looming larger—closer.

Then. . .the soft feel of meadow grass, cool and dew-fresh. We had not dashed ourselves upon the canyon floor after all. We had found ourselves in a mountain meadow. Scents of wildflowers filled the air. Birdsong trilled. Wind soughed through the trees. Stream waters bubbled.

I looked to a sudden movement along the tree line. A white horse stood pawing the grass. The great stallion whinnied, shook his full mane and came to stand beside me.

Bill rose from the grass, mounted the steed and pulled me up behind him. And together did we ride through the idyllic surround and into the enchanted woodland. All round us life thrived and sounds were magical.

Laughing stream. Happy birds. Joyous windsong. Gentle hoof beats.

Hoof beats. Hoof beats. Hoof beats.

My eyes shot open. My spine tingled. *Hoof beats!*

Bill bolted from the bed. Yanking back the window curtain, he angrily spouted, "Damned spirits *never* do what they're supposed to do! He's *outside* the perimeter!"

This was not good. Not only was the entity waiting for us, we hadn't had time to adequately prepare. Our physical systems were groggy and our minds were reeling from trying to activate them after the deep sleep we'd been in. We needed to be at peak performance on all levels, and we were missing the mark by a mile. Our confidence was not high, but we had other matters to attend to, so it wasn't an issue to dwell on.

We grabbed our jackets and pulled them on. And without a word spoken between us, we each settled down to mentally prepare. It was not easy concentrating while the outside sounds pierced our efforts.

Twigs snapped. Hooves, impatiently pawing the ground, grated on our nerves. The intermittent lulls of silence were even worse. It was nearly impossible to block out the audio interference and the strong vibrations that were being felt from the stalker. Yet I suddenly found myself within a warm void where no exterior irritations could penetrate to annoy or distract me. I had managed to duck behind the shield of protection and enter its circle of invincible Light. There, within the strong fortress, I energized my forces and honed the senses.

When I opened my eyes, Bill was waiting. His demeanor had lost its former frantic attitude. He was within his own power. . .now he looked like the warrior he was. Strength radiated from his being. We came together and hugged one another, quietly voicing our commitment of love and psychically bonding the male and female aspects of our power into a unified mantle of force.

We were ready.

Stealing out of the camper, we made our way into the thick of the forest where we could keep a watchful eye on the clearing. In our heightened state, every sound was magnified. Across the open expanse, bushes rustled.

We crouched down behind some boulders and waited for our man to make the first move.

Like twins, our heads turned to the right.

A dry aspen branch snapped. In the deathly stillness it sounded like a rifle crack.

Psychically we followed the vibrational field that silently reconnoitered around us. Our heads went left now.

Hoof sounds disturbed the ground to the left. The stalker was good. He was playing psychological games—trying to wear on our nerves and confidence.

It wasn't working. We were still at peak perception.

Then all movement halted. There were no more vibrationary fields to follow. No sounds were created for our benefit. We barely breathed with the effort of straining our senses to listen and perceive. We waited. Poised for quick action, we waited for a great length of time. Night wind began soughing through the tree boughs.

I dared to whisper in my companion's ear. "Something's not right."

When he turned to me, moonlight played on the whites of his eyes. It was unsettling until he blinked.

"Think he left already?"

"I can't say. Sure seems like he did. Maybe we slept too long and we came in on his departure."

Bill furtively looked around the clearing, searched the bordering tree line and checked behind us. It was eerie.

"There's just nothing here now," he murmured.

"Think it's a trick?"

"Could be."

Silence. We'd wait and see, for neither of us felt it was over.

But the longer we waited, the stronger we doubted our theory. The night mountain air worked against us. Cold settled in our crouching bones. A shiver trembled through me. After nearly forty minutes of frozen surveillance, I had to move.

As if on cue, we both straightened up. My hand went to the small of my back.

"You okay?" Bill softly asked.

I nodded. "Just getting old, I guess."

Together we stood tall and peered around.

Nothing.

I upturned my hands in a gesture of futile confoundment and stepped away to lean against a lodgepole. The action had been like tripping a booby trap. We heard it coming, but before we could react, a rock came flying from somewhere behind us.

Bill instinctively ducked.

I spun for cover behind the tree. The projectile grazed my hip and I went down. It hadn't done any real harm other than putting me off balance.

"*You son of a BITCH!*" Bill bellowed angrily, rushing to my side. Bending low, he was both deeply concerned and infuriated. "Where'd he get you?" he asked, checking me over.

I rubbed my hip. "It just grazed me," I said, not wanting to think about what the rock could've done if I'd reacted a second slower.

"This is *asinine!*" he fumed. "No spirit is worth this! I'm not going to stand by while some deranged lunatic takes pot shots at you." His head then jerked to the trees and he shouted into them. The veins of his neck throbbed. "This is *my* woman you *creep!*"

"Shhh," I said, trying to calm him. "He doesn't care, remember?"

"Well *I* care. Goddammit, we're getting out of here."

I grabbed for his jacket sleeve. "No! Wait. I've got an idea."

Through his irritation, he impatiently listened to the new plan. He didn't like it. He didn't like it at all.

"No. There's no way in hell I'm leaving you exposed to this maniac in any way." His head shook. "No. I won't do it. We're leaving."

My hands grasped the ground as if it had handles to hold me there.

"I *know* it'll work. I *feel* it."

Silence.

Waiting.

I couldn't believe what he did next. He bent low and picked me up in his arms.

"What're you doing? Put me down! Your *back!*"

"Forget my back. If you think the 'injured woman' bit will

work, then you'll *be* the injured woman! Start moaning 'cause here goes nothing."

He'd refused to leave me where I was while he carried out the ruse. He wanted me right with him every step of the way. And truthfully, I was glad he did.

I was carried to the center of the clearing and set down in the prickly weeds. Feigning severe injury, I lay down and kept still, for the plan called for my partner's action—not mine. Although I was to appear passive, I was strongly active. My energies raced to give forceful reinforcement to my partner's power. They fed his field and strengthened him. When he spoke again, his voice was full of lethal vehemence.

"*Show* yourself, you coward!" he bellowed, while turning in place to spy the camouflaged stalker.

Underbrush snapped as the horse was urged forward.

"Come *on!* You *afraid?*"

More bushes rustled. Hooves stomped to a stop. For the first time we got a look at our adversary. He was an imposing sight mounted so tall in the saddle. The dark beard and glaring black eyes were menacing. He stared at us. Flaming anger was now directed at his screaming tormenter.

"You fight like a *woman!*" Bill taunted.

The black orbs flared.

"Get down off that horse and fight like a *man!*" Then Bill pointed to his feet where I lay barely able to breathe with the high drama that was unfolding. "This is *my* woman! This is *Summer Rain!*" If you *want* her. . .*fight* for her!"

The stalker remained motionless.

"What's the matter?" Bill sneered. "You forget your *broom?* Is *that* how you fight? Like a *woman?*"

The huge man dismounted. Bill had succeeded in accomplishing the first step of the plan.

Now the stalker heaved a great breath and began striding forward. He was a massive bulk of muscle. The fringes on his buckskin swayed and he fondled a knife at his belt. I was getting very nervous, but the fact that Bill had transferred the man's combative energies from psychic to physical was tipping the scales in our favor. So far my plan was working and I continued to send my partner additional power while maintaining the exterior attitude of complete helplessness.

The man in buckskins approached toward Bill with calculated steps. Each stride was slow and deliberate. The eye contact was hard and deadly.

Bill held his ground, for the rage he displayed was not an

act; it was emanating from deep within the core of his being. It was real.

The stalker stopped in front of his tormenter. He fiercely glared into the steel blue eyes that were cold with challenge. Then the black eyes lowered to settle on me.

Bill backed away, purposely drawing off the man's attention.

"You ought to be real proud of yourself the way you pick on poor innocent women!"

The stalker turned to the voice while pointing down at me. He spoke for the first time. The tone was icy.

"I came for Calf Woman! I came for my *wife! Her!* You took her from me."

"Take *another* look, idiot! That's *my* woman! That's *Summer Rain!*"

A chill passed over me when the trapper bent down low to peer through the moonlight. His gaze inspected my hair.

"Calf Woman wears *rabbit!*" And he spun to face Bill.

My hand flew to my hair. Oh God, I'd forgotten to remove the piece of rabbit fur and feather. I rose up on my elbow to watch the scene that had intensified. My bruised hip ached and I winced.

The stalker swung back to me. The trembling fingers fondled the knife handle.

Bill shouted at him. His voice startled me, for I'd never before seen him in a combatant situation. His body literally shuddered with the violent fury of his wrath.

"Hey YOU!"

Again the hulk spun around. Now he was intent on getting rid of the mocking person who stood between him and his target.

I worked hard to support the man who slowly backed away from the threatening one that advanced toward him. Bill's voice rang out across the clearing as his hands came up and the fingers wriggled.

"*C'mon* brave man! Where's your *slingshot?* Aren't you going to throw stones at *me* like you do helpless *women?*"

Bill's feet slowly back-pedaled through the tall weeds.

The trapper advanced and unsheathed the Bowie. The blade glistened in the moonglow.

Still the taunting was relentless.

"Oh! Now the big *man's* got a *knife!* Look, big man," he shouted, showing his empty palms, "I *have* no weapon!"

The stalker leered.

What happened next occurred so fast I couldn't tell what transpired. Either Bill stumbled on some dead wood and fell or the stalker advanced so quickly that he took Bill by surprise and he tripped trying to get out of his way.

My heart pounded to see the two suddenly scuffling on the ground. I could hear a volley of swearing from both men and the sight of the stalker's arm raising and stabbing down turned my stomach. It all happened so fast it was over before I could get up. A retched cry froze me in place.

"AHGGG! SACRE BLEU!"

The scene became a stop-action frame. Nothing moved.

Then, in slow motion, the attacker stood to stare down at his victim—his *intended* one. The knife dropped; it just vanished, and the victim rolled over and rose to his feet. The two rivals just stared at one another.

My thundering heart beat furiously within my chest. The confrontation was over. The stalker's rage had turned into shock and disbelief, for his weapon had had no effect upon the man who now stood before him.

I would've liked to have seen the look on the trapper's face when the reality of his actions struck. Yet I could well envision the horror of his expression. Now he stood numb of mind and body. In awestruck shock did he watch his former adversary rise and slap at the dirt of his pants.

I heard Bill talking, but couldn't make out the words. The woodsman glanced back at me then listened intently to what my companion said.

I thought I saw the shoulders of the buckskins slump. Yes, the man now had a definitive reversal of mood. He followed Bill back to where I was left in the grass. I rested back in the prickly ground cover. Now it was my turn to share center stage.

The sounds of their approaching footfalls seemed louder than normal and my heart skipped a beat or two as the trapper came up to kneel beside me. The new smells were potent. Buckskin. Sweat. Dirt. Animal. Woodsmoke.

Nobody spoke.

Then the man's face neared mine. Recognition illuminated his sharp features that softened with regret and genuine sympathy. I pulled my neck in like a turtle when the large hand came up to touch my hair. But the touch was gentle and the eyes were soft—they expressed pity.

"Poor little Summer Rain," he crooned with a thick accent. "Now Jacques sees you are not Calf Woman." He sighed heavily. "Jacques has been a foolish man to have injured you." His eyes scanned my body. "Is it bad? The pain?"

I nodded slowly.

He moaned with his own pain of his actions.

"Summer," Bill said, "this is Jacques and he's sorry for what he did to us."

"Oh oui, Summer, Jacques is sorry. What can I do? *Anything!*"

My eyes went up to search Bill's.

He knelt down beside us and nodded in response to my unspoken question. The trapper was indeed aware of the reality of the situation. He realized he was dead and that his revenge was a futile cause.

I then gave the grieving man my full attention.

His eyes were anxious—pleading.

"Can Summer Rain ever forgive Jacques?"

I nodded.

"How can I repay this terrible foolish deed? How can I make up for the hurt I cause you?"

My heart was smiling with the formulating answer.

"Jacques," I whispered through the terrible pain, "I forgive you but I want you to have peace."

His bushy brows creased. "You want peace for Jacques?"

"Yes. For too long have you lived with your hate. That makes me sad. I see that in your heart you are a good man. You don't deserve to go on any longer without your peace." I searched his eyes. "I want you to end your search and go home. Calf Woman is not here."

The unruly hair blew in the breeze that had stirred.

"Oui. She is not here. Jacques knows that now."

In the distance, a coyote howled—just once.

I noticed Bill's gaze turn to the woods at the haunting sound.

Jacques smiled. "I do a bad thing tonight," he said with a voice heavy with guilt. "But Jacques is done. No more foolish Jacques." He smiled warmly. "I go now. Now I go home." His eyes firmly locked on Bill's. "Take care of your woman."

And he rose.

Together Bill and I watched the trapper walk from the clearing and vanish into the tangle of trees. A horse snorted. Hoof beats tramped through the brush.

"Do you think he's really going home?" I asked hopefully.

"Shhh, listen."

Nothing was heard but the wind whispering through the trees. Jacques was tired of the endless stalking. He was ashamed of his foolish actions this night. He was anxious to grant my wish for his peace. The stalker now had a new target—home.

Bill was concerned about my hip as he helped me up. "Can you walk? Does it hurt bad?"

I smiled and leaned on him as we headed back toward the truck.

"Yes and no, but I think a certain part of me is going to be rather colorful for a few days." I rubbed the sore hip. "It could've been a lot worse."

Back in the camper, he quickly lit the heater and we snuggled down beneath the quilt. This time he remembered to take the inside. It felt so good being warm and secure again, and for a while we talked about the encounter. I had asked what had happened when Jacques charged him and my companion chuckled.

"Your macho man tripped over a log."

The corners of my mouth lifted in the darkness.

"You're no macho man; you're just brave. I think you did great out there tonight."

"Yeah?"

"Yeah."

"Well for one thing, I don't think I've ever been so angry. That guy really got to me. I guess my natural emotions carried it all."

"Honey?"

"What."

"Were you scared when he took out the knife?"

"I think for a minute I was, but then I remembered that this wasn't an ordinary situation. His psychic energy could hurt but the etheric knife couldn't. It was then when I realized I had him good."

"Well it sure scared me. It was frightening seeing him stab at you so many times. Didn't that seem weird to you?"

Silence.

"Honey?"

"I'm sorry, I'm just tired. Yeah, that was real weird."

I thought about how it would feel having someone stab at you and not feel anything. I still thought it'd be a very terrifying experience. Then I wondered about the conversation they shared that I couldn't hear.

"What'd you say to him after the attack?"

Silence.

"Honey?"

Deep even breathing.

I sighed and pulled the covers up to my chin. The camper was suddenly shadowed in total darkness. Moonglow vanished and thunder rolled across the angry sky. It was going to rain like hell.

I smiled. There was no way I was going to collect my winnings. My mate had outdone himself this night. I had been the damsel in distress and he had been my brave champion. He deserved to win the wager.

I closed my eyes and mentally made a shopping list; brown sugar, apples, flour, cinnamon. . .

Axe Man of Miner's Creek

The two-lane road stretched out before us. For miles and miles did it trail toward the distant horizon. The black line cut through spacious rangeland that seemed to sweep into infinity. The magnitude of expanse was immense and it gave one the feeling of being somewhat diminutive. The vast openness of the West's terrain frequently became overwhelming and created within the human perception a sense of being a microscopic life form of the grand design of life. One is often plunged into the realm of the infinitesimal while traversing some of nature's more spectacular panoramic vistas.

Now, with nothing but open rangeland spread on either side of the black velvet ribbon of road, it generated a queer sense of timelessness. Time and distance didn't appear to be reconciling. Our mileage seemed to never gain. It was like being trapped in the frustrating dreamscape, running for your life and never moving an inch because your efforts are nothing more than slow motion. The vastness of the open landscape had caught us in a web of timelessness. The distant mountain range was like a shimmering mirage: The more ground we covered, the farther away it appeared to be. And for a heart that wildly beat for the exciting terrain of mountains and pine trees, streams and wildlife, my wavelength reading was nearing a flat line. I slumped in drowsiness and closed my eyes.

Like a sodden autumn leaf slipping below the glistening surface of a high mountain pool, my consciousness floated deeper and deeper through a shimmering golden void where all sounds became muffled, then silenced. So quiet was the drifting. So peaceful was the gentle descent. Tranquility and serenity came in waves of warmth. Like an iridescent bubble did I alight upon the depths of the pool bottom, and gently did I bounce in slow motion before settling within the buttery sun rays that pierced down through the sapphire blueness. And there, within the depths of silence, did I dwell in eternal repose to ponder the beauty and purpose of existence.

Waves of blackness came in ripples that disturbed my

esoteric contemplation. Gently did they nudge my thoughts away from their exquisiteness. Ripples gained in strength to become forceful pressures of turbulence that disturbed the quietude and disrupted my meditations. The outside force agitated the serenity. The silence was breaking up in a hundred fragments. I shuddered.

"Honey? Wake up," came the faraway voice.

Irritated, I opened my eyes and straightened myself up in the seat. Squinting with the suddenness of the daylight glare, I reached for my sunglasses. We were easing onto the shoulder of the road.

"This isn't Miner's Creek," I muttered, peering out the passenger window.

The driver's eyes sparkled. "No, but look over here," he said, pressing himself back into the seat so I could look out his window.

I'd been annoyed that he'd shocked my psyche so suddenly out of its beautiful journey state. Now I eyed him suspiciously.

The blue eyes were smiling.

I dubiously leaned forward to peer around him.

"Buffalo!" I squealed in sheer delight. "Can we get out?"

"Why do you think I pulled over? I knew you'd want to stop."

We scrambled out and scampered across the asphalt. Picking our way through a tangle of tall weeds, we walked right up to the fencing. A great herd of the massive creatures were grazing about the range. The sight touched my soul.

"Just look at them," I moaned with a heavy heart. "They're all penned in. And to think how mighty they are and how the ground once shook with the weight of their racing freedom. Now their existence means nothing more than pounds of juicy buffalo burgers."

"Hey! I didn't stop so you could get morbid."

I gave him a wry smile. "I know, but it is sad. Why, I feel just like cutting this wire and letting them all out so they can. . ."

"Be run over by a semi," he finished.

I sighed. "Yeah. They don't even have anywhere to go anymore."

Then, as if to uplift my heart and comfort my sadness, a baby meandered over to me. Its spindly legs trembled as it nosed the fencing.

I knelt and crooned to the infant. Its eyes were so big and bright. Its muzzle, so fuzzy and prickly, quivered at my scent.

Wanting very much to hug it, I had to settle with a simple touching. My hand reached in through the barrier as I softly murmured to it. A rough pink tongue lapped across my palm. My heart giggled with the sweetness of the four-legged's infantile innocence.

Then I was swiftly jerked away. I fell back into the weeds just seconds before the baby's mother charged the fencing. My heart stopped, for her massive head filled my field of vision. She loudly snorted her anger.

Bill slowly and cautiously helped me up and we backed away to the edge of the road. I released a long breath of relief.

"Whew! I forgot about its mama."

Bill grinned. "Good thing I wasn't as intent as you were. I don't think a flimsy bit of wire would've deterred her very much."

We stood and watched the baby teeter after its retreating parent. They were moving toward the main body of the herd, and I felt that the little one was getting one heck of a lecture about being friendly with strangers—especially the two-legged variety. How pitiful that was to me that we two peoples couldn't trust one another.

We got back in the truck and, as Bill started the engine, I craned my neck to get a good last look at the herd.

He moved his head to block my view.

"We'll come back this way. Maybe they'll be around again." My heartlight brightened.

Then he frowned in a disciplinary manner. "But no more *petting.*"

"No more petting," I repeated like a good student. Yet we both knew that I'd probably try it again; only next time, I'd keep one eye on the mama.

A half-hour away from the buffalo, the road before us rose. From our low vantage point, we could see how it snaked up into the foothills and twisted in hairpin curves up the mountainside. Forests, lush and green, smothered the slopes.

"Is that Star Mountain Pass?" I inquired with a measure of new apprehension.

"That's the start of it. Miner's Creek is down on the backside."

It looked rather threatening to me.

"Did you know it was that steep?"

"No."

Worried, I slumped back in the seat and stared up at the dizzying height.

"Old Betsy's going to have to have an awful lot of energy for this one," I said with a note of doubt mixed with hope.

"Not to fear, not to fear, she'll make it just fine."

I wondered if that bold statement was generated by solid fact or shaky optimism and I didn't bother asking, for we were already nosing up the incline. And as the transmission was dropped into low gear, the roadside shoulder abruptly sheered off into a plummeting cliff. The narrow road became a high rampart that twisted around the lofty turrets of the mountain.

Creeping up the narrows of new passes never failed to give my heart pause, for behind every blind curve, the unexpected had to be anticipated. A boulder could be in the road or another vehicle could be coming and, frequently, in order for the two to pass, there'd only be inches to spare.

I tensed when I saw the asphalt end.

"Dammit," Bill grumbled beneath his breath, "now we got dirt." And "dirt" meant a whole new host of undesirable conditions that were possible. Luckily though, the going wasn't that bad and the pavement returned.

The grade leveled off and the road became a winding lane that meandered through dense old forests. Firs and spruces grew to record heights. Aspens had wide barrel trunks and competed with the conifers that stretched skyward. Crisp woodsy scents waited through the cab. I was in heaven.

My mate was grinning. "If you can pull yourself away from the woods, you might want to think about lunch."

I glanced at my watch then looked up the road. "Is there a town ahead?"

"It's just a speck on the map but it should have at least a diner or something."

Checking the map, I found the spot. He was right; it was just a speck called Timber Gulch.

"Well if it doesn't have anything decent we have those sandwiches in the back."

The driver cringed. "Maybe we'll just wait until we get to Miner's Creek. I know they have restaurants."

That sounded more than fine with me. I wasn't exactly in the mood for peanut butter an' jelly anyway. Then, enjoying the peaceful setting, a new thought on an old theme cropped up.

"I wonder how many people live around here."

Bill passed me a suspicious look. "No, this isn't our spot. It's too cut off."

"I like remote."

"Remote's fine, but the access has to be good. That road back there will be history at the first sign of a tremble. You'd be stranded up here."

"What about the back way? The way we're headed. Isn't that a lot different?"

"Yes, but then that only leaves one access and we were told to have at least two that'll remain solid."

"Well, just the same, it's still pretty up here."

"Can't argue that point."

"So do you think there's many people living around here?" I asked, repeating my former question.

"Nah, it's just too secluded and. . .well I'll be!"

A motel came into view.

We pulled into the paved parking area and Bill whistled low.

My narrowed eyes kept their sights on the building. "What an awful place!" I gasped.

While the engine purred, we leaned forward to survey the eerie motel.

"Think it's haunted?" Bill asked.

My head shook. "Not that simple," I whispered in fascination.

"What do you think it is then?"

"I can't tell, but I'm certainly going to find out. Wait here."

Not being one to run from a good mystery, I left the security of the truck and strode toward the building that was emitting extremely negative vibrations. It literally reeked of them. The aura was frightening.

The strange thing about the whole matter was the outward appearance of the place. To hear us talk about its evil aura would quite naturally conjure up terror-filled visions of the Bates Motel. But no, not here. This was more like Hansel and Gretel's candy cottage. It reminded me of the exquisite beauty of a poisonous flower. Irresistible. Tempting and deadly.

Freshly painted, the office centered the sprawling complex. Four individual units spread out on either side of it. Cedar roof shakes accentuated the colors of the bright green flower boxes that hung below all the windows. Brilliant petunias overflowed each to trail their variant hued blossoms. Cheery curtains adorned the windows, and above each door frame, Dutch hex symbols were painted in gay colors. At the outset, the overall tone hinted at an attempt to emulate the architecture of a Swiss chalet. Its style resembled those found nestled deep in the valleys of the Alps. The outcome was a bit strained, but still remained pleasant to the eye and certainly tempting to the unsuspecting traveler.

Adding extra bounce to my step, I jaunted across the lot toward the office door. I was already solidly ensconced within my chosen character role. Behind the self-created facade, my protection had slammed in place like steel doors lined in lead.

I opened the cross-hatched door and, with a saucy smile, greeted the woman behind the desk. She appeared to be deeply engrossed in her glossy magazine, yet I noticed that the page was an automotive display ad. She had obviously just flipped it open to any page. I figured she'd been watching us through the window.

The woman was a matron who clearly thought she was twenty. Long nail tapers, perfectly manicured, were lacquered in a wine shade of gloss. They were also false. Hair, fluffed in frizzled ends, was the color of burnished copper. Green frosty eye shadow shaded the lids that were loaded up with layers of heavy black mascara. Lashes reminded me of spider legs— Black Widow legs. The woman's complexion was good, I think—beneath the thick powder and cherry red rouge, it was hard to tell.

When she saw me, her eyes rounded with joyous surprise— also fake. And that was all right with me because I too was play-acting—only I had a reason—she didn't.

"Hi!" I bubbled, crossing the carpet to the desk.

"Well, good afternoon, young lady. You folks need a room?"

So she *had* been spying on us. Why else would she use the plural?

"Oh no, we're just out for a weekend drive. We've never been up this way before and we thought we'd look it over."

The jaded eyes slid to the window then came back to rest on mine.

"You don't say," she crooned.

I felt Bill's power enter my circle of protection. It felt reassuring, for in order for me to get a solid fix on the woman, I needed to keep her talking, and my mate's unseen presence was added comfort.

"We just came up Star Mountain Pass. That's one scary road!"

A painted brow arched. "Scary? I rather like it myself. Of course, I'm used to it."

"Anyway," I prattled on, "the woods are so remote around here. I was saying to my husband that I didn't think anyone lived way up here. Then we saw this place and was I ever surprised! It's so cute!"

She gave me a patronizing smile. "Why thank you, dearie. We're very proud of our little spot here."

Now I knew there was more than one of them.

"Do you get much business?"

The eyes narrowed. "More than you'd imagine. Mostly groups of people stop here."

She had emphasized the word "groups" and I temporarily filed that away.

"Don't you get a lot of snow in the winter?"

"Oh yes! There's been times when we've been snowed in for days. We don't mind though."

My eyes widened in disbelief. "You mean you live up here all year? It's so *remote!*" I exclaimed in exaggerated surprise.

A sneering smile spread the ruby lipstick. "That's the way we like it, honey. It's private."

I wished she'd stop with the "honey" and "dearie" bit. I hated that sort of condescension.

"But aren't you awful lonely?"

"Oh my no. There's more of us that live here. We're quite a cozy little group. We have plenty to do."

I bet they did. Finally the impressions were coming at a fast and furious pace. I crossed to the window, bent over the Windsor bench and pulled back the curtain. Peering into the deep woods across the road, I sighed.

"Got any *wild* things around here?"

The voice was dripping with dark red menace.

"You *afraid* of wild things, dear?"

I turned to see her pleasured smile. "Well. . .yes."

The eyes widened to saucers. "We got coyotes and mountain lions. We got wolves and *bears.* "

I smothered the temptation to say, "Oh *my!*" Instead, I exaggerated a chilling shudder.

"No thanks! I need my crowds of people and bright city lights! This would be too lonely and scary for me."

"Well," the woman chuckled, "everybody has their druthers, I guess, but the woods has got all *kinds* of surprises."

"Oh?" I said, moving back to the desk. "Like what?"

She laughed. "Honey, you wouldn't believe me if I told you. Nice city girl like yourself has no idea what's in them woods." The eyes ominously narrowed. "Or what goes *on* in them for that fact."

"I guess not. Like I said, I'm out of my realm up here.

Anyway, I think this place is real nice. It's a lot different than most we've seen."

"Yes, it *is* different, isn't it?"

"Well, I'd better not keep my husband waiting. Thanks for the info." I put my hand up in a combined gesture of gratitude and farewell.

"Bye, dearie. Have a nice drive."

"We will. You have a sunny day too," I said, turning to open the door.

She was expecting me to walk out and was already headed toward the window to watch us.

I reeled around and caught her off guard.

Her countenance was hard and calculating before it flashed into false pleasantness.

I sparkled a wide smile. "Geez, I almost forgot what I came in here for. We got to talking and I completely spaced it out."

"Oh?"

"Yeah. It's getting late and before we spotted this place we were talking about getting something to eat. Then the motel came up and we thought somebody here would be able to help us out. Isn't there some little town not too far from here?"

"That'd be Timber Gulch and I'm glad you stopped because my best friend owns the Stew Pot there." Her red talons waved at the air. "My dear! Aggie creates the most delicious meals! You go into the Stew Pot an' tell Aggie that Cassandra sent you. She'll treat you real special like."

"Great. Thanks a lot." And I left.

"Don't look at the office," I advised, getting back into the truck. "Just smile and pull away."

The driver grinned and mumbled between his clenched teeth. "Well? What'd you find out?"

After we were squared on the road, I took a moment or two to shed the protective barrier. A deep breath returned me to normal functioning.

"She's dark. She's real dark."

"For real?" he questioned. What he was actually referring to was the *source* of negativity—whether it was actual or imagined. Some folks played at dabbling and then believed they were the all-time adepts while others truly were proficient adepts.

"For real," came the disappointed reply.

Now my partner was concerned.

"She didn't read you, did she?"

"No. She didn't suspect a thing."

Then the corners of his mouth tipped up. "Don't tell me you pulled that scared bit."

I just grinned.

His head shook. "For someone like you to pretend that the woods scare you, you must really be a good actress."

"It's easy. The woods do have scary things. I'm just familiar with them, that's all."

Silence.

"What are you thinking?"

"I'm wondering what your excuse was."

I told him then added, "But I don't think I want to stop at the Stew Pot. I can wait for lunch until we get to Miner's Creek."

No argument issued forth on that score.

A few miles from the motel, the road that trailed through the verdant woodlands crested the summit of Star Mountain Pass. The point wasn't as marked as most passes were and if it wasn't for the sign we never would've noticed it. The downside was a gradual descent that spiraled alongside high timbers and Jade shadowed forests. Deer and elk were plentiful in the region, for twice we spotted them standing in groups within the dense high brush.

Our descent from the summit took forty minutes. Normally it would've been shorter, but we were not your normal travelers. Slow and easy was the set mode of speed, for always did we take great enjoyment in new and beautiful regions. At normal speed we would've missed seeing the four-leggeds in the thick tree line. At normal speed we would've passed right by the fox we'd seen.

At the bottom of the pass, the road split. We went right. Our destination was just ahead. And as was customary on our exploratory excursions, Bill coasted through the entire town so we could gain our impressions.

Neither of us had previously heard anything about Miner's Creek, nor had we any beforehand knowledge as to its appearance. I can't speak for my mate's expectations, but mine had been one of deterioration and depressed economy as most century-old mining towns were. Knowing I was guilty of being within Expectation in the first place, I should've naturally drawn some form of lesson from the Sweetwater experience. Although I was not in Expectation back then, the reality of that town totally surprised me. Now, upon entering the main street of this little remote hamlet, I was again given a most pleasant surprise.

The overall tone of it resulted in a successful blend of an Old West town with an underlying atmosphere of a Mark Twain setting. In front of the Miner's Creek Mercantile was a parked surrey. I half expected a woman to come out complete with long dress, flowered bonnet and twirling parasol. Across the street, two youngsters peered curiously through the cracks in the wooden sidewalk. Becky Thatcher and Tom Sawyer looked as mischievous as ever.

The buildings themselves were not of the Sweetwater colors, but were rather more representative of the browns and greys of old. Still, the various wood stains gave the lustrous effect of well-cared-for structures that bespoke community pride.

As we cruised along Main Street, people bustled about doing their Saturday shopping and chores. Pickups, older cars and even a horse or two waited along the street for their owners to complete their designated errands. Whenever we were noticed, hands waved and smiles lighted up faces. Strangers were not viewed suspiciously but were clearly welcomed. It gave us a warm feeling of congenial camaraderie that certain mountain folks shared.

Nearing the final buildings, we passed a livery stable. Beside it was a blacksmith. The double doors of the smithy's wooden shed yawned open to the summer day and a gentle breeze gave him welcome respite from the glowing embers he labored over. The man in the heavy apron was not sweating over horseshoes, but was busily exposing a masterpiece that had hidden within a shapeless piece of iron. It looked like he was creating an ornate lamp post. Our creeping vehicle caught the blacksmith's eye. He looked up and quickly waved before returning to his ancient craft.

We smiled and waved back. Seeing the artisan, I thought about one of our friends back in Woodland Park who had given up much to dedicate his life to the goal of reviving the fine craft of true blacksmithing. Lee Pavlica had a strong will and had sacrificed much to stick with his chosen profession, and finally it seemed that it was paying off for him. People were beginning to recognize his talent and the fact that he made no compromises when it came to maintaining the pureness of quality.

"Do you think Lee knows that guy?" I asked my companion.

"It's probable, since they occasionally get together for meetings. Lee's been all over."

I thought about the many journeys our friend had been on, frequently having to hitchhike because his vehicle was down.

Yet never seeming to mind because of the honorable goal to become a master of an ancient art.

The scenery drew my attention back to the town. The buildings ended abruptly. A new symbol of the Old West stood out in stark relief before us and we stopped to consider its unexpected presence.

Beside the road, in a small clearing, was a long dead tree. Its trunk was twisted. Its branches were tangled in a skeletal frame of bleached bones. And hanging from a thick limb was a noose that swayed menacingly in the light breeze. The morose object was eerily sobering.

"How odd," I commented. "Why would they want to mess up the nice mood of the town with something like that?" I shuddered at the more than intimidating sight.

Bill snickered. "What's the matter? You don't like the *real* West?"

"I don't see Doc Holliday around anywhere."

"That's because he's in Leadville. Seriously though, they probably just wanted to add a little bit of authentic drama to the place. I think it's kind of unique. Spices up the place, if you know what I mean."

"Unique? Spice? Some folks carry authenticity a mite too far, don't you think?"

Swinging the truck around, he conceded. "Maybe you're right. The local kids probably use it for a swing."

Now that *was* morbid.

Heading back through town, we looked for a good place to satisfy our grumbling stomachs. Now we noticed that not only had the town strived for authenticity, the entrepreneurs also had little imagination. It was that or they just plain liked the name of their town.

We passed Miner's Creek Hardware, Miner's Creek Haberdashery, Miner's Creek Dry Goods, and on and on until. . .Bill announced the black sheep. He whistled low.

"Will you look at that."

I leaned to peer beyond him. What I saw made my blood run cold, for I was looking at a cafe called Poor Joe's. That in itself would not make my hair stand on end, but *who* poor Joe represented did. There was an axe painted on the weathered sign. Poor Joe was our *axe man!*

Words weren't necessary. We knew where we were going to eat and the driver swung around to ease into a parking space in front of the cafe.

Inside, we were quickly transported back in time as we

stepped into the replicated interior of a prospector's cabin. This was definitely authentic. The lighting was low because of the flour-sacking curtains that blocked out the light of day. Miners' lanterns softly glowed on the tables. The barn wood paneling supported a myriad of antique tools. The pewter plates were shaped like gold panning tins. Sawdust was scattered over the plank flooring. But what magnetized one's attention was the lighted painting that hung on the far wall. Poor Joe dominated the room in all his powerful menace. I was fascinated.

Bill escorted me to the table beneath the portrait and I stared in hypnotic captivation at the imposing figure in the painting.

Eyes like twin coals glared down at the onlooker. The artist had been a master, for he'd made the eyes appear to be looking straight at you—no matter what angle you viewed them from. They seemed to move. Joe looked like the typical prospector. Thick and unruly black hair, full beard, and a weathered and craggy face stared out from the canvas. His buffalo plaid shirt was worn and dirty. Baggy pants were held up by wide suspenders. Boots were heavy and crusted. . .so was the axe he held.

I couldn't pull my eyes off him. There was something obscure about him that the artist had deftly captured and I concentrated on trying to define the nebulous characteristic.

"*That's Joe!*"

I jumped at the waiter's sudden voice.

He chuckled. "He scares you, huh."

Bill was smirking and I ignored his amusement, for he'd seen the young man's silent approach.

The tousle-haired youth smiled.

"Wanna sit somewhere else? Or maybe change places with your boyfriend here? You don't hafta face old Joe."

"I *like* facing old Joe," I blandly stated.

That was not an expected reply.

"Well, most ladies don't."

I didn't bother informing that I wasn't exactly within the norm of the mean when it came to "most ladies."

"This is fine," I said as he placed the menus before us.

He looked over at my "boyfriend." "She's gonna have nightmares," he tried to warn. "You might wanna switch places." Then he left.

I eyed Bill, grinned, then gave the menu my full attention. When we folded them up, the waiter returned to take our orders.

"You passing through?" he asked, starting the small talk.

Bill handed back the menus. "Thought we'd spend a little time browsing around."

"Ahhh, tourists."

"No," Bill corrected, "just out for a weekend drive."

"Oh, then maybe you already heard about old Joe here."

"Can't say that we have."

The young man's eyes fired with excitement, for he was going to be the first to tell the strangers all about Joe.

"You wanna hear?" he asked, nearly busting his buttons to spill the tale.

Bill looked over at his lady.

"You want to hear Joe's story, honey?" he asked for the waiter's benefit.

"Sure."

The man standing at the table literally trembled with excitement.

"I'll go give your orders and then when they're ready I can tell you all about it. I got a break comin' up anyway. That all right?"

We both nodded and he rushed to the kitchen.

While we waited, I'd gone up to the front of the cafe and taken a local paper from the stack by the door. After returning to the table, I scanned it and made frequent comments to my dinner partner about various tidbits I thought were interesting. Before I could get halfway through the thin tabloid, our food arrived. So did the eager beaver.

Our meal came so quick I hoped it was cooked through—I hoped it was even warm. It was not only both. . .it was downright tasty. Wanting to dig into the steaming food, my eagerness was stayed by the loitering presence of the waiter.

I self-consciously set my fork down and slid my gaze up to him.

Quick to please, he inquired if we had everything we needed.

Giving the table a once-over, I said that we were all set and thanked him.

He remained glued to the floor and cleared his throat.

"I'm on my break now. I can tell you that story." The young man wasn't aggressive; he was just bursting with impatience.

I had thought we'd have time to privately enjoy our meal before we had company, but evidently it had been wishful thinking.

Bill inclined his head to the extra space beside me.

"Sit down, son."

Full of nervous excitement, the waiter slid into the seat before I had a chance to scoot myself over.

"Whoops, sorry," he muttered.

I smiled weakly and pulled my plate in front of me.

Bill caught my eye and winked. He knew I would've preferred having the young man sit with him, not because I didn't want the stranger beside me, but because my impressions came easier when I could look him in the eye and have a better perspective to read his body language.

I flashed him a subliminal frown before turning to the youth next to me.

"What's your name?"

Anxiously working his palms over his knees, he replied with a smile. "Mark. Mark Davis."

We introduced ourselves to Mark and asked how long he'd worked at Poor Joe's. The answer became more involved than was necessary. We learned that his family owned the business, he'd lived there in Miner's Creek most of his life, he attended the high school that was in the big city "down the road a stretch" and that the cafe was going up for sale soon because they were moving out of state. The recitation of his autobiography gave us ample time to down most of our meal before Bill turned the conversation around.

"So what about that story?"

Mark's eyes fixed on my half-filled plate.

"Well maybe I should wait," he suggested, "because it gets real messy."

"Messy?" I repeated.

"Uhuh. It's kinda gory, if you know what I mean."

I wasn't into gory—tales or otherwise.

"Well, we just want to know the main facts; we don't need the gory details."

He looked at me, then nodded his head as if I were depriving him the recounting of the best part.

"Well, Joe walks around in the woods and he always has this big ol' axe with him. He prowls around draggin' the thing an' it's all bloody. So is he. Then people have seen him. . ."

"Mark," I cut in, "we're really interested in the story, the *whole* story. Could you take it from the top? Like who Joe was, what you know of his life? That sort of thing."

The air seeped out of his balloon when he heard we wanted to know the dry and uninteresting parts instead of the spooky ghostie stuff.

"Joe an' his wife came here over a hundred years ago.

Nobody knows for sure just when, but it was right around the time when gold was discovered in this area."

I frowned. "There must be record of that," I commented, insinuating that an approximate date could be reasonably established.

"Well," he sheepishly admitted, "I'm not too up on my history."

"Okay, that's all right. I guess it's not important. Go on."

"So anyway, Joe built a cabin and he looked for gold."

"Is the cabin still standing?" Bill inquired.

"Oh no. That burned when the forest fire went through. There ain't nothing left of it now."

My companion then urged the man to go on. "Then what? Did Joe ever find his gold?"

"Yeah, he did. In fact, that's what the story's all about." Finally the boy was getting to the good part. We could tell by his quickening pace of delivery.

"Okay. Joe hits paydirt an' he tries to be real cool about it. He don't tell anybody. . .but one of his friends gets real suspicious."

I hated to keep interrupting the flow, but I needed more information.

"Do you know this friend's name?"

"Let's see," he pondered, "It was one of them real old-timey names," he mused, rubbing his chin. "Jared? Zeb? No," he said, shaking his head, "I think it started with a K."

I tried to think of some old-timey male names and offered a few as suggestions.

"No," he mumbled in frustration. Then he started. "Caleb! It was Caleb!"

We smiled at the discovery and listened while Mark got back into the mood.

"Caleb found out that Joe had a secret cache and he wanted a cut of the action. He wanted to know where Joe was getting it all. Since Joe wouldn't tell, Caleb had him watched. The stream was the source. Once Caleb discovered that, he an' his buddy paid Joe a late night visit." Mark's eyes rounded. "An' it wasn't no *social* call either!"

My eyes locked onto those in the portrait.

Mark noticed. "He's a mean one, ain't he."

The intent gaze lowered to the boy's. "Go on, Mark."

His voice lowered to accommodate the spookiness. He was milking it for all it was worth.

"One night. . .when it was real dark in them woods. . .Caleb an' his friend snuck up on Joe's cabin." The tale was being described as if it were being told to imaginative kids around a midnight campfire. "They was real quiet 'cause Joe an' his wife was sleeping."

The storyteller paused for optimum fright effect.

"Then the two busted through the door and rushed to the bed. They had *knives* out! But old Joe wasn't so dumb. He grabbed his axe from the wall over the bed and swung hard!" Pause. "Caleb's buddy got it right in the neck. . .*square* in the neck. What a mess. The blood started pumping an' spilling all over the woman an' she screamed an' screamed while. . ."

"Mark," Bill halted after seeing my grossed-out expression. "The lady's still eating. Could you tone it down a little? Not be so graphic?"

The waiter's eyes rested on my plate. "Sorry, I told you it was messy."

It would've been a passable tale if it wasn't for the hard fact that I'd been taught to make all sensory perceptions a total experience. Because of that singular lesson, whenever people talked, I was extremely visual with their words. My inner reception of the spoken word mentally interpreted into automatic and simultaneous visions. For me, people's speech was synonymous with viewing a film. I had become extremely visual and it was a knee-jerk reaction. Words were vivid pictures to me and my companion knew that. He didn't think I needed to "watch" the action the boy was describing.

Mark noted that I'd pushed my plate away. Although he noticed, he forgot to take Bill's cautionary advice.

"So with all that blood runnin' all over Joe's wife an' with all that. . ."

"*Mark!* The *graphics!*" Bill reminded, inclining his head over to me.

"Oh yeah. So Joe takes his axe and starts across the room for Caleb. Caleb raises his shotgun and blasts it right at Joe. He goes down and so does his wife."

We waited for the rest of the story.

None came.

"And?" I prompted.

"And that's it."

That was "it" for the gross part, but that wasn't it for the whole story.

"A murder was committed, Mark, a double murder. In fact, there were *three* left in the cabin. What happened then? Was Caleb ever caught?"

"I don't think so, least nothing in the story says that."

I thought on that. "How do you know Joe's friend was named Caleb?"

Mark shrugged. "That's the name, that's all I know."

Something was suspicious.

"How come nobody knows whether or not he was caught? And if there were no witnesses to the crime, how do we know Caleb was the perpetrator in the first place?"

Mark peered at me. "What's all this third degree? You guys talk like you're detectives or something. You cops?"

That would be hilariously funny if it wasn't for the boy's sudden fright. I'd previously picked up the telltale smoke aroma on his shirt when he first sat down. I think he was a little more than nervous about his marijuana habit.

I smiled warmly. "No, we're just curious and want to get the story straight, that's all."

He was visibly relieved. Then shrugged again over the mystery.

"Aren't there records of any land? Old newspapers? Historical Society journals?"

Mark's face brightened. "Now I see what you're getting at. No, all that went up with that fire I was telling you about. Newspaper went too."

Bill's brow furrowed. "So essentially, this is a word-of-mouth tale."

"Yeah. It's kind of a ghost story around here. Most folks laugh it off an' others swear by it. Some are so scared of it they never go up in them woods after dark."

I eyed him. "Which one are you?"

He laughed. "You gotta be kidding! It's just *spook* stuff."

"You don't believe it?" Bill said.

"Come on. Look at that picture," he groaned, "how campy can you get. *Axe* man. Brother, what a crock."

"*You* sounded pretty convincing," I challenged.

"Lady, that's part of my job here. It adds flavor, know what I mean?"

"I know what you mean," I said. "Then the town could take or leave the tale."

He sneered. "They wish they never heard of it. I mean, who wants their town to have a mascot like that?"

"Then why the painting? Why the Poor Joe's cafe?"

"Like I said, it adds a little something different. Maybe you haven't noticed yet, but everything in this town is called Miner's Creek—real creative people. So my dad, he came up with the brainy idea of capitalizing on some old story he'd heard. When folks seen what he'd done, they gave him all kinds of flack, especially since it's just an old rumor."

"Then Joe's ghost isn't real?"

The young man's head tilted. His look was incredulously mocking.

"As real as flying saucers an' E.T."

We both grinned at the youth's innocent sarcasm. He took our expressions for one of mutual agreement. And that made it even more amusing. How little he knew.

After the gaiety of the moment began to wane, I asked our young friend if he knew the location of the rumored haunting.

"Sure I do," he bragged, "but it's way back in the woods on old unmarked trails. It's kind of hard to find."

"If you drew us a map could we find it without too much trouble?"

Mark laughed. "What do you want to go out there for? Ain't nothing there. And there sure as hell ain't no ghost. You'd never find it anyway—even with a map."

Bill's voice was light-hearted on the surface, but underneath, I detected a tone of apprehension about the boy.

"Could you show us where it is then?"

The following moments of silence were awkward. And when I saw Mark's face flush with the unexpected question, I too had doubts about his pretense of bravado and disbelief.

"We could come back when you're off your shift," I offered. "We'd really appreciate seeing the spot."

The boy's hands trembled. He shoved them beneath the table in an effort to conceal their revealing tremors.

"There's nothing out there," he insisted. "If you're interested in that kind of stuff, I'll show you where the old graveyard is. There's probably a spook or two moaning around there at night."

Our young waiter was desperately trying to wheedle out of our request. He really did believe in the story and he didn't want to go anywhere near the axe man's territory.

"Look," he said, realizing a refusal would reveal his underlying attitude, "my sister's in the back. She can take over for me. If you want to see the spot that bad I'll take you right now. . .I got plans for later."

Of course he would have plans; later meant dusk. Dusk meant almost night. Everyone knew what night meant—even the axe man.

My eyes lit up. "You sure you can take off like this?"

He was already sliding out of the seat.

"Hey, no problem. Me and my sister cover for each other all the time. This won't take long anyway. It's not that far, just up into some bad roads."

We followed our tour guide through the kitchen and out the back exit. An open Jeep was parked by the door and we piled in. The engine chugged and coughed for a minute and then, with a jerk, we were off to see the wizard.

Bill sat beside the driver and they were in a position to do all the talking. It was a breezy afternoon and their words were carried away on the wind. While they chatted, I took the time alone to take in the scenery. I was always interested in the vitality of new places and I surveyed the tree line for signs of health or ill. We were traveling through some magnificent specimens of virgin forest where the finely-balanced ecosystem was precariously holding its superb balance.

The Jeep bounced and pitched over weed-choked paths. It turned this way and that up roads that weren't even recognizable as roads. I was just about ready to feel like I was getting lost when we abruptly halted. The first thing I noticed was the eerie lack of birdsong and. . .no breeze.

"Well, this is it," announced the driver. "Right over there is where folks claim to see him." He was pointing to his left where the trees were especially tall. One could walk beneath the bottom layer of the pine branches.

I peered around past Mark to see where he pointed. I jumped out.

"What're you doing?" he asked in an anxious tone.

"Looking around!" And off I went.

Bill scrambled out of the vehicle next.

Mark didn't like what was going on.

"Hey!" he shouted after us. "I thought you just wanted to *see* the spot!"

"We do!" I hollered back. "We'll only be a few minutes." Before I turned my attention back to the forest, I noticed that the young man was nervously looking through the trees around him. He was clearly uneasy to be sitting alone and so exposed.

Soon I heard a hurried tramping sound behind us and I turned to Mark.

"We're almost done," I soothed. "You could've stayed in the Jeep."

"That's all right. I was getting bored." He followed us around in the wildgrass. "Not much to see, is there?"

"No, there sure isn't," I agreed. But there was plenty to *feel*.

Mark, hands on hips, was cool. Shifting his weight from one foot to the other, he scoffed bravely. "Well, I don't see any axe man." He wouldn't have said that if he'd felt Joe's powerful impressions.

"Neither do l," I said with a genuine smile of amusement.

He raised his brows at me. "Ready to head back?"

I looked to Bill. Behind the boy's back, my partner shook his head.

"Ohhh, in a minute," I chirped. Then, to ease his discomfort, I got him talking. "Was Joe's cabin around here, Mark?"

"I don't know where that was. It burned so long ago I guess there wasn't much left. . .it probably got all grown over."

I mulled that statement over. "Well, I wonder why Joe's been seen here then. I would've thought he'd appear around his cabin where the violence took place."

"Lady," the boy spouted with impatience, "Joe's out *looking* for Caleb. There's a *reason* for that axe of his."

The boy's quick response proved he believed in the ghostie part of the story. And as soon as he realized what he'd said, he moved to cover his tracks.

"At least that's what those fools in town believe."

"Uhuh. Well, why right here?" I pushed.

Mark shrugged. "I suppose because this is where Caleb had his place."

Great! Now we were really getting somewhere solid.

I looked around. "I don't see any cabin."

"And you won't either."

"Oh?"

"Caleb didn't have one. He had one of those other things. You know, like a lot of the mining towns had at first."

"Oh, you mean like a tent with a wooden floor."

"Yeah. He had one of those."

"How do you know that?"

"It's in the story."

I saw Bill nod and I was about to save our driver further uneasiness when he spoke up before I could say anything.

"Can we go now? I really gotta get back."

"Sure," I said.

The relief was a visible thing.

Driving back, we exchanged small talk. It was small talk to Mark and it was revealing talk to us, for he rambled on about how the town would really like to see poor Joe gone—the believers, that was.

That made me curious. "Why do they refer to him as 'poor' Joe?"

Mark grinned. "Anybody who can't rest in their grave's gotta be some poor old soul."

Then he remembered to qualify it again. "Least that's what they say."

"So," I concluded, "the believers would like to see Joe at rest."

"Guess so. . .the nonbelievers too. Then there'd be no more stupid story."

That was music to my ears because those on both sides of the fence wished Joe would just disappear from their lives. And those wishes were right up our alley.

Mark pulled in behind the cafe and we walked through to the register. By now the place was buzzing with the supper crowd and we thanked the waiter for all his trouble.

He had a final question. "What brought you folks up here? Was it the ghost?"

Sorry to say, I left that one for my partner to answer.

"We have an old friend up this way and, with this great weather, we took the time to look him up."

"Oh. Well, have a nice day."

We paid our tab and left.

Within the privacy of our truck, we sat for a few minutes to discuss our next move. Then I asked my mate a frivolous question.

"What would've you said if Mark had asked you who our friend was? What could. . ."

He held up his hand to postpone the answer. He was rolling down his window.

Mark appeared beside the truck.

"That friend you mentioned?"

"Yeah?" Bill said.

"Well, I know just about everyone around here, even the ones way back up in the boonies. Maybe I can help you out."

"I don't think so," I heard the driver hedge.

"Well, is he located in town then?"

"No."

"He must be in the boonies."

"Yeah, Mark, he's way back in the boonies.

"What's his name?"

My heart drummed to hear the answer. When it came, I couldn't believe my ears.

"Joe."

A queer silence fell like a lead curtain.

"Oh," Mark mumbled. "I don't know any Joe though. Sorry." "That's okay," Bill said. "Thanks for everything. You've been very helpful."

"Sure thing." He hesitated beside the pickup. "Ahhh, you folks gonna look for your friend tonight?"

"That's what brought us here," Bill said.

"Think you'll find him?"

The verbal cat-and-mouse game continued.

"Probably."

"Well. . .you have a nice visit."

"We didn't come to visit," came the shocking response.

"Oh?"

"No. We came to talk Joe into going back home. He's got family who misses him. He's been in the boonies far too long."

Silence.

Waiting.

Heart drumming.

Mark's voice quivered. "Think he'll go?"

"I dunno. That's up to him."

"Well. . .good luck," he stammered.

Bill just nodded and Mark scampered back to vanish into the cafe.

"Jesus!" I blurted. "Why'd you have to tell him our friend's name was Joe?"

"Well, isn't it? What was I supposed to say?"

"Anything! Now you got him all scared. Now the whole town will know why we're here. Dammit, Bill, you just blew our cover."

"How'd I know the kid would think our Joe was their Joe?"

I rolled my eyes in frustration. "Oh come on. Don't you think it was rather a bit obvious?"

He started up the engine and shoved it into gear.

"Well hell with them. Let them think whatever they want. We got work to do."

What more was there to say? The damage had already been done and now we had to concentrate our efforts on the job ahead. I was prepared to do that until my mate groaned.

"Oh-oh. Don't look over at the cafe. Just turn and face me."

I did as bid. "Why?"

"There's a dozen pairs of eyes watching us out the window."

"Oh damn!" I moaned, slumping down in the seat. "See what you did? Mark told everybody in there about us. They're probably all shaking their heads and wagging their tongues about the two crazies."

He grinned. "Nope. Their expressions are more like awe. I think they're more fascinated than anything."

We pulled out of town.

I furtively straightened up.

"I don't *want* awe," I bitterly complained. "And I certainly don't want fascinated wonder either. Now we'll probably have a slew of gawkers up there tonight."

"You kidding? You forget what Mark said? Half the town's afraid of those woods at night. They'll probably all go home and work their worry beads or light candles and say prayers that we succeed."

That thought of positive energies sent our way was not at all uncomforting.

"Well. . .I just hope you didn't screw this one up."

A hand settled on my knee and squeezed.

"C'mon, babe, loosen up."

And with a heavy extended sigh, I allowed the frustration to ride the breath out of my system. The way was cleansed and the mind was reset and cleared. Immediately we began analyzing all the information we had gathered. And our energies were directed toward formulating a persuasive plan to get Joe back home.

Once we reached the turnoff, Bill nosed the truck up and down the near-hidden roads while retracing our previous route. Soon I felt just as lost as before, and I wondered if the driver was too.

"Do you know where you're going?" I stammered, trying to hold on while the vehicle pitched and bounced.

The driver, intent on the rough road, didn't answer.

My attention went back to the overgrown woodlands. I was beginning to understand what a stone felt like while it tossed around in a polishing tumbler. Stream beds cut across the boulder-strewn trail and I prayed that we wouldn't get stuck in the water or get high-centered.

Finally all movement stopped and I scanned the unfamiliar scenery.

"This isn't the spot."

"I know that."

"Are we lost?"

"Nope. We can't go any farther though without a four-wheel. We'll have to settle for this and walk a little ways in."

That may be a problem, I thought as we climbed out of the disabled vehicle. Going around to the driver's side, I frowned.

"How'd you remember the way so good?"

He'd been busy checking his bearings. "I kept track of Mark's odometer between turns."

"Hey!" I praised, "That was real clever."

My mate grinned at me. "Like the young man said, even a *map* wouldn't have been any good. Way I saw it, counting was the only way to find it again. It was the only *logical* thing to do."

"Well, Mr. Spock, where to now?"

"This way," he said, taking my hand and leading me off to the left.

Within ten minutes of woodswalking, we were back in the familiar territory and began to walk the area. Taking individual readings, we each concentrated on the incoming impressions. When I was finished, I sat beside an aged aspen to wait for my partner. Watching him, it was clear that he was having some major difficulties.

He wore a puzzled frown while walking back toward me.

"Strange," he muttered.

"What's strange?"

"Did you pick up on him?"

I nodded that I had.

"Well, that's what's so strange. I couldn't get anything other than the basic presence of him."

I mulled that oddity over. "Did you at least feel his strength?"

His eyes slid over to mine. "That much I did get. We've got another nightstalker type on our hands."

"How do you figure?"

"I wasn't necessarily talking about our method. I was just referring to the power he's capable of wielding. We still need to talk about a good plan. This one's a tough one." That brought his thoughts around to me. "What'd you get? Anything useful?"

My face wrinkled up. "It might be useful if we can figure it out. My impressions were contradictory. I felt his strength too, but there was also some weakness that was there. His determination is real strong, but there's an underlying sense of conscience—maybe guilt?"

"Guilt? Over what?"

"That'd be pure speculation. Maybe that'll be our clue to the resolution. The man's definitely in the throes of self-conflict."

"Think he knows he's dead?"

I shrugged. "That could be one answer. That'd either mean he realizes his mission is futile or else he feels compelled to keep doing what he's doing."

"And that'd mean he's driven by his insatiable vengeance. Then again, we're assuming those are his motives."

"Yeah. And there's no room for assumptions with this stuff."

He sighed. "Did you get anything else we need to toss around?"

My eyes met his. "Nothing more on *him*," I whispered dejectedly. "What I got was on *me*."

"Oh? Having to do with what?"

"My own feelings." I shrugged. "A great fear overcame me. Something about this guy really scared me."

Now Bill was deeply concerned. "Was it his power?"

I shook my head. "It didn't feel like that kind of source. I can't explain it other than a kind of stomach-turning terror."

"Honey," he said softly, "want to go home?"

I had a sick feeling churn within me.

"I don't know. If I could just pinpoint this stupid feeling I'd probably be all right. The worst part is not knowing its cause."

"Want to leave it or try to go into it?"

Silence.

"Hon?"

"I really don't want to run away from any of these. We'd better try to sort it out."

He jumped right in. "Does his power frighten you?"

"No. I don't feel any threatening probabilities with that aspect."

"Okay. How about fear of failure on this one. That'd possibly make you feel real bad inside."

"No, that hasn't even occurred to me. That's not it either."

My companion brooded over the mystery my feelings created.

"Well, if it's not coming from his power or the outcome, and you feel confident neither of us will be harmed. . .what's left?"

Our eyes locked.

"I can't imagine," I sighed, "and maybe it's just as well."

His gunmetal eyes were intent upon mine.

"Let's skip this one. If you're sensing a terror about it then maybe we should leave well enough alone."

I hesitated before responding.

"We were led here for a reason. That reason may be something I have to face—learn to get over. If I renege on this one I'll always wonder what it was I needed to gain from it."

Although he understood my viewpoint, he still held deep reservations.

"Are you absolutely sure this is what you want to do?"

I nodded.

"And you're sure this terror doesn't have anything to do with our safety?"

"I'm sure."

Silence. . .thinking.

As far as I was concerned, there wasn't anything else to talk over.

"C'mon," I said, "let's get back. We need to get some rest."

When he looked at me, his countenance was full of doubt, yet he accepted my decision. And, hand in hand, we strolled back to the comfort of the camper.

The high mountain air of the late afternoon brought a new crispness of clarity to the senses. It was drawn deeply into the lungs, refreshing and cleansing the inner being with its pureness. The breeze, soft as a slumbering baby's sigh, exhaled the woodland's sweet essence and soughed scents of pungent evergreen. The fragrance of pine and spruce wafted through the window screens to fill my head with their inebriating spirits of intoxicating magic. In the silent quietude, Bill and I rested side by side. My drugged state of nature-induced euphoria wasn't hard to perceive.

"You slipping away?" came the soft whisper.

I let a pleasure-filled smile curl my lips.

"No, I'm not going anywhere. It's just so serene lying here in the forest like this. It's so incredibly peaceful."

My mate inhaled deeply of the conifers' heady perfume.

"Almost as good as woodsmoke," he commented with an amused light in his eyes.

"Just as good," I gently corrected. "It's just as good."

I pulled the quilt up over my shoulders, and, snuggling down into the protective warmness of my companion, I found a safe haven that was free of my former frightening images. No terror. No fear. No axe man. just a womb-like warmth.

Peacefully, we slept. For hours did we remain oblivious to the outside world.

A biting chill caressed my cheek. Furtive movement stirred within the enveloping blackness of the camper. In the ebony surround, Bill was quietly fumbling with the heater.

"If you turned on a light you could see what you're doing," I whispered.

The lantern suddenly illuminated the interior with an eerie fluorescent glow.

"I didn't want to wake you with it," he said, finally lighting the heater pilot and adjusting the burner.

"Why's it so cold?" I chattered, tightly tucking the cover under my chin.

"Wait 'til you see. Stay under the covers until it's warm in here." He cranked the windows down and sat on the floor beside the bed. We were face to face and his eyes held a fair measure of trepidation. "It's clouds, babe. They're hanging to the ground. It's like clam chowder out there."

"No wonder it's so cold." I stuck my hand out to test the air. It was still heavy with the remaining moisture that the heater hadn't yet burned off.

"You should get back under the covers until it's warm in here."

"Nah," he said, brushing off the idea, "it won't be much longer now. It's already heating up. Anyway, we need to talk about later."

I rolled over on my side and rested up on one elbow. The spreading heat felt good on my face as the tiny portable heater labored to keep away the encroaching mist of coldness that wrapped around the camper.

"Bill," I sighed, "I have no idea how to approach this one."

That didn't surprise him because neither did he.

"Honey, have you noticed that each case was different? I mean each one had to be handled by separate methods of resolution."

"I noticed. What I'm wondering is how many methods there are. No-Eyes just said that there were many ways. She never enumerated them specifically. I guess the circumstances of each encounter are what determines the method. Trouble with that is, we don't know that method until we're well into it. Plans don't mean much at all."

He chuckled. "Kind of like going out for Chinese and then finding yourself in Mama Leone's Little Italy. You don't know what to order until you're there."

"Yeah," I grinned at his amusing comparison, "only No-Eyes didn't exactly use that analogy. She said it was like not knowing which blanket wrap to wear until you went outside to test the air. We need to test the air with each of these before we know which trail to take."

"But you know what?" he asked without pausing for a reply, "that trail always becomes clear. No matter who the entity is, and whatever the circumstances are, there's always a solid path that opens for the spirit to leave on."

I smiled warmly. "That's comforting, isn't it."

He just smiled back and nodded.

I became quietly pensive. "I wonder what new trail this one will resolve itself with?"

"I have no idea," he muttered, "no idea at all."

"We've come full circle. That's what I said when we got on this subject."

And it was good our discussion had concluded, for it was then our psyches tingled. . .Joe was afoot.

Bill's eyelids quickly shut as he began his inward journey.

I shot up to a sitting position and followed suit.

After twenty minutes of intensive preparation, we donned our outerwear, shut down the heater, and took a few extended moments to emotionally embrace. We were one.

The transition from warm, bright camper to cold, dark night was like leaving the womb. The etheric mist had lightened. Now, instead of the opaque white shroud, it swirled about in ectoplasmic layers of vapor.

As we willfully advanced through the ghostly tentacles that coiled around and beckoned us deeper into the woods, a peculiar sensation came over me. My scalp tingled with the suddenness that *deja vu* had struck. And I was reminded of the misty morning with my teacher. The mind rationalized and became strong with the inrushing flood of new thoughts. Fear fled. This spectral surround was not some frightening portent; it was an omen—a good omen. I secretly smiled with the instant realization. I half expected Joe Red Sky to silently walk out of the preternatural mist. And I reached out into the waiting whiteness to swirl the moisture around. Like an owlet's downy feather riding the shifting air currents, the foggy entity drifted and danced with a grace of its own.

"It's friendly," I whispered. "It's good medicine."

My companion squeezed my hand in accepting response.

"Know why?" he hushed back.

"No, but I think I'm going to be glad it came."

We plodded on, picking our way nearer to our target's territory. We were almost there.

The haunting environ had stunted our distance perception. We had miscalculated and had gained more ground than we'd realized, for our psyches soon began detecting random signals.

Sporadic at first, they suddenly escalated into a volley of furious blips. We had breached the axe man's perimeter.

We halted and listened.

No sound pierced the deep night. A solemn funeral stillness stalked like death among the trees. Not a branch wavered. Not a creature roused. Nothing even breathed.

I looked up at the spired firs. Like great standing stones did they tower as sentinels marking the spectral home of our adversary. So utterly unnatural. No coyote call. No owl hoot. Just the Stygian silence and the rolling mist that prowled at our feet and caressed our faces.

Together did we strain our ears for sound—for the sound. We turned our attention to our right where the pines huddled tightly together, for, from there, a muted disturbance pierced the deathly soundlessness.

Our necks craned forward, heads cocked to turn a discerning ear. An axe was being dredged over a stony ground.

The sound was incongruous and I whispered in Bill's ear. "This is all weeds and wildgrass. "

Without daring to pull his eyes from the direction of the grating noise, he whispered back. "There might've been some crude road here back in his day. It was probably gravel or real stony."

The scraping became louder. The distance between us and Joe was lessening. Our man was heading straight for us. And, without a word uttered between us, we both began advancing through the mist.

The nebulous figure, surrounded by the pallid surround, at first appeared apparitional. Then, as both sides advanced, the prospector's substance congealed. Finally, seeming as solid as we were, he stood before us.

Immediately I knew why the mist was good medicine, for when I saw Joe's face, his clothes and weapon, the blood drained from my cheeks. I felt like my knees were going to buckle. I felt like I was going to faint, for Joe's cadaverous face was splotched with blood and the clothing was splattered. I dared not lower my eyes to the instrument that trailed at his side.

Bill's hand tightened around my arm for moral support. He was deep into my head. He knew now what had prompted my former feeling of terror. It wasn't Joe's power nor his threat—it was his appearance. He knew I'd have to get past that in order to do any effective work. He also knew that the friendly mist was helping to veil our target's grotesque presentation.

"We're friends," I managed to sputter in spite of the sickening sensations that were threatening my weak stomach.

The man's ebon eyes glared into ours.

"No one comes into these woods after dark," came the icy response.

"We came to help you," Bill said with confidence.

The black eyes narrowed in suspicion. "Why?"

Bill started to reply, then stopped as Joe menacingly hefted the weapon up and cradled the blade in his other hand. It was clear that my companion had no intentions of playing the taunting macho man with this one. I heard him nervously clear his throat.

"Joe," he began sympathetically, "it's time to resolve your conflict."

The man slowly nodded as his thumb caressed the wet blade edge.

"Time for that is long overdue. Tonight I finish my business."

That would've sounded encouraging, but I knew that Joe's business and our business were not exactly the same.

The deep voice issued forth in a calm and deliberate manner.

"Tonight I finally settle the score."

"How?" I dared to ask.

When he shifted his eyes to mine, starlight momentarily reflected off the glassy surface of their depths. Some unknown trait speared through and it gave me a subliminal spark of hope.

"Tonight I collect a debt. Tonight I make *pieces* out of Caleb."

"Caleb?" I questioned, drawing the man into conversation.

"Caleb," came the weighted reply.

"What has he done?"

Dumb question.

The man flung out his arms. The axe swung down like a pendulum. The barrel chest expanded in a manner of display.

"This! This is what Caleb has done."

The shirt glistened its vile evidence.

The mist swirled to veil the macabre sight.

Joe again fondled his axe. "I do not mean to frighten you, but you have come to where you knew I'd be. You must have information for me."

Bill re-entered the scene. "Yes, we do have information. We know where Caleb is."

Joe's eyes rounded like new moons.

"Ah! I have prayed for this night! Tell me now and I will end this business."

"First we need to talk," Bill slipped in.

"No! *Business* first!"

Silence.

"Caleb's dead," I whispered.

The shock on Joe's face was one of profound disbelief. "*No!* He lives to feel my revenge."

I sadly shook my head. "I'm sorry, Joe, but Caleb died when the fire came through."

The coal black eyes narrowed. The thumb became a trigger-itchy device as it slid back and forth to smear the wetness of the blade.

"You lie," he said calmly. "You lie to deceive me. Caleb *lives!*"

Now the path that we must take opened before me. Joe's own words had brought us up to its trailhead.

I exaggerated a feigned sigh of defeat. "I do not lie, Joe, but we are both right. Caleb is dead, yet also does he live. We can't bring him here, but we can take you to him. Will you let us do that?"

The eyes gleamed with the deeply satisfying thought. He grinned and nodded.

I could feel Bill's rising anxiety after he perceived the trail I intended to take. Trying to shut out his interfering impressions, I spoke again.

"We'll take you to Caleb if you do one thing for us."

Joe squinted down at me in distrust. "What is this one thing?"

"Can we talk about this over by those trees over there? I really need to sit down."

He glanced to the tree line, then agreed.

When we reached the aspen stand, Bill sat in the damp grass, rested his back against the trunk, and raised a doubtful frown. This was going to be a method we'd never attempted together. It was chancy to tread an untried trail in the middle of such a serious encounter.

I rested against another aspen and Joe sat between us. The weapon balanced on his knees.

Maintaining a sense of congeniality, I forced my sight away from the ghastly object that nearly touched my own leg.

"Joe, Caleb didn't just injure you."

The man sarcastically chuckled. "Don't you think I know that?"

"Then you realize you're dead."

"And you're not," he summarized neatly.

I smiled.

The man grinned, but just for a moment before looking over to Bill, then back to me.

"What's this all about? What's this one thing I have to do? You said you'd take me to Caleb."

"Yes, we will do that for you, but because we're different, we need to meet on common ground. That's why we first had to make sure you understood that you're spirit and we're not. Obviously you can't change, but we can. We need to have a few minutes to meet you on your own level. Will you give us that?"

Joe pondered the idea. "If I give you this time, will you then take me to Caleb, 'cause I got business with him. I been waiting a long, long time for this night."

"I know, Joe. We promise you'll see him if you want."

"I want," he half-growled.

"So how about it?"

He hem-hawed a second then nodded with a heavy sigh.

"All right, but just a few minutes; I got me a score to settle up."

"Thanks," I said, smiling up into his messy face. I eyed Bill. Already his eyes were closed and I wondered how he was doing. Then, shutting my own, I worked to make a speedy exit. The time-factor involved created an irritating sense of urgency. I had to force the exit, yet it needed to be a smooth transition. There was some frustrating difficulty at first, but after a time of deeper concentration, the time aspect dissipated and I entered the core of my being. I was out.

And so was my companion. He was grinning with the heady success of the feat.

Joe saw us and stood. Now our communications would be more clear between us. They'd be natural.

Bill and I, standing on either side of our man, slowly closed in. And before Joe could react, the love meld was already in motion. He was totally enveloped by the pulsating rosy glow that radiated its compassionate warmth around and through the three joined spirits.

And Joe cried. In great tension-releasing sobs did he cry.

Together, Bill and I drew up the man's rage, his revenge. We effectively absorbed his hate and his vile intent. The man was left without a purpose. Now he was ready to go home.

When we separated, Joe was euphoric. His expression was

a mixture of shock and inner peace. Fascination glowed from his soft eyes. Then, suddenly, he raised his hands and searched around him.

The axe was gone. It just was no more.

I smiled. "We'll take you now."

"What?"

"I said we'll take you to Caleb now."

A puzzled frown creased the heavy brows. "Oh. Well. . ."

I cocked my head. "Well what?"

Clearly, his new attitude confounded him.

"Well. . .I don't seem to care about him no more."

"Doesn't matter," Bill informed, "we're still taking you because Caleb wants to see *you*."

Silence filled the space between the etheric trio before Joe found his voice again.

"But I don't want to see him. I'm tired. I've wasted more than a century caught between my foolish hate and revenge. I don't want to see him." Then his head tilted curiously. "Why'd he want to see me?"

"Retribution. He's been waiting for you all along. While you wasted time looking for him in the physical, he was also forced to wait within the reality of his crime. He too has suffered much these many years. Now. . .all that is left is the release of his pain. He needs to apologize to you."

Joe's attention was splitting between my words and the wavering surround that was closing in. The physical mist had drawn itself up to condense into a slowly rotating vortex of etheric matter. Enclosing the three of us, it turned and pulsated. It encapsulated us in a living tunnel of light. Joe didn't realize it yet, but his clothing was becoming cleaner. His face now had a freshly-scrubbed appearance.

The altered scene was too confusing to him. He forced his eyes to mine.

"Caleb wants to. . .he, ah, he *wants* to see me?"

"Yes, to make amends that will conclude his years of suffering."

"But. . ." he began, then stopped to squint at the brightening mist.

"Joe," Bill said softly, "there is another who has also suffered much during your absence. There is another who waits for you."

The substance of the tunnel walls thickened. They brightened more.

With Bill's last cryptic words, Joe needed no further explanations.

"Andrea! My Andrea!"

We smiled.

"Take me to her!"

I cocked my head in hesitation. "What of that unfinished business?"

"It's *finished!*" he swore.

"And what of Caleb? What do you feel for him?"

He hung his head. "Pity."

I smiled.

"Please!" he pleaded, "take me to Andrea!"

I glanced over at Bill. He was frantically motioning for me to finish up. The tunnel was going through another metamorphosis and we had to exit immediately.

"We cannot go further, Joe. We must return, for this trail is not for us—not yet."

"But. . ." His head suddenly jerked to face the illuminating brilliance ahead. Then he quizzically looked to me in amazement.

I grinned wide and nodded. "Yes! That's *her* calling! She's waiting. *Go* to her!"

He stared at me. Eyes flooded with unrestrained happiness. "Andrea! Anndreeeaaa!"

I opened my eyes. My body was cold, very cold.

Bill wasn't back yet and I waited in frozen silence for his safe return. I waited for what was too long a time. He should've lowered right back in. I worried.

Not wanting to make a disturbing sound in the brush, I remained where I was and considered going back to check on him when his eyelids slowly opened.

He smiled.

I smiled.

"That was really something," he sighed.

"Yeah, another trail taken." I then moaned with the aching effort of unfolding my stiff bones.

Together we stood. His arms encircled me and we turned to scan the woodlands. A gentle breeze soughed through the conifers. We gazed up into the night sky. Spired treetops swayed. Stars winked down. Celestial light silvered the forest. All was clear again.

All was blessedly clear.

Madness in Bogan Flats

The weeks of the dusty summer trailed through the entity of time. They ambled their somnambulant way into the month of August. Little rain had fallen and the forests were becoming parched. Fire danger was high. The radio announcers continually cautioned their listeners to be careful with their matches and campfires. The warnings of Smokey the Bear whispered behind the minds of every camper and hiker—nobody wanted to be caught in a blazing forest fire.

Before sunrise on this beautiful August morning, my eyes opened to scan the semi-darkness of the bedroom. Beside me, my mate mumbled in his colorful dreamscape. My gaze slid to the greyness that began slipping through the slats of the wooden window blind. I smiled. Yes, it was truly a beautiful day, one of good omens, for it was pouring rain and drumrolls of thunder rippled across the sky. Nature would take a long thirsty drink this day. Mountain ponds would be freshened. Trees would be glistening from their new washing. The earth would be pungent again. Four-legged people would be quenched. And all of nature would breathe easier, for the fire danger would be alleviated. I smiled.

A whisper-soft voice rent the fragile fabric of my private thoughts.

"A good omen. A summer rain for Summer Rain."

I turned my head to look into the sleepy eyes beside me.

"I'm so glad we finally got rain. I was beginning to worry. The mountains were too dry."

He kissed me and climbed from the bed. Rolling up the blind, he studied the view.

"Been pouring like this all night," he concluded after seeing how sodden everything was.

"Are we still going?"

"Of course. This thing will have already passed through that area. It'll be sunny and the woods will be nicely dampened down."

Overhead, a sharp thunder crack vibrated through the frail

house. Bill's profile was momentarily illuminated. His eyes lifted to rest on the roiling clouds.

"Wish we were back in Rainbow Valley," he commented with a measure of underlying disappointment.

"Mmmm, I miss it too. We don't get to join with the Thunder Beings anymore."

Every time a particularly angry storm system moved in, Bill could be counted on to say the same thing. Although I could always anticipate hearing the wishful thought voiced, I always sympathized with the sensitivity that generated it. Our little log cabin in Rainbow Valley had sat on a high mountainside at ten thousand feet, and whenever a powerful storm blew over, we'd stand on the deck and join with its electrifying power. I'm not suggesting that that was the most intelligent thing to do in a bad storm, but somehow we actually felt protected by its dynamic omnipotence. To stand tall while the thunder cracked and rolled, while the jagged bolts of blinding lightning zigzagged down out of the blackened clouds, was a spellbinding experience like no other. It was akin to walking into the incredible power of God—a magical encounter that left one feeling radiated with His energy. A mystical union. The grandest drama of nature.

For me, this sharing was one of bonding my being with that of nature. For Bill, it was a highly mystical union and communication with All That Is. He'd experience it as a high esoteric touching. For him, it was very moving for his spirit. The forceful side of nature had always fascinated him. I think his favorite occupation would be that of a pilot who flies into hurricane eyes, or a tornado chaser.

Another crack trembled the wood-slab house. Rainbow, ears plastered to the sides of her knobby head and tail tucked down between her legs, nosed our door open and scrambled under the bed. I slid off the bed and crouched down to peer into her safe hidey-hole. The tail swished in clear communication.

"Thank you so very much for your deep concern, but if it's all the same to you, I'll just stay where I am, thank you."

I crooned a little to our scared baby, then got up to pad off into the kitchen.

Bill peeked his head around the doorway. "What're you doing?"

"Starting breakfast."

"We'll go out. Just make some lunch."

Forty minutes later, while the rain still pelted Woodland

Park, we drove up to the restaurant. Godmother's Kitchen had their lights on and Bill lit the table candle. With the dark, wet day, we felt extra cozy in the corner booth. While we ate, our conversation naturally flowed to the encounters.

"I have a question," I said.

"Shoot."

"It's a technical question about our last case. How can a spirit be carrying around something like an axe?"

"Isn't that like the horse bit we talked about?"

I was quick to shake my head.

"Animals have minds, memory and energy. An axe is an inanimate. It's just an object. Yet Joe's axe was etheric. I'm not sure I understand how that's possible."

"You *saw* it. . .that makes it possible."

"I know what I saw, but I want to understand what I saw."

He eyed me. "Weren't you informed that some technicalities have no explanations?"

"Yes, but this is different. This is just a factor intrinsic to apparitions."

"You're right. Now I have an interesting question. What makes an object like an axe any different from other objects like clothing? Buttons. Jewelry. Shoes. Shirts."

He had a valid point and I considered it.

"Well," I began. "We know that spirits are pure energy, so when they wish to manifest, they utilize that energy to create a representational configuration with exterior raiment. They present an image that contains significance either for themselves or for whomever they're manifesting to."

"So? Let's go deeper into that aspect. Let's narrow this down and get into specifics. What of the *wayward* spirits? What constitutes *their* individualized image?"

"They present themselves as they were in their last physical existence."

"Go on," he prompted.

"They do that because they don't know any better. Since most of them don't even realize that they're dead, they retain *memory* of their appearance; therefore, they don't let go of the energies that molded that appearance. Their physical characteristics remain the same, unaltered. . .right down to the ragged moccasins, blanket wraps, suspenders and. . .axes."

My companion smiled. "Those wayward ones are clever, but they are not so clever. They automatically perform the fascinating feat of molding their energies into images and they don't even realize they're doing it."

Silence.

"Now what're you thinking about?"

"They way you worded that made me think of something else. No-Eyes touched on something a lot like that—the use of one's energy to mold an image or form."

"I think I know where you're going with this, but go ahead."

"She mentioned the secrets some Indian people had to alter their physical form. She said it's been done. Isn't that trans-figuration?"

He nodded in agreement. "There're all kinds of terms for that. Transmutation. Transformation. Shape changer. Per-mutation. Well, you know them all. Take your pick."

A curtain of silence hung between us.

"So?" he said.

I sighed. "So there's so much more I want to learn."

"Why would you need to learn how to do that?"

"I didn't mean to actually *perform* transfiguration; I just meant to *know* more about it."

He shrugged. "Many Heart probably knows about that sort of thing. Didn't he say your paths would cross again? That you'd spend time together again in the future?"

That thought both depressed and hurt me.

"Yeah, he said that, but he also said it wouldn't be until after we're located on our sacred ground. Who knows when that'll be?"

"Well, at least it's something you can look forward to. In the meantime, don't you think you've got your hands full?"

"Speaking of that," I reminded, "we'd better head out. Looks like the storm's lifting."

And it was, for a blue Colorado sky smiled down on us just ten miles out of town.

"There's a little something for you in your side mirror," the driver hinted.

I leaned over to peer into the glass and saw a brilliant double rainbow.

I fawned over its spectacular beauty of vividness. Then it struck me as being more than a mere natural phenomenon of nature.

"Another good omen," I beamed.

"Yep. One more and we'll have the triad. We couldn't ask for a better sign. Guess this one's going to be another success."

"Hey, don't go getting *cocky*," I teasingly jabbed.

"Touché," he playfully grinned. "You sharpen that rapier tongue of yours this morning?"

"No, but you set your own trap with that one. I just thought I'd spring it."

"Smartmouth," he grumbled.

There were few couples who could freely banter with each other the way we did without it slipping into a full-fledged heated argument. Our playfulness warmed my heart. Our complete openness was a beautiful and sacred thing. And with the reminded realization of that, I snuggled in closer beside my driver and got comfy within the companionable melding of our flowing auras.

This encounter would take us deep into the territory of the Western Slope. If we drove without stopping, we wouldn't reach our destination until four hours later. And if we had been making this journey on a weekday, it'd be another hour longer due to the two traffic stoppages going through Glenwood Canyon to accommodate the construction work on the super-highway. That was a trucker's nightmare that played havoc with schedules.

But this wasn't a weekday; it was Saturday. Although we always liked to get to our destination as quickly as possible, our mood was more relaxed this time and we weren't in any great rush. . .motor homes passed us. And that in itself was a profound statement made by my driver.

When we neared Wilkerson Pass, Bill asked me if I wanted to stop to feed the critters again. I would've liked that moment of sweet respite during the journey, yet when I saw the parking lot full of RVs, I declined the offer. With so many city people noisily tramping about, I knew it'd be impossible for an enjoyable communion to take place. I slumped back in the seat and we drove past.

On the descent from the pass, our eyes naturally squinted to survey the panoramic view of the lowland that stretched out before us. The last time we'd taken this route was when our destination was St. Elmo. Our eyes searched for the mysterious eagle, yet, much to our disappointment, we covered the long stretch of land without seeing him.

At Hartsel, we headed north. Now we'd be going through some of the state's higher country. After passing the towns of Fairplay and Alma, the road that climbed to the summit of Hoosier Pass was straight and steep—the downside was a different matter, for it twisted back and forth in tight hairpin curves before uncurling to lead the traveler into Breckenridge, then Frisco. Frisco was always our gas-up point, for it was right before the Interstate that would take us west over Vail Pass and all the way through nonstop to Glenwood Springs.

Once on the Interstate, my thoughts became seriously weighted by the upcoming encounter. There was an oddity about it that bothered me. I asked Bill if we could talk about the case, and he admitted that he thought the facts were somewhat confusing too. He was anxious for me to hear his thinking on it before I voiced my own. Before going into any individual thoughts, I decided it was best to review what we knew of the case just to make sure we were both aware of the same information.

"The entity manifests itself as a wagon train scout. While he was far ahead on the trail, Indians attacked the wagons and carted off his wife and daughter. When he returned, there was no one left alive."

"Right," the driver said. "Now get out the map. I want you to see something."

I unfolded it, then waited.

"I'm sorry," he sighed, "I meant the national forest one."

Setting the state map aside, I opened the White River National Forest one and refolded it to expose our destination.

"Now follow the red line from Glenwood down to Redstone."

"Got it."

"Go down a little more to the broken line that veers off to Marble."

My finger traced the line but never made it to Marble. Just in a ways along the broken line, Bogan Flats was marked in red letters.

"Okay, I've got Bogan Flats."

"Notice anything out of place?"

"Bogan Flats isn't located along a major road. It looks as if McClure Pass might've been the original trail the wagon train was on."

"That was my guess too. So. . .why is this character in Bogan?"

I thought on that. "He could've scouted in that direction. That could've been where he was when the attack took place."

"Or?"

"Or he could've mistakenly led them there and that's the actual location of the attack."

"Or?"

I sighed. "Or he could've deserted and hid out there."

"So which one is it?"

I studied the map. "Guess we won't know until we talk to him." I paused a moment to ponder the possibilities. "I don't think Bogan is where the attack occurred. It doesn't really make sense for an experienced scout to veer from the main trail."

"That was my thinking too. So he either deserted or he was scouting there."

My attention on the map was distracted by the change of engine sound. It was laboring. I looked up and noticed we were ascending Vail Pass. We were nearing the summit. Heading west over Vail Pass was a breeze, but going back the other way was tortuous on engines.

"We're not coming back this way, are we?"

"No, we'll take the Leadville exit then. I don't think Vail would do the engine in, but why put it under all that strain if we don't have to?"

Relieved that we'd be taking another way back, I returned to our former discussion. Another possibility came to me.

"Honey, what if Bogan was where the Indian encampment was? It'd make sense for the scout to try to track his family down."

"You're right. I never thought of that. It makes a lot more sense too. And another thing, how did the scout die? Was he keeping himself hidden while spying on the Indians and then got caught?"

That sounded logical to me. I closed my eyes and went deeper into it. When I was done, I verified our last hypothesis.

"Bogan Flats isn't where the attack occurred; it's where the encampment was. It's where the scout met his demise."

My mate grinned. "Now that *my* confusion is all cleared up, what bothers *you* about it?"

"The 'why' factor. *Why* is he wayward? What purpose holds him bound there?"

"I don't think he's searching because, if your information was right, he'd already found the women. How about revenge? He could be looking for Indians for revenge."

A psychic chill caused a tremor to ripple through me.

"That's very probable, but what makes him mad then? No-Eyes said he's all mixed up. It seems to me that if he's looking for Indians to take his revenge out on, that isn't crazy at all, that's as logical as logic gets."

Silence.

"Well?" I prompted.

"Well, then I guess we have to think like a crazy person."

That idea really helped a lot. I sighed.

"All right," I began, trying to think it out, "a crazy mind thinks in illogical patterns, right?"

"Wrong," came the contradictory reply. "Mental hospitals and prisons are full of very clever crazies. Very complex and detailed crimes have been plotted and carried out by crazies. You can't assume that just because this scout is supposed to be mad that he's also thinking illogically." Bill was pensive for a silent moment. "No, there's some other reason for the madness. What else would *seem* illogical on the surface but still *be* logical?"

"This whole discussion is illogical. I'm so mixed up now I don't even know where we're at in all this."

The driver laughed. "Hey, this is nothing compared to some of the psychology discussions we've been through. This should be a piece of cake!"

I glared at him.

"C'mon," he grinned, "don't give up now when we're halfway there."

"Let me think about it for a while."

The pickup nosed into Glenwood Canyon where the Colorado River once rushed over boulders and sang its freedom song. Now, because of the massive and grotesque construction going on, there were lengthy stretches where the singing waters were diverted, exposing the dry, rocky river bed. The sheer canyon walls rose high above the road. It made my stomach turn to see the hideousness of modern technology that was taking millions of dollars to build, when, one day, the Earth Mother would send it all tumbling down like a child's Lego set. How clever and wonderful does man believe he is in his ignorance. What utter work of folly.

Clearing the canyon and tunnel, we pulled into the Village Inn for lunch. Bill didn't ask me again about the encounter confusion. He probably thought I was still thinking on it. And he'd be right too because I was. I hadn't stopped thinking since we stopped talking about it, for a vague theory was temptingly flickering through the currents of my brain—the nebulous idea remained a slippery irritant, and I kept trying to grab it by its swishing tail.

Bill talked while we busied ourselves with lunch. Ordinarily I'm a very intent listener; however, this time his voice was no more than a melding of the restaurant's monotone murmur. It was far off and disconnected, yet I'd managed to elicit all the right nods in perfect responsive timing.

The nefarious theory that continued to evade my efforts of

capture had to be caged. Fragments of it flickered and taunted just beyond my conscious reach. I couldn't pull it in. It was like an ice fisherman watching his prize continually swim back and forth past the opening, yet never getting it to take the bait. It was frustrating. Then—

"I *got* it!" I blurted, slapping my hands down on the table. "That's *it!*"

Bill jumped. His forkful of salad missed his mouth by a mile. He stabbed his chin and lettuce toppled back onto the plate.

Heads turned.

Ignoring the effects of my sudden outburst, my eyes twinkled with excitement.

"Honey! I know what makes him act mixed-up and crazy!"

My dinner partner's eyes furtively scanned the faces of those around us. The people were returning their eyes to their plates. My mate leaned forward and sternly whispered.

"Do you *mind?* Did you *have* to upset half the restaurant?"

I shifted my gaze to the diners. None seemed interested in us. And, in my undaunted exuberance, I grinned back at his flaming blue eyes. "He's *transposing!*" I said in a more dignified tone.

My companion was nonplussed.

"Want to explain that or do I have to guess?"

The sarcasm went unchecked.

"Listen," I said, getting into it, "the guy's transposing the entire scenario. He's acting like he was *there!*"

The bland face that stared back at me mildly suggested that perhaps I was not making sense.

"Okay, okay," I soothed, "just bear with me a minute while I try to make this clear. First of all, it's not *revenge* he's caught up with—it's *guilt!* He's feeling a great guilt for *not* being there when the attack came. So. . .he's transposing the circumstances of the event by transferring his purpose from *revenge* on Indians to *protection* of ladies—just like he was *supposed* to be doing in the first place." I was beaming. "Get it?"

He was not beaming. "I get it, but if this is what he's doing—this 'protecting'—why isn't he manifesting at the attack site?"

"Because that isn't where he last saw his family. . .the encampment was."

Expressionless silence.

"Well? What do you think?"

A brow arched. "So how come you can figure out a crazy person?"

I grinned. "The world's full of 'em. Sanity rests with those who 'figure' 'em. . .not with those who join 'em."

He grinned back. "No-Eyes say that?"

"None other," I proudly replied.

Then he mysteriously leaned forward and crooked his finger for me to do the same. He had highly secret things to say that were for my ears only.

"Are you done with the outbursts? Because if you are, I'd like to finish my salad without maiming myself."

Now I was embarrassed. "I'm sorry. I'm done."

"You sure?"

Duly chastised, I nodded weakly.

"Good," he said with an exaggerated smile.

The rest of our meal was enjoyed in peaceful conversation about the new theory. Bill concurred with the new conclusion and the reasoning behind it. All aspects of the case reconciled nicely with it. We would proceed on the basis of the scout's intent to protect. The entity would be out to prove his salt. He would want to protect me—a woman—for his purpose had nothing to do with a race factor as we had initially supposed; it had to do with gender. Either way, one of us was going to be his target. At least now we knew who. . .and it wasn't me.

A couple sitting near us got up and gave us parting smiles of amusement before passing to the register.

Bill teasingly glared at me in his embarrassment.

I grimaced in animated apology. "Sorry, I didn't mean to be the featured entertainment here."

"More like comic relief, wouldn't you say?"

I pouted and bowed my head.

"Oh God," he laughed, "let's get out of here before you have the whole place snickering again."

When we left, we headed directly south through the heart of Glenwood Springs. Ever since our first excursion through there I couldn't get over the uniqueness of its warm valley location, and I kept it filed in the back of my mind for future reference. The only thing about it that was a personal distraction was the volume of summertime tourists that flocked to the famous hot springs that were once held so sacred by various native tribes.

Now as Bill merged the truck into the heavy main street traffic, I gave the surrounding topography more serious scrutiny.

"Bet I know what you're thinking," sang the driver.

"Just looking."

He didn't buy that one at all. "You're not just looking. By

the way you were studying those mountains, I'd say you were *shopping.*"

"Yeah, but you can relax; you're safe. I didn't bring any money. I don't think I'll buy a mountain today. . .maybe tomorrow."

Clearing the town, we continued to the Carbondale turnoff. If we'd gone straight, we would've ended up in Aspen.

As we made our way along Highway 133, the surrounding topography gradually changed. We were ascending a gentle rise that was taking us from one climate zone to another. Cottonwoods were giving way to tall conifers. Sagebrush yielded to rich green kinnikinnick and squawberry. Arid became moist. Sun-dried land became jade-shadowed woodlands. Hot turned to cool.

A roadside sign pointed into the trees.

Redstone.

My driver let up on the accelerator. "Want to see what Redstone's all about?"

I leaned over to inspect the scenery past him. There was nothing to see but tall pines and a wooden bridge that narrowly spanned the rushing waters of the Crystal River. That in itself tantalized my nature-hungry appetite.

My eyes danced.

We veered off the highway.

Redstone turned out to be just my kind of town. I wasn't even sure it was an official town because I hadn't noticed any of the usual civic buildings. What I did notice was its absolute serenity and aesthetic quaintness. Its strategic position between the heavy forest and the surging river was most unique and gave one the feeling of a hidden place out of time. A picture book hamlet. An entity entirely separate from the hustle-bustle of the world.

I liked Redstone—I liked it a lot—and I had Bill pull up to an unimposing real estate office. With a pounding heart, I inquired about house rentals—there were none. A few were for sale, but that didn't do us any good because we couldn't afford to buy yet. Deeply disappointed, I returned to the truck.

We came out of the hamlet via another bridge that brought us back onto the main highway.

My heart ached, and, with a hangdog expression, I voiced my disappointment.

"How come every place I want to live there's never any room in the inn?"

He flashed me a dubious look. "It's not time yet, I guess," came the old response to the old question.

"That's baloney. Other people get in, why can't we ever seem to?"

Silence.

I went on to reinforce my premise. "Look how many months we looked for something around Glenwood and Basalt. We had all the real-estates looking and nobody could come up with anything."

The driver chuckled under his breath.

"Who wants to rent to seven people, a dog and a bird?"

"Well, I know it sounds like gypsies-come-to-town, but we had great references. My God, Bill, we leave houses in better shape than we find them!"

"You know that, and I know that, but they don't know that. We pull up to a real estate office in this dented truck and it's all over before we walk through the door."

I sighed.

"Look," Bill pointed out. "Marble."

We turned off to the left and headed into a verdant forest. The road followed alongside the rushing Crystal and my attention was swiftly swept away from our housing dilemma. A sign on our left caught my eye.

Bogan Flats.

"It's a campground!" I groaned in surprise.

"That's what the map says."

I stared at my companion. "I never noticed that. Now what do we do?"

"We do what we came here to do. We go down and park it."

Peering down through the conifers, I made out parking spaces beside the river. There were only two occupants located in the tree line—one was a tent, one a small RV. Doubts were playing havoc with my rational sensibilities.

"We can't do anything with campers here!"

The pickup nosed down into the campground, then it eased into a spot that nestled back into the tree cover. The engine was cut. Sounds of the roaring Crystal played musical strains of peace in my ears and carried the resonating notes into my heart. Calmly, I grinned.

"I know, I know, you don't have to say it. The timing's right and the people won't matter."

There was no need for any response. We both knew the truth

of the matter. If the time was right for us to help the scout, then help him we would.

We got out of the truck and began strolling over to the water. I furtively checked the two occupied spaces. No cars were there. No one was home. I hoped it would stay that way.

Reaching the bank, we sat on the ground and watched the river flow. Its effect upon the senses was mesmerizing. I allowed the water spirit to wash through me and carry all my negative attitudes downstream with her.

"I hope our land has a rushing stream like this," I softly mused.

"This is a river."

"Don't get technical; you know what I mean."

Bill tossed a stone into the current. "Many Heart said we'd have water. Don't you believe him?"

Reclining back on the softness of the earth, I rested head in hands and stared up at the lacy sunlight that floated lazily through the boughs.

"I believe him. . .it's just been so long, that's all. And we've had such a hard time finding an opening over in this area. Sometimes it all seems like a pipe-dream."

His serious face lowered to mine and I looked into the color of the blue eyes. They were scolding. They reminded me of an overcast sky—one that bodes the coming of darker, angrier storm clouds.

I laughed. "Don't you go lecturing me. You know you feel the same way I do."

"Well," he softened, "if we've learned one thing out of all this, it's been that we can't force things. Destiny's a determined lady. She yields to no one."

That bit of wisdom brought a smile to my face. "Time is her only partner. She waits for time to catch up with her before she makes her next move. It's all in the timing. Time is Madam Destiny's master."

"So. . .in the meantime, instead of beating our heads against all the walls, we wait in acceptance for Old Man Time to shuffle forward. Right?"

I eyed him skeptically. "Yeah, right. You just remember your own great words of wisdom next time you smack head-on into one of those walls."

A raven cawed and swooped through the trees. Its sudden appearance halted our conversation. There wasn't any more to discuss anyway, for it was one of those trying subjects that just ran in continual circles that spiraled into infinity and never went anywhere conclusive.

We remained stretched out on the bank. The spoken word sounded discordant next to the pureness of the sweet river voice.

We listened as we entered its magical power.

The water song was more deeply hypnotic than we thought, for both of us had been gently lulled to sleep. When I opened my eyes, the slant of the sun rays had elongated and a breath of a chill whispered in the air.

Bill stirred. When I glanced over at him, he was staring up into the pines. He was deeply immersed in thought. I sat up and watched the churning Crystal.

"What're you thinking?" came the curious voice from behind me.

I turned and smiled. "Nothing."

The smile was returned. "Sell that to someone else," he scoffed, raising himself to sit beside me.

I hesitated by toying with a few blades of grass.

"Oh. . .I don't know. I was just thinking about what people will think."

"About what?"

"Us, about us and what we do."

"What about us and what we do? You're not getting to the point.

"I know; that's because I'm not sure there is a point. I was thinking that we were like double agents—we work both sides of reality."

"Yes, but the difference is that we don't work one against the other. Go on with your thought."

"Well, most people know us as plain old Bill an' Mary. We're your everyday common folk, know what I mean?"

"Let's say I can see where you're going with this."

Raising a cautioning finger, I quickly continued.

"So this common couple, this so neighborly and down-homey pair is discovered to have a most shocking secret life. One that. . ."

"Everyone has a secret or private part of their life. You make us sound like a couple of Walter Mittys."

"You interrupted me," I playfully admonished. "Didn't your mother ever teach you that that was rude? Anyway, I was wondering what all the people who know us well will think when they find out about our rather unusual sideline."

"Who cares? Besides, nobody knows *anyone* all that well.

Ever stop to think that one of our upstanding neighbors may be a wife-beater, another could be dealing drugs, and maybe the old widow behind us is a closet mobster."

"Now that's dumb," I snickered. "You know what I mean."

"Yeah, I know exactly what you mean and, again I say, who cares? And it's not dumb at all. If we can have some secret aspect to *our* lives, why can't the little old lady down the street? That's my whole point. There's not a person walking this earth that doesn't have a skeleton or two in their closets. But honey, that doesn't make everyone a double agent or a hypocrite just because others aren't aware of their more private lives."

I thought on that. "Yes, but. . .*ghosts?*"

He chuckled. "I admit it's a bit far removed from the ordinary, but, just the same, it's like someone with a unique hobby or special interest."

"Well. . ."

"Well nothing. Look," he said, taking my hand in his, "what we do is nobody's business; it doesn't hurt anyone, nor does it interfere with anyone's life. Why should anyone think us any different than we were before they found out?"

I shrugged. "I just think we'll get some funny looks."

"So what if we do?"

Silence.

"Honey, you and I know we won't be any different. We'll always be us. I love you and you love me. That'll never change. So if folks look at us differently then that's because their viewpoint has changed—not us." He shook his head and squeezed my hand. "Nope, it's you an' me, babe. You an' me together—just like always."

And, just like always, his special way never failed to soothe my troubled heart. He was right—always, it was "you an' me". . .you an' me forever.

We left the riverside and returned to the camper where I busied myself with spreading out our gourmet repast—peanut butter sandwiches, coffee and fruit. While we dined we talked about the oddity of our camp neighbors' absence, for it was well-nigh time they should've returned to their home bases. Speculating on the various possibilities as to their whereabouts, we wondered if sweet destiny was planning on detaining them until our job was done. That was a nice thought, and it was also a hugely optimistic and presumptuous one.

At twilight, when our meal was concluded, we closed up the door, cranked down the windows, and snuggled beneath the bed quilt for the prescribed rest period. We closed our eyes and let our conscious minds drift within the water current's roar. Just before sleep overtook me completely, I heard a raven caw out from somewhere in the forest depths. I smiled at hearing the beautiful spirit sound that now completed the triad. And my last conscious thought was a warm and comforting one—no matter how people's view of us changed. . .*we* never would; we were a bonded pair. . .always and forever a pair.

In my sleep, a massive body twitch brought me to wakefulness. Drowsily, my mind took note of the complete darkness that had enveloped the camper. I wondered what time it was, for it seemed very late. No sounds came from the campground except for the incessant rushing of the river waters. In the near-ebony blackness, I stared at the window and considered getting up to see if our camp neighbors had returned. I was too groggy and didn't want to expend the energy to move from my warm cocoon. If I had been asleep, I would've thought another body twitch had struck, but now that I was awake, what I felt was no involuntary physiological spasm—the entire camper swayed.

"What the hell?" Bill muttered as he shot up in the bed. "Is it windy?" he asked.

I was already at the window. In the starlight, the silvered branches were still. My neck prickled.

"It couldn't be calmer out there," I said coldly. "It's our man."

Bill scooted off the bed to join me at the window. "Do you see him?"

"No," came the whispered reply, "but we felt him."

Then Bill peered out through the pearly moonlight.

"Still no sign of anyone around those campsites. No cars yet."

"Maybe they're out doing the town and a late movie."

He clucked his tongue. "Could be, then again. . ."

His thought was sliced off by another sudden jolt to the camper. It rocked and I fell back from the window.

"You all right?" he asked.

"Yes, but why do I have this feeling the scout wants us out of here?"

"Your guess is as good as mine and we're going to find out right now before we have an upended truck. C'mon."

Quickly we grabbed for our jackets and pulled them on. Taking a few additional moments for our bonding procedure, we made it out the door just as another rocking wave of energy hit. Once completely outside, all was deathly still.

"What now?" I said, wondering which direction we needed to take. "We don't even know where he is."

"Comforting thought, isn't it?" came the quiet response.

"Maybe we should head over to the bank."

We got halfway there when my partner halted.

"Damn!" he spat. "I forgot to lock up the camper."

"What? Now?"

"Got to. The rifle's there."

"Leave it. Nobody's even around."

He hesitated, then shook his head. "No, I gotta lock it up. Look, you sit right here and I'll just be a minute."

Shocked at his insistence, I sat alone and watched him race back to the truck. Even more shocking was seeing him climb into the camper. Maybe he wanted the lantern, I thought. Being separated made me nervous and I furtively looked around. The lone tent and the vacant RV now appeared eerily desolate and abandoned. Trees seemed like still-lifes on a canvas. Nothing moved but the river, and I had an awful sense of foreboding creep through me.

Then—

Cursing and shouts came from within the camper. The door was shut and Bill's anger was muffled.

I stood. "What's wrong?" I shouted.

He had to literally scream for me to hear his words.

"I can't open the door or windows! He's got them all sealed! Get over here!"

I started to run and was abruptly stopped. Some force prevented me from advancing. It was like a dream—a nightmare. Bill was ranting in a rage because we'd been separated and I wasn't able to get to him. My mind raced in a frenzied search through its banks for a solution. Had No-Eyes covered this sort of possibility? Yes. And the solution was. . .was. . .damn! I couldn't remember! I was too frustrated and unnerved to think straight. I glanced around. Our man was nowhere in sight. And now my fright and frustration had turned to anger, and anger was not a clear-thinking emotion.

I realized that and sat in the wildgrass. In the distance, I could hear my entrapped mate caterwauling his angered protests at me and yelling what the hell I was doing sitting down. Ignoring his furious outrage, I listened to remembered voices of wisdom from the days with Many Heart.

"Exit the frustration," they echoed. "Exit the fear. Exit the anger."

I closed my eyes and eased away from the present tumultuous situation. Soon Bill's clamorous swearing faded away and I was no longer within any emotion but peace. When my eyes opened again, I held to my attained state and warily reached out my testing hand.

Nothing. No force was there to block my way; at least if it was, I could now pass through it unaffected. Slowly standing, my feet slid forward, one hesitant foot at a time. I was moving. As I maintained the psychic attitude, I felt a subliminal sense of inner rejoicing. It was a good feeling that was felt as if it were somewhere far in the recess of my consciousness.

Once Bill realized what I was doing, he became silent and watchful.

Carefully and cautiously, I advanced to the back of the truck and we both cheered.

But the moment of celebration was short-lived.

As soon as I reached my hand up to the door, it met with the force that imprisoned my partner. Although I was able to dissipate it from myself, it remained a powerful energy field surrounding the vehicle. The scout was still in complete control.

Knowing I couldn't maintain my present altered state much longer, I tested the effects of its release. Slowly I let it go while holding my hand out. I'd half expected the field to return around me, but it didn't. Evidently, once the scout saw that it was ineffective for me, he never bothered to reinforce it. And, for that bit of luck, I was grateful. I released a great sigh of relief and stepped over to the louvered windows on the side of the camper.

Bill and I were nearly nose to nose with the glass and the force field between us. His face was crimson. Eyes flared with a fire I'd never seen before.

"I'm gonna *get* this bastard! He's *still* a God-damned *coward!*"

"Shhh," I mouthed to him. "We'll get you out."

"Don't shush me, damn it! Just wait 'til I get my hands on that son of a bitch! Just *wait!*"

"It's not doing any good getting all riled up. You've got to settle down."

"How in God's name can you expect me to settle down when he's got you out *there* and me in *here?* Jesus Christ, I can't *believe* this shit. What are we gonna do?"

"Let me think about it," I said.

"Oh, wonderful, that's just wonderful; now we have to *think* about it. Don't you *know? You* were the one who went through all the lessons! You're supposed to be *ready* for this kind of shit!"

His sarcastic attitude wasn't helping the situation and I turned my back on him to pace beside the pickup. For a while longer I heard him swearing up a torrential storm of expletives. Once or twice he struck the wall. Then he settled down.

Silence from within.

Outside, a lot of heavy thinking was taking place.

After a few minutes, I began to worry about his silence.

"Bill?" I called.

"Leave me alone," he yelled back. "I'm thinking."

"I just wanted to know if you're okay."

"I'm just *fine,* honey. Everything's just real *fine* in here," came the thick sarcasm.

How could I expect to hear anything else? And I thought about how frustrated he must feel being in a forced separation from the one he loved. Loved? Love? Love!

My eyes lit up and I spun around.

"*Bill!* I *got* it! I know how to *beat* him! *Bill!* Come to the window!"

His exasperated face appeared.

I grinned up at it. "Bring up the *rose!*" I blurted excitedly.

Exasperation brightened to hope. "I love you!" he shouted. "I love you more than *anything! I* love you more than life *itself!* I'd do *anything* for our love!"

"I *love* you, Bill. You mean the *world to* me! I couldn't *live* without you! You're my heart and *soul,* my very *breath!*"

We both repeated the endless litany that proclaimed our eternal devotion to each other. We echoed them over and over as I inched to the back door and he waited there for me on the inside. Voicing our chain of endearments, my fingers rested on the force field by the door.

It was weakening. It was no longer a solid barrier. It now felt more like putty.

I shouted to signal the effectiveness of our maneuver.

"Our *love* conquers *all* adversity!"

He maintained his fervor of love in a tone of renewed excitement, and as he pushed, the door cracked open.

Relentlessly, we kept up the amorous barrage.

The opening widened and my arm pitched through. Before I knew what was happening, the seat of my pants was grabbed and I was yanked into the camper. Bill pulled me to him and hugged the breath out of me.

"Oh God! *God!* I love you so *much!* Jesus, I was so *scared* for you out there."

After smothering each other with kisses, we finally managed to settle down. I poured us some coffee and we sat on the bed.

When I next spoke, my voice was calm, yet serious.

"He was trying to protect me—nothing more."

Silence.

"Honey? That was the only way he knew."

Silence.

"We have to be rational about this. You can't take it personal."

When his eyes came to rest on mine, they were murderous. Still he remained mute.

"Please, honey, please," I pleaded gently. "You have to realize that he. . ."

"He *separated* us," came the chilling voice. "I take that *very* personal."

"But. . ."

"But nothing!"

Silence. For a long while, silence was a living thing between us.

Then his voice melted. "Mary?"

I looked up into the soft misty eyes. "What, hon?"

"I couldn't live without you." The voice was barely above a whisper. "I really couldn't. Without you by my side, life would be an empty shell. I'd have half a heart. . .half a soul."

Tears stung my eyes. "Oh, honey, don't." And I pulled him to my breast to comfort him. We remained that way—frozen in time—until, out of the corner of my eye, I saw a movement.

The door soundlessly swung open. The field was gone. We both looked out into the blackness of the night that the gaping opening exposed. Then we questioningly eyed one another.

I smiled. "See what our love does?"

A widening grin greeted me back.

"Well?" I chirped. "Now that we won the first round, are you ready to face him?"

Sheepishly, he nodded. "I'm ready."

I arched a curious brow. "You going to punch his lights out?"

Bill couldn't hide the smile. "No. . .but that's what he deserves."

I playfully tousled his hair. "C'mon, we got us a scout to confront."

Moving toward the door, I was jerked backward.

"This is one time *I'm* going out first," he said, not wanting me to be the one locked out again.

Once outside in the night, he took firm hold of my hand. We glanced over at the camp spaces. Noticing they were still unoccupied, we headed upstream for the riverbank. After picking our way through the trees, we spotted our target.

Sitting on the bank, he was hunched over in a defeatist attitude. He stared at the churning waters.

"I knows you're there," he suddenly spoke. "You can have no fear. I ain't gonna do you no harm."

Bill's grip tightened over my hand as we approached the man and sat near him.

The scout gave us no more than a passing glance before returning his attention to the starlit river. He chuckled sarcastically beneath his breath and shook his head.

"Another dumb move. I'm all the time makin' all the wrong moves. Shoulda known *better* this time. . .shoulda known better."

I thought it was time to speak. "Shoulda known better about what?" I asked softly.

The man looked over at us. "Shoulda seen that light right off. I shoulda seen it 'cause it's plain as day."

He was making no sense.

"What light?"

"Why, that rosy light 'round you two. That 'bout explains it all, don't it." His head drooped from side to side again. "Shoulda seen that you two was lovers."

Bill entered the scene. "We're man and wife."

"So. You're still lovers. What's the big difference? Point is, I just shoulda seen it. That there light shoulda tol' me."

I looked around us and didn't see any light. Before, we'd worked hard to generate the rose-colored aura of love, but now we didn't perceive it as the scout had. It was possible the aura surrounded us all the time and only certain sensitives picked it up.

I was curious to nail down the man's rationale for remaining in the physical.

"We're friends," I began.

"I can see that, ma'am."

"I'd like to know why you're here in this place."

The scout glanced at me as if I should know.

"Why. . .I'm here to protect the womenfolk!"

He didn't know he was dead.

"I see," I hedged. "And how do you know when they're in danger?"

The question confused him. "I jest knows, that's all."

"Have you rescued many?"

"Not for some time now. Nope, not no more." Then his eyes rested on Bill's. "I'm right sorry for the trouble I caused you back there, mister. Guess my ol' eyes ain't so good no more and I do apologize."

I squeezed Bill's hand in caution, but the warning gesture wasn't needed, for he'd already softened to the poor soul's pitiful situation.

"Apology accepted," he said in a sincere voice. Then his next words surprised me. "We've come to give you a new job."

The scout's eyes brightened with expectancy and hope.

Mine widened with question.

But my companion was grinning.

"I hear you were once a pretty good scout, in fact, the best."

Our man seemed to blush. "Well, now. . .I was considered better than most in my day."

"And I hear tell you liked your work too."

I was beginning to get the picture now and I silently acknowledged my understanding with a wink and a grin. My mate's idea was nothing less than brilliant.

The scout bragged about how much he liked his work and that there didn't appear to be much call for it no more.

"Oh!" Bill interjected quickly, "but there *is!* That's why we're here. We came looking for you because there's a job for you."

The man couldn't believe his ears. What a stroke of luck!

"Me? You came lookin' for me? Mike Dawson?"

"Yep. We were told to go find Mike Dawson because nobody else would do. We were told nobody else was good enough for this big job."

"No foolin'?"

"No foolin'."

Then Mike's eyes narrowed to slits. "Jist what sorta job we talkin' 'bout here?"

"Well? Seems some big new territory's been discovered. Lotsa folks are wanting to be heading up that way an' the wagon master in charge won't hire anyone but the best to scout it for him. He says to me, 'you go an' get me ol' Mike Dawson 'cause he's the best in the business.'"

"No *foolin'!*"

"No foolin, Mike."

"Hot damn!" he shouted, jumping to his feet. "I got me a *scoutin'* job!"

We stood and smiled.

"Kinda looks that way, Mike," Bill said.

"Well, what're we waitin' for? Let's go!" said the over-anxious scout. "Lead the way! Can't keep the wagon master awaitin'!"

"Ahhh," Bill hesitated.

I took up the sudden slack.

"We have more to do here," I said. "We're not going that way just yet, but the wagon master said for you to wait for his guide—he'll lead you there."

That seemed to placate him. Then he frowned. "You sure you two don't wanna come an' see this new territory?"

I smiled at his simple naivete. "Oh, yes, we do! Someday we'll make it there, but we have a lot to do here first."

Mike Dawson shook his head. "You folks'll be missin' out on some mighty fine opportunities. Ain't *nothin'* like settin' eyes on a new frontier. No ma'am, ain't nothin' like it in the whole world."

I smiled. "I know, Mike, I know. We'll look you up when we get there."

"Hey, you do that. I'd be right proud to see you too—maybe show you around."

"I'd like that, Mike."

The scout smacked his first into his other palm. "When's this guide due?"

Bill responded. "Soon after we leave, Mike, and we have to get going now. We're real glad we found you."

"Me too."

We congratulated Mr. Dawson on his new job and said our farewells. After we walked away a few steps, he called to us.

"Hey!"

We turned.

"How can I repay you two?"

I put up my hands. "No pay needed, Mike. We're just doing our job, but if you think it'll make you feel better, you can repay us by doing a good job in that new territory you're going to."

Mike bowed low in a gentlemanly manner. "Ma'am, I will do that for you. I'm gonna be right proud to do that for you."

I smiled. "That makes me very happy, Mike, *very* happy."

And we left the scout. But even before we were out of earshot, we heard Mike talking to someone.

"Hey! You that wagon master's guide that's come for me?"

We didn't hear any more of the conversation. I don't think Mike Dawson was in the mood to hold to no needless chatter. He was in the mood to hightail it to his new job—he had new territory to see.

We stood by the stream for a while, then returned to the camper. Our neighbors pulled in just as we were climbing into bed. I was grateful for their consideration, for they were quiet and soon were also abed themselves. The night was hushed to sleep by the water spirit's lullaby song.

I pulled the quilt around my neck and stared out into the blackness.

"Bill?"

"Mmmm."

"What made you think of a new job for the scout?"

"Oh. . .I don't know. It just came naturally, I guess."

"I thought it was brilliant."

"Yeah?"

"Yeah."

Silence.

"Bill?"

"Mmmm."

"He wanted us to go with him."

"I know. That part was kind of funny."

"Well, I just want you to know that you did good. And I wish I could've seen Mike's face when he finds out who his new wagon master really is."

"Yeah, the great Wagon Master Who leads us all home. . .home to our real territory."

"Bill?"

"Now what? Aren't you tired?"

"Yes, but I just wanted to say one more thing."

"What."

"I've never said I love you so many times in one day."

"Maybe we can do it again some time—only under better circumstances."

"That'd be fun."

"Goodnight, babe."

"Night."

Silence.

"Bill?"

"Mmmm.

"I love you."

Psychic Inferno and Hell Demons

On a crisp September evening, Bill and I sat in Godmother's Kitchen. The restaurant lights were dimmed low and candle wicks flickered within the red glass holders on the tables. Over a quiet dinner, we were preparing to discuss our next encounter when one of our friends tapped on the window beside me. He gestured if we'd mind his company and Bill motioned him in.

Eric quickly appeared and, after again making sure he wasn't intruding on our little private tête-à-tête, he slid into the booth beside me.

"Haven't seen you two for awhile," he said. "You two still involved in that spirit stuff.?"

Bill nodded.

"Mind a few innocuous questions on the subject?"

We said that we didn't, since Eric was well versed in the matter of metaphysics and his interest in the spiritual aspects of the paranormal ran high. We always welcomed the more analytical questions from someone of his intelligence and depth of thought.

"Since we talked last about this whole issue," he began, "I've done a lot of thinking and I'm having trouble with a few glitches in it."

"Glitches?" I frowned.

The waitress came over to the table to see if the newcomer wanted to order. All he wanted was coffee and he patiently waited until the woman brought it and departed before going into his theoretical problems.

"Okay," he began, "spirits are pure energy, right?"

I smiled. "You're starting out pretty basic, but yes, that's right."

"Well, I know that's real fundamental, but that's where I have to start with this. Anyway, next I want to state that a spirit has a mind." He paused for verification.

"So far, so good," Bill said.

"All right. And that mind is highly intelligent. It knows the score regarding its own dimensional reality."

He was correct so far, but I felt he was creeping into a gray area. I was beginning to see where his glitches came from if he continued along these lines without bringing in more clarifying factors. He didn't.

"So one of my problems is this—if a spirit has total intelligence and comprehension, why do some get confused after the physical death of their last vehicle? Wouldn't that intelligence automatically be operational—at its optimum?"

I set down my fork.

"Eric, you started out good, but then you took off without bringing in the rest of the main factors. Your confusion stems from working with only one-third of the whole."

His brows creased.

This could be a complex concept to adequately explain if I didn't get the words or the sequential order right. Sometimes my mind's pace was far ahead of my tongue, and issues like this would ultimately have to be backtracked over to insure absolute clarity. I tried to keep reins on my racing mind.

"You're really asking about wayward spirits, and the technicalities that create them are unclear for you."

He agreed. "Yes, because if a spirit has the high intelligence, how can it *not* know where to go or where it belongs?"

"Okay, we'll get all that straightened out, but before we can do that, we first need to go back to those basics you started out with. You were doing good, then you splintered the facts and left two-thirds behind you. That's why your conclusion didn't wash for you."

I pulled notepaper and pen from my purse. Crudely sketching a human head, I divided the forehead into three parts and labeled them.

"On top is the superconscious. This is the 'high intelligence' of the spirit you talked about. Below that is the subconscious. And below the subconscious is the consciousness. Are we together so far?"

Quickly nodding, he was anxious to hear the rest.

"All right," I said, circling the pen around the three levels. "Enclosed in this circle is the *totality* of the spirit. The spirit encompasses *all* the mind levels." I looked at him.

"I realize that already."

A cautioning finger came up. "But you *fragmented* the spirit's totality, Eric. When you had the spirit leave the physical vehicle, you had it taking only *this* part with it," I said, pointing to the superconscious segment of the mind.

He was getting the picture.

"Eric, a spirit takes all *three* with it when it crosses over." I paused a moment to sip on the hot coffee. "Sometimes I explain this another way." I flipped the page and drew two stick figures standing side by side with a line connecting them. "This one is the physical, three-dimensional body," I said, labeling it. "This one is its spirit. And this line in the middle is the connecting cord. The body is the *conscious* segment of the mind, the cord is the *subconscious*, and the other form is the *superconscious*—all parts of the whole."

"I get what you're saying, but if the physical body is the consciousness, how can it also be taken with the spirit? Consciousness is physical. It remains with the physical at all times."

"Does it?"

"Yes."

"Are you sure?" Bill questioned, finishing the last of his dinner.

Eric slumped in a slightly sarcastic manner and sighed.

"Well, we can't very well be walking around without it, can we now?"

"Why not?"

Our guest frowned.

"Think about it," Bill encouraged.

After a few minutes of expending mental energy, our friend put up his hands.

"Guess you got me. As far as I'm concerned, the physical is the consciousness. It can't exist without it. If you say it can then we're at an impasse."

Finally finishing the last of my own meal, I pushed the plate aside.

"We're not at an impasse at all," I said, patting our friend's hand. "Listen, if we go on your premise, every unconscious person is dead, every sleeping person is really dead, every comatose person is dead."

"Well, you know I didn't mean those types of conditions."

I raised a warning brow. "But that's exactly what you said. You maintained that people just don't exist *without* consciousness. We're not conscious when we faint. We're not conscious during sleep state or operations either."

"So maybe what I really meant was that we can't *animate* without consciousness."

Bill smiled. "I don't think you 'really meant' that either, Eric. What about sleepwalkers?"

"Oh shit, I forgot about that."

We all laughed.

Again the waitress came to remove the dinnerware. We ordered a half liter of rosé. This was getting very interesting and it looked as though we'd be heavily involved with it for a while longer.

Our friend eyed us. "So where the hell were we?"

Bill obliged. "We were with the sleepwalkers."

"Oh yeah. So. . .if the conscious segment of the mind isn't necessarily required for physical animation. . .if the conscious part leaves. . .if states like sleepwalking. . .Christ, I don't even know where I'm going with this. You two sure know how to confuse a simple question."

"Eric," I grinned, " *you're* the one who lost his train of thought. We're right with you—we didn't lose anything."

"So find it for me."

"You want to know what consciousness is if it isn't the primary factor of physical animation."

"Sounds good. So? What is it?"

"Awareness. Consciousness is awareness."

"Ahhh," he moaned as the light dawned.

"Now," I said, "that should've naturally generated the next question."

It did.

"Where does consciousness go during unconsciousness? Where does the 'awareness' go during sleepwalking?"

"Good!" Bill praised. "Now *you* tell us."

"C'mon," Eric groaned.

"I'll help you," I said, smiling. "Remember when you told us about the time you recalled where your spirit went one night during sleep?"

Now the light bulb was really putting out wattage.

Eric beamed. "During all unconscious mind states the conscious part always flows into the *subconscious,* the *cord!*"

"Yes! And the factor that determines what is consciously remembered of a spirit experience during the unconscious state of sleep is how *far* the consciousness *traveled* along the cord."

Eric shook his head. "No wonder I got this confused to hell—this is heavy stuff."

"It can be, but it doesn't have to be," I said.

Bill refilled our glasses. "Now that the basics are over with, we need to get back to your initial question—the wayward spirits."

It was amazing how easily we got sidetracked with this material. That's probably why I talked for hours and hours whenever our little groups got started on the metaphysical subject. One thing always naturally led off in a dozen different spinoff directions. I was always glad when Bill had hung onto the beginning thread, especially now with this one, or I could've branched off again and again.

"Yeah," Eric repeated, "the wayward spirits. So," he realized, "now my original question's not valid."

"Let's go over it anyway, just to be sure you've cleared it," I suggested, ready to start at the top.

Eric wanted to do the honors himself.

"Let me. That way I know I'm clear."

"Okay," I readily agreed. "Go for it."

The man anxiously resettled himself in the seat. He was eager to gain the issue's comprehension. He began at the beginning.

"Consciousness is physical *awareness*. During states of unconsciousness, the conscious part of the mind joins the subconscious part—which is within the cord connecting the two to the superconscious, the spirit."

I stopped him. "The superconscious being the *high intelligence* aspect of the spirit."

"Yes. And all *three* levels of the mind too."

I nodded. Now he had it.

"Okay," he continued. "So when the physical vehicle dies, all three levels of the mind flow through the cord that, for want of an adequate term, retracts into the energy of the spirit." He raised a brow. "Right?"

"Close enough," Bill said.

"Okay. So now the spirit is completely separated from the useless body. Now it has its fully functioning intelligence." At this point Eric hesitated with confusion. "So. . .why the hell doesn't it know what's what? Aren't I right back at the beginning again?"

"Sort of, but not quite," I smiled. "When you started with this question you only had one-third of it, remember? You had the spirit existing with the 'high intelligence' of the superconscious, but not with the *rest* of its total mind. Now you know it has all *three* levels with it—that's what's going to make the big difference here."

Eric considered what I'd just said. "Now I see. The spirit isn't operating with just the superconscious. It's got it *all*."

"Yes," I said, knowing my dear friend still had a long way to go with it yet. I waited.

Silence.

Waiting.

He rubbed his beard. "So how come I'm still confused? I still don't get how a pure spirit could ever become wayward when it has full mind capacity when it's free again."

Bill sighed. "You're still unclear because we've only covered half of the concept."

"*Half?*"

"Yes, but the second half is easier."

"I hope so," our friend exclaimed.

Bill tried to explain it.

"You clear on the first half—about the mind levels?"

"Yes."

"All right, keep it separate for now."

Eric rolled his eyes. "I'll try."

"Now the second half of this issue deals with more basics. You know that all spirits are not at the same level of development, right?"

"Right, because they're all at different stages of advancement, like school grades."

"Yes. So naturally, their 'high intelligence' aspect would also be at differing levels of comprehension, knowledge, and other wisdom attainments. Are we clear so far?"

"Yes. It'd be like teachers who have more education and comprehension than their peers."

Bill nodded. "So one spirit's 'higher intelligence' will be higher or lower than another's. That's the primary basis we're going to build on here. Okay?"

"Gotcha."

"For purposes of clarification, we'll use the example of a spirit that is more or less on the lower end of the scale as far as its superconscious goes—its 'high intelligence' is not the highest. Follow?"

Eric nodded.

"So here, on a 'high intelligence' scale of one to ten, we maybe have a four. It's cognizant of a lot of spiritual realities, but it's not *fully* aware of them *all*." Bill paused.

Again our friend indicated that he understood.

Bill continued. "This spirit, with its four rating, exits its body and now brings with it its other two mind levels. These meld with the superconscious to create the total mind of the spirit. With me so far?"

"Go on."

"Now this level-four superconscious has been joined by the subconscious and the conscious. If, during the spirit's last physical life, it experienced a highly emotional lifetime or violent death circumstances, the *conscious* fragment of the mind will tend to *dominate* the other two. It will *override* the more intelligent aspects of the *higher* parts. Therefore, the conscious part will *retain* the spirit emotions and, if they are very strong, they will even *detain* the spirit's advancement. . .it becomes wayward."

"Whew! So basically, it all comes down to which level of the mind is strongest at the time of the spirit's transition."

"Essentially yes," I said. "If the spirit was a highly advanced one though, say at a number eight level of advancement, there's no way the conscious aspect could detain it to become wayward. It would automatically go where it belonged after physical death."

Eric tossed all that over. "That's because a more advanced and developed spirit couldn't be held back by the strong emotions still retained within the conscious part, like revenge and such."

"Right. Hey, I think you've got it!" I beamed.

"Yeah, finally," he sighed. "I feel kind of dumb now."

I frowned at him. "No. . .it's not a simple concept. It's a very complex set of principles. The precise technicalities of the whole thing are difficult to even explain."

"Yeah, I guess so, but once they are explained, it's easy to see how a lesser advanced spirit could get caught up in the residual emotions of its last conscious physical experience. Now it's easy to see how a spirit could be wayward."

"Well," Bill soothed, "at least you're clear on it now. You had another question on this subject, didn't you?"

"Hey!" Eric said, holding up his hands, "I've taken up enough of your time. It can wait; besides, now I see how I need to think a little deeper on this stuff, maybe I'll come up with my own answer once I give it a little more thought." Then he expressed a curiosity. "You two going out on another one this weekend?"

"Out in Phantom Canyon," Bill said. "At least it's not too far this time."

"Mind if I ask what it's about?"

"Not at all," I said. "It has to do with some kind of fire that's occasionally seen. Also there's something about hell demons."

"Hell demons! You kidding?"

I shrugged. "That's what No-Eyes said. We haven't the slightest idea what it's all about."

"Not *real* demons," he said skeptically and a bit nervously.

I raised a doubtful brow. "I hardly think so. It's probably something somebody sees and fantasizes about or exaggerates as being demons. People love to blow things way out of proportion. They don't stay around at the scene long enough to use their rational minds."

"Well, you two be darned careful. You couldn't pay me enough to do what you do."

Bill chuckled at that. "Yeah, pay's pretty poor."

Our friend shook his head. "You guys ought to write a book about your spook cases."

Little did he know that it was already planned, only not to capitalize on the "spooky" aspect.

I grinned. "What for?" I said, upturning my palms. "Nobody'd believe it."

"Well then, sell the stories to television! People love to be spooked by a good scary story. Maybe Ray Bradbury or Hitchcock! They'd love them."

I laughed. "No thanks, Eric. I don't do fiction. . .at least not that kind. If I ever do get into fiction, Bill and I would work together on the more spiritual stuff, probably stories woven around native American mysticism and spiritual beliefs."

Our friend didn't agree. "You're missing out on a wide-open market for this kind of thing."

"Like I said, thanks but no thanks."

"Well. . .I gotta get going." He dug into his pocket and set five dollars on the table. "Least I can do is leave a tip. Thanks for the wine and clearing things up. Good luck this weekend. I'll be anxious to hear about those bad hell demons. Okay if I give you a call Sunday night?"

We said that'd be fine.

And although our friend wanted to stay to discuss more, he respected our private time and left the restaurant.

When we got home and I was passing through the kitchen, the phone rang. I picked it up and immediately my spine tingled. The woman's voice on the other end of the line was trembling with confused hysterics.

"Bill? Is this Bill?" she stuttered.

"This is his residence, but he's unavailable right now," I said, rather than stating that he was detained in the bathroom.

An emotional sigh of relief came through the receiver.

"Is this his wife? Mary?"

"Yes. Who is this?"

"Oh my dear, you might not remember me, but you came out to my house in Green Mountain Falls one day with your husband. I remember you both so well; you were so kind."

The woman's shaky voice worried me.

"Was this for a service call? Did he fix your furnace?"

"Oh yes," she breathed in short, shallow puffs, "he fixed it real good. But I need his *help!*"

"Is the furnace acting up? Do you have heat?"

Great wracking sobs came then.

"Honey? Mary? I'm just an old woman and my kids are gonna put me *away!* They're gonna take me outta my *house* and if they *do* that, I'm gonna *kill* myself. *Tonight!*"

Oh dear God! I thought, what do I do with a *suicide* case on the line?

Finally, through forty minutes of talking to her, she eased down out of the tangle of overwrought emotions. She had felt alone and abandoned, and up against a wall—completely powerless to stop the devastating plans her family had to put her in a nursing home—away from everything she identified with and loved as home. I didn't break the connection to hang up until I was confident of her stability.

Immediately after talking with her, I called the Woodland Park Crisis Hot Line and spoke to the operator, who said they'd get right on it. The following day the psychologist called me for a review of the former conversation. He was going out to the woman's house within the hour and needed the background information. Monday morning, Bill and I took a flower bouquet when we visited the distraught lady at her house. She was now nearly completely bedridden and we could see the writing on the wall. She eventually went to the nursing home where she died within a year's time.

But that initial unexpected call was greatly upsetting to me, and, as Bill and I sat on the couch and discussed it, he succeeded in calming me down. What made it so devastating to me was remembering her words, "Bill said that if I ever needed anything to call him. He was such a nice young man and I remembered what he said." How heartbreaking that we couldn't do a single thing to help her, for she actually was infirm and really did require round-the-clock nursing care. It was a no-win situation for both of us, and those were hard to take. It must have been very difficult for her family, and my heart pained for them as well.

As we were talking it through after the call, I jumped when the phone shrilled for a second time that evening. Bill got it and winked over at me—it was Eric.

"Sure, no problem," I heard Bill say. "No really, we could use a little company right now. Mary just had an upsetting call and needs to get her mind off it. . .no, nothing like that. I'll explain when you get here. Right. See ya."

Bill came back into the living room. "Seems old Eric wants to talk some more. I told him we could use the distraction. He's on his way over. That all right?"

I sighed and grinned. "That's probably the best relaxant I could have right about now. I'll go make some coffee."

By the time the brew was done, our friend came through the door, and while I poured the coffees and cut pieces of coffee cake, Bill explained the excitement to the newcomer. We spent time discussing it, then, when there was no more to say about it, I looked to Eric.

"So. . .your curiosity got the best of you, huh?"

Boyishly, he admitted that it had. "And I was itching to know more about your case tomorrow."

"Gotta watch that curiosity, Eric," I teased. "It'll getcha in a heap a trouble if ya don't watch out."

He grinned. "I know."

It was good therapy to have our friend with us now. Even though we needed to get to bed, I knew thinking about the upsetting call would keep me awake anyway. A good in-depth discussion was just the thing to wear me out and make me more receptive to the idea of sleep.

"So?" I nudged. "What's on your mind? Those hell demons gotcha?"

"No. As a matter of fact, I wasn't particularly thinking of them at all. I was more or less wondering about that fire you mentioned. What exactly is that?"

I looked to Bill, then back to the frowning questioner. I shrugged.

His look was one of incredulous disbelief. "You mean to say you don't know?"

Bill smiled. "Not exactly, but we have some basic theories."

"More basics," Eric said, shaking his head. "Your basics are not what I'd exactly call simplicity. Dare I ask what these 'basic' theories are?"

"Of course," I quipped, "you can always ask."

"Okay, so what are your theories behind the fire?"

Bill downed a healthy bite of coffee cake before responding. "Actually it's *one* theory because there can only *be* one. The fire's an imprint."

"Oh. That's nice. What the hell's an imprint?"

I tilted my head to give our friend an innocent look of admonishment.

"C'mon Eric, you know what an imprint is. A psychic imprint?"

He suddenly realized what we were talking about. "Oh sure. Those are energy impressions imprinted within a specified atmospheric periphery."

"Exactly." I grinned. "But most people think what they're seeing is a full-scale apparition—a living ghost."

Silence ensued.

Bill asked our guest if he disagreed with what I'd just said.

"No. . .no, I agree, but how does that theory apply here? mean, a ghostly manifestation that's a replaying imprint is one thing but. . .a fire? How does that apply?"

"I don't see the difference," I commented. "Any action can be replayed again and again. If an event can imprint itself by the very nature of its powerful energy output, why not a fire that happened long ago?"

"I don't know. I suppose I never thought that hard on it. . .that extensively."

"If people sight a moving human form that's an imprint, why not a moving fire?"

"I see your point."

Silence.

"So?" Bill said. "There's a problem?"

"Well yeah. How can you help an imprint? An imprint's just a recorded event that keeps replaying until it eventually fades from lack of energy to feed it."

My answer wasn't one that was born of absolute assurance.

"Well so far, all our cases have presented differing circumstances that required different resolutions. Various techniques had to be applied. It's as though we're being given a broad spectrum of technicalities with each of them. Now we think we're going to be up against something totally idiosyncratic."

"Say what?" Eric muttered.

"Totally unique," I paraphrased. "We believe this case has not only a psychic imprint, but also the incongruous factor of a living manifestation. This would make it clearly divergent from all the previous patterns we've been exposed to so far."

The theory snagged our friend's high interest.

"Can that be, though? I've never heard of the mixing of the two."

"Neither have we," Bill admitted. "But there's no other logical explanation for it. A recurring fire that doesn't burn anything—that leaves no physical effects on its surroundings—has to be generated by a release of energy. . .the spurt that spells an imprint."

"I agree with you on that point, but what makes you think the entity involved isn't also part of the imprint replay scene?"

I looked him hard in the eyes. "Because No-Eyes wants us to clear it. If all factors involved were nothing more than a simple imprint, then there wouldn't be a thing we could do with it. It'd just have to fade away in time on its own. Besides, you're forgetting something else here. That fire *would* be fading by now if that's all it was. But it appears just as brilliant and as explosive as the night it originally happened." I paused. "Eric, why isn't the imprint fading by now?"

"Because it was so violent it's still too strong."

I shook my head. "Of itself?"

Our friend then turned to Bill. "Because. . .ah, it's not fading yet because. . .what'd she mean, 'of itself'?"

"You said it wasn't fading yet because it's too *strong*. She asked *what* was keeping it strong? Since all imprints always fade, *something* must be generating the continued supply of energy to maintain its visual intensity."

Eric's eyes narrowed. "Don't you mean some *one?*"

"Now you got the picture. The manifesting spirit empowers the imprint with enough energy to maintain its initial visual magnitude."

Eric was thoughtful. "So if you can clear away the spirit, what happens to the imprint? Does it go too or does it now begin its phase of fade-out cycle?"

"We believe it will vanish with the entity. That's because the spirit is the only factor holding it. The imprint's long past due to have completely faded by now."

"How is that determined?"

"What determined?" Bill asked.

"The length of time it takes an imprint to fade."

"Actually," my mate said, "each one would be different. The actual block of time required to completely dissipate a psychic imprint depends on several contributing factors; that of original cause, the intensity of degree of exuded force, the emotional impact, and the dimensional sensitivity of the flashpoint."

"Run that last factor by me one more time."

"Mmmm," Bill groaned, "I was afraid you'd ask about that one. It's not a concept to easily define. Fundamentally, we're talking about the sensitivity of the atmospheric quality at the time the event in question occurred. The initial event, when it's violent and quick, is termed the flashpoint. . .so is the beginning of the imprint's replay. About the best analogy we've come up with is a photographer's lab. When he utilizes high resolution paper and solutions, his end product is the best it can possibly be—it's crisp and clear; colors are so intense they jump out at you. But if he utilizes lesser quality materials, the product isn't so intense or beautiful. So too does the dimensional quality of the atmosphere at the time of imprint, or flashpoint, affect the clarity and longevity of the replay event."

"How'd you learn all this?" Eric asked, shaking his head.

Bill chuckled lightly. "Lots of trial and error. Years of marathon discussions. Mary's days with No-Eyes and people like her. This kind of thing isn't exactly what you'd find in your local library."

"So. . .you think this one's got an imprint *and* a real entity."

I smiled. "That's what we think. But we'll try to verify it before we get into it."

"And you usually get that sort of thing out of the impressions during the preliminary scan of the location?"

"Usually, although sometimes the impressions aren't as clear as we'd like them to be," I said. "It's hard to say just what we can actually pull out from the preliminaries. Hopefully we gain enough to at least substantiate the existence of a living spirit's presence. I'd hate to think we've wasted time on an absolute imprint, but I suppose that'd be a possibility some day."

Silence.

"Got another question?" Bill asked.

"Nah, not really. I just think it'd be something to watch one of your encounters sometime. But I know you don't want anyone else hanging around."

"You know why?" Bill inquired.

"Sure. It's private. What you do is a very personal interaction between you and the spirit. It's no sideshow for gawkers."

"And?" I prompted.

"And it could get hairy," he grinned.

"Yes. It could get very hairy. We can't risk the possible

dangers to a third party. So far, thank God, we've been able to handle them. We've been lucky."

"Do you expect this one to be difficult?"

"We don't go into these in expectation, remember? Awareness, peak awareness, is what we have to maintain to catch the unexpected before it catches us. These cases have been so divergent there's no way to anticipate anything concrete about them. And as to your question. . .I don't know; we *never* know until the moment arrives."

"Well, like I said before, you couldn't pay me enough to do what you do." Eric smiled wide. "But I'm sure glad somebody does it. Maybe if I ever become wayward you'll still be doing your thing and you can come show me how dumb I've been."

"I hardly think that would happen," Bill said. "But just in case, you can bet you'll be seeing us again."

"Geez," Eric teased, "and here I thought I'd have a little fun after I kicked the ol' bucket. You know, hang around and scare the pants off some of my old enemies, maybe do a few boos here and there."

My head was slowly turning from side to side.

"Sorry my friend, you'd better do all your mischief now, 'cause when you're gone. . .we'll be watching."

"Spoil sports."

And with that, our discussion concluded. Eric gratefully thanked us for allowing him to come over. He wished us well on our imprint case and bid his farewell.

Later, when we were in bed, we talked for a while in the darkened room. We talked about the suicide call and we reviewed portions of our two conversations with our friend. Then, when all was said and done, we snuggled together and journeyed away to dream our separate dreams.

When we awoke Saturday morning, we lazed in bed for a while. Our encounter destination was only a few hours away and there wasn't the need to be up and on the road so early. Rainbow nosed our door open and padded into the room. Tail wagging, she leaped onto the bed and greeted us with excited whimpers. One by one the girls made their appearances and Aimee was in the middle of announcing that she was going to serve us breakfast in bed when the phone rang.

It was for me.

After talking to the psychologist about the previous night's call I'd received, going back to bed wasn't appealing anymore. I busied myself with helping Aimee. Soon the country kitchen was filled with tempting smells. Coffee brewing. French toast.

Blueberry compote heating. Cinnamon. And all five of us ate at the table while Rainbow, putting on her most pitiful orphaned expression, sat staring at us in hopes some juicy tidbit would fall her way—several usually did.

After breakfast we got right to the chore of gathering together our emergency supplies for the trip. Phantom Canyon was a long stretch of lonely road that wasn't well traveled and we needed to be well prepared for every eventuality. I then made us sandwiches and filled the two thermos containers, one with fresh coffee and the other with ice water. And after making sure our girls had all their usual instructions, we were on our way once again.

Bill pulled into a gas station and topped off the tank. After getting back behind the wheel, he gave me a peculiar look.

"We're all filled up, oil's fine, transmission fluid's good too. We going to be all right?"

"You mean with the truck?"

A brow arched.

"Yes, we're all set."

"No surprises?"

"No surprises."

"Okay then, I'd just hate to be stuck in Phantom Canyon, that's all. That place is deserted as deserted gets come nightfall." He pulled out into the traffic. "You know what we need for these trips? We need to get a good C.B. I've been thinking about that for some time now."

"How much do those cost?"

"It's been a long time since I priced them; they've probably gone up since then, but we'd need a pretty good one that'd handle those remote areas we find ourselves in."

"Well. . .price them again and we'll work on saving up. I think it's a good idea too."

The driver turned left at Divide. Now we were nearing our old stomping grounds of Rainbow Valley where we used to have our little log cabin that I missed so much. Seeing the region again renewed my desire for the remoteness that the mountain forests once provided us.

"It hasn't changed much, has it," I mused aloud.

"I noticed a couple new houses here and there, but generally it looks about the same."

We rounded a curve and, down in the valley, to the right, a red house stood alone on a hilltop. We'd once lived in that one too. From our present high vantage point on the ridge road, the house appeared to be a solitary dwelling amid pine-covered hills and valleys. It looked very serene. And, as always, tourists had pulled off onto the shoulder to peer through their binoculars down on the peaceful beauty of Rainbow Valley and the little red hilltop house.

Another hairpin curve in the snaking mountain road took me away from the good memories of a time past. Now we were approaching the one-way tunnel and fortunately it was clear for us to proceed through. Fifteen minutes later, we were driving down Bennett Avenue, the main street of Cripple Creek. Not so many out-of-state people were milling about the shops this day, but in a couple weeks, when the free autumn-color jeep tours began, there'd be no parking spaces left anywhere.

Bill pulled up in front of a shop called the Brass Ass.

"We've got some time to kill; want to browse a little?"

I couldn't believe the words that'd come from the world's greatest anti-shopper.

"You serious?"

"Let's just say that it'd be better roaming Cripple Creek than Phantom Canyon. I thought that, since we made such good time, we'd use up some of it here, because once we're way out there there'll be nothing to do after the preliminaries. We can roam around here, maybe have lunch, then head on out."

After seeing what was new in the Brass Ass shop, we headed up the street to see which curio places had closed and which were new. It didn't take me long to discover a gold mine. The Trading Company was full of Indian goods and I marvelled and fawned over the delicate shawls and colorful rugs. A black bear lamp caught my eye. The paintings that hung on the walls were mesmerizing, and I stared at one in particular that bore a striking resemblance to No-Eyes. It also took Bill by surprise. He bent his head to my ear.

"You think the artist knew her? Maybe was one of her students at one time?"

"Could be," I mused. "But then again, if that were so, I think the eyes would show much more depth. I think if one of her students could paint this well, the portrait would literally scream with power. It couldn't be any other way."

"Well, it sure is close," he said, moving on to study the others.

Remaining behind to consider the painting, I had to agree with my companion's opinion. Yes, it was a close likeness, but without the feeling of power, without the impact of great wisdom her portrait would exude, this one just wasn't close enough. And as I walked away from it, I was surprised at my feelings, for I found that I was actually disappointed at not finding another possible student of the visionary's. What I would've given to be able to make that connection—even if it was secondhand—through a painting.

After roaming through the animal museum, Bill led me across the street. "Let's grab a bite," he said. "It's almost lunchtime."

"I'm not eating in there," I sputtered, pointing to the popular restaurant we were headed for. "There's a stuffed buffalo head on the wall and they serve buffalo burgers. No thank you, sir."

"I wasn't headed there. We're just crossing the street. Can we do that? Just cross the street?"

I grinned. "As long as we don't go in there."

My mate smiled and shook his head. "Good thing *I* married you—I don't think anyone else could *begin* to understand you or cope with all your little quirks."

I sucked in my breath. "Quirks! What quirks?"

"Ohhh, like skinny-dipping in streams, disappearing in the woods, taking off without telling anyone. . .just simple little things like that."

What could I say? So I came up with something brilliant. "Let's go eat."

The cafe we ended up in was small and nondescript, but locals sat around and the place had the mouth-watering scents of homemade delights and freshly-baked goodies for the most serious sweet tooth. I postponed thoughts of my waistline and we ordered black coffee with fresh German streusel. It came hot with butter melting over the crumble topping. The portions that were set before us made my eyes bug.

"How am I going to eat all this?" I raved to my partner.

Getting ready to slide a forkful into his own mouth, he winked. "Oh I'm sure you'll find a way."

And I did. I was just thankful that I hadn't ordered the Baklava that had at first tempted my palate.

Over coffee, we eased into the main topic of the day—the encounter. We spoke in low tones, but evidently not low enough.

A pair of old sourdoughs leaned out of their chairs. Our conversation was suddenly comprised of four people instead of two.

One of the grey-whiskered men cleared his throat.

"Excuse me folks. I couldn't help but overhear your conversation there, but are you talking about that there funny business down in Phantom Canyon?"

We indicated that we were.

The man's blue eyes widened. "I dun *seen* it!"

"Me too!" perked his more timid companion. "Yuh, me too."

What luck.

Bill reached over and pulled a chair out from our table.

"Would you men mind joining us and telling about what you've seen down there?"

Without need for further prompting, the two men rose so quickly they nearly toppled their chairs. Once settled in their new spot, Bill introduced us to the strangers.

"An' we're George an' Jake," one of them said, while pointing from one to the other.

"You live here in town?" I asked them.

"Oh no, we come up from Cañon City. We're up visitin' friends for the weekend."

I scanned the small cafe for their friends.

"But they wasn't home," George clarified with an impish glint in his eye. "But we're stayin' all weekend just the same. The missus ain't gonna know no different." With that, George grinned and jabbed his elbow in his pal's side.

"George, these here folks don't wanna hear about all that. They invited us over to hear about that there ghost fire."

"Oh yeah. Sorry."

I was really enjoying our new company. It tickled me to see the old timers getting away for a weekend from the little women. And I wondered just what sort of rip-snortin' things they were planning for their freedom time, especially since I'd caught the mischievous glint still sparkling in the old codgers' eyes. I bet they were a real lively handful of trouble in their younger heydays. I hadn't realized it at the time, but my amusing wondering thoughts had me smiling.

George pointed at me. "You're sittin' there just as antsy as can be to hear that story, ain't that so, ma'am."

"Oh yes," I agreed. "I'm very anxious to hear it."

"Let's see now," he reflected. "How much do you know already?"

"Not nearly enough," Bill informed. "We know that there's a strange type of fire there, but that's about the extent of it."

The man grinned wide. "Well! In that case, I reckon we need to start at the beginnin'." Then George turned to his pal. "You wanna start?"

"Nope."

"You sure?"

"Yup."

"Okay then," George shrugged, turning his attention back to us. "Anyway, the tale goes like this. It all began when, way back when, this frontiersman brings his wife and baby daughter out here to the wild west Colorado territory. He builds them a cabin—nice one too I hear. Then one day whilst he's out hunting, the cabin catches fire. I don't know what caused the fire though. D'you know, Jake?"

"Nope. Coulda been the fireplace or maybe a kerosene lamp."

"It was most likely the lamp," George concluded.

"Probably the fireplace," Jake interjected.

"Well anyways," George sighed, "this fire breaks out an' for some fool reason, instead of the woman takin' the babe out the front door, she hides down in the trapdoor space beneath the floor. Didn't do no good o' course, 'cause they burned anyway. So then the man comes back an' digs out the bodies. He buries 'em then shoots hisself."

That was tragic. No wonder the fire remained as an imprint.

I had a question. "What have you actually seen?"

George's eyes rounded like full moons on a clear alpine night.

"That *fire!* Whuwee! What a sight! Then I seen the man come and he searches all around in them ashes. Then he just up an' disappears in the middle of all that rubble."

"Nope," Jake calmly contradicted.

George stubbornly turned to him. "Whadya mean, nope?"

"Nope the guy don't disappear in the middle—he goes over to the woods *then* he goes."

"That ain't so."

"'Tis too."

George looked at us and winked knowingly. "Jake sometimes gets to tipping the jug a little more 'an he should. You been drinkin' down there in Phantom?" he asked Jake.

"Nope," came the deadpan reply.

"Well, hell you haven't. That ghost out there *always* disappears right smack dab in the middle of all that charred cabin."

"Nope. No he don't."

"Jake! How the hell are these folks gonna know what's what if I say one thing an' you say another?"

Jake shrugged. "I seen what I seen, that's all I know."

George looked us in the eye and shook his head. "The man disappears *inside.*"

"Outside."

George didn't even bother to respond verbally; he just sat there and sent his head from side to side in a gesture of finality. Jake never saw his friend's last word on the matter.

"Anyway," George said, "that's the story and that's what we done seen."

"When did you last see this?" Bill inquired.

"Ohhh, let's see now. Guess 'twas about two months ago now."

"Three months ago," Jake mumbled his correction.

"No it wasn't. I remember when it was cuz that's when we. . ."

"Gentlemen," I said softly, "it really doesn't matter. You've been very helpful."

Curiously they looked at me. George wanted to tell more.

"Don'tcha wanna hear 'bout that there fire? About how strange it is?"

"No thank you, George. We were mainly interested in the story behind it."

"Oh. Well, you folks headin' down there? Maybe try an' see somethin'?"

"We gave it a passing thought," Bill hedged.

"Well, if you do go down there, you be sure to watch yourselves. That there canyon's real deserted. I heard many a strange tale 'bout that place. That's why me an' Jake here only drive it in daylight."

My curiosity got the best of me. "Would any of those strange tales have anything to do with some kind of hell demons?"

Both men's eyes popped.

"Hell demons, you say?"

I nodded.

George looked to Jake then back to us.

"Now that's a new one. But lady, I wouldn't put it past Phantom Canyon to welcome the devil hisself. You two be mighty careful down there, ya hear?"

We said that we'd heard and, yes, we'd be mighty careful.

"Well, Jake? What say we mosey on an' let these two alone."

Jake stood and tipped his fishing hat to us. As they shuffled over to the register, they argued over whose turn it was to foot the bill and who was to leave the tip.

I smiled at the man across the table from me.

He grinned back. "I wonder how they ever agree on how

they're going to spend their weekend freedom? Then again," he reconsidered, at their age, there's probably not a whole lot of choices."

I disagreed with a raised brow. "You see that spark in George's eye? I think those two aren't that far over the hill. I bet they try their darndest to flame up their old embers. Don't kid yourself; there's still enough for them to rekindle and I bet they have a dang good time trying."

"You think so?"

I glanced out the window. George and Jake were talking to two elderly ladies. They appeared to be old friends and they strolled away together. Bill had seen them too.

"Well, son of a gun," he spouted in surprise. "Those two still got it after all. How'd you know what they were up to?"

"I can spot that special eye twinkle a mile away. It gives them away every time."

"Them?"

"Yes. . .dirty old men," I said in feigned disgust.

My companion then leaned far over to the center of the table and gestured me to do the same. He had a secret.

I tilted my head at him in suspicion, then leaned forward to hear.

His eyes narrowed as he whispered, "Someday I might be one of those old men."

"Oh God," I sighed, "I hope so."

"And I'm gonna need an old woman. Will you be my old woman?"

"Hold that thought, big boy. Ask me again in thirty years."

"It's a date."

"You still gonna whisper sweet nothin's to the old woman?"

"You bet, sweetheart."

"Then you just reserved one wrinkled old woman."

"Promise?"

"Promise."

Now that all our tomorrows were taken care of, we needed to bring our attention back to today. We left the cafe and Cripple Creek to head toward the town of Victor. And, after clearing that, we found ourselves at the entrance to Phantom Canyon. The beginning section of the road appeared innocent enough, but soon the open spaces narrowed, and the rest of the way was a long and lonely ride.

We had taken Phantom only once before. It had been a mid-summer day and we were going from Victor to Cañon City. That drive left a distinct impression on my mind, for it was one that seemed like it would never end. We never passed another vehicle along the entire route. And when we stopped and pulled over a couple times to walk around, the stillness bothered me. Nothing moved but the huge deerflies. It was darkly eerie, even in the brightness of the midday sun. I didn't like Phantom Canyon at all then and, as far as I knew, nothing had occurred to change that opinion.

Now, as we again drove through the area, the silence was deafening. It reminded me of a living thing—one that waited and watched all who passed through.

The driver was pacing our journey so that we wouldn't miss the emanating signals that pinpointed the location. Earlier we had admonished ourselves for neglecting to ask George or Jake about the exact area. My insights suggested that the locale was a ways back from the road and into the woods. If that impression was accurate, then our job was greatly simplified, because much of the land on either side of the road was not that expansive.

"How're you doing?" Bill asked.

"Depends what you mean. If you mean impressions, there's nothing yet; if you mean comfort range, that's a little shaky—it's definitely questionable. I never did like this area."

"At least it's not in the middle of summer this time."

"Oh for heaven's sake! There's a real estate sign!" I shook my head. "Can't imagine why anyone would want to actually live down here."

"Maybe a hermit," the driver chuckled.

"Yeah, a hermit who likes having deerflies for constant companions." I sighed. "It's just so desolate. . .too desolate."

"Some folks want desolate."

"I can understand someone wanting to be relatively remote, but not really desolate."

"Each to his own."

My hand suddenly rose to signal a halt to the conversation. Bill slowed the pickup.

My eyes searched the changing terrain.

"This it?" he whispered.

"Not quite. Keep going."

And just a little farther down the road, we pulled over and stopped. Thick woods were to the right. We had reached our destination.

Getting out, we scanned the scenery and general characteristics of the land. A gentle breeze moaned through the trees.

"Dusk is going to come early here," I said, noting the high

western mountain ridge. "It's going to be like switching off the lights."

My companion agreed as he guided me through the wildgrasses and into the tree line. "How far in do you think we'll need to go?" he asked.

I said I didn't know, but felt it would be a ways.

After nearly twenty minutes into the forest, both of us began picking up the sensations we were now familiar with. We'd come to a small clearing and split up to walk the perimeter. The toe of my moccasin hit a rock and I stumbled. Catching myself, I put my hands out to break the fall.

Bill shouted across the clearing to make sure I was unhurt.

"I'm fine," I called back. But then a chill came over me. One that didn't have anything to do with natural physical causes. My fingers tingled and I peered down at the rock they were resting on. I frowned, then shuddered.

"Bill?"

"What?"

"Can you come over here a minute?"

He tramped through the tall wildgrass and came up beside me. Kneeling down, he had a look of concern.

"I thought you said you were all right."

"I am, but I wanted you to have a look at this." I pointed to the nearly buried stone. "What do you make of it?"

Even before his hand made direct contact, his palm hovered above the grey surface and he frowned. Then, actually touching the rock, he began inspecting it.

"This what you tripped over?"

I nodded.

"You know what it is? It's a foundation stone." His eyes scrutinized the rest of the area. "Yeah babe, that's what it is, and you're sitting right inside where the cabin was."

I shot to my feet. "I don't feel so good."

"What's the matter, that streusel too rich for you?"

"No, it's up here," I said, pointing to the center of my forehead. "I need to move away from here for a few minutes. I'll be okay; I just need to regroup a bit."

"You sure you'll be all right?"

I reassured him and suggested that he finish whatever he was doing before I interrupted him. He strode back toward the tree line and my gaze returned to the stone.

What could have possibly affected me so badly? Something, some residual vibrationary impression had clutched at my senses—my very soul. I'd never quite experienced such intensity before and it literally made me feel sick—it turned my stomach and drummed my heart. Upon deeper thought, I realized that my powerful reaction had not been one born of danger nor evil, but had, in fact, been one generated by great sadness. It was not fear that sickened me—it was empathy. And, for me, one was just as devastating as the other.

I inched closer to the stone. Stepping within the area of the former cabin, I slowly walked its invisible interior. Each step opened a floodgate of clear impressions and flashback frames of visions.

The fireplace. Wood cookstove. Table—flowers on it. A wide bed. Laughter. A barrel of flour. Singing. A crib. Two cribs.

Then. . .the trapdoor.

I stared with unseeing yet seeing eyes. I stared down at the pinewood door that only the psyche could see.

Bill was shaking me. "Honey! *Honey!* Come *back!* Why are you crying?"

His voice seemed very far away and I slowly raised my gaze to him. He wasn't in clear focus and I merely stared at him.

"*Jesus,* Mary, snap *out* of it!"

Then he slowly came into focus and my eyes locked onto his.

"There were two babies," I whispered, glancing back down to the grass where I'd seen the trapdoor. "There were two babies. . .and they both died with their mama down there."

Bill looked down into the weeds at my feet.

"It's not there anymore," he softly said. "There's nothing there but weeds now."

Mesmerized, I couldn't tear my eyes from the scene I'd witnessed. "Yes, just weeds."

Bill gently pulled me to him and guided me out of the area. We sat beneath some aspens and he hugged me while I eased back into myself—my complete awareness.

"It was awful," I moaned, "just awful. Their screams. . .the fear, the pain. It just made me sick. She lay on top of her babies to shield them but it didn't work." I turned to look into my mate's sympathetic eyes. "They were twins. They were so tiny. . .so helpless."

And for a long while did we sit together beneath the quaking aspens of the forest. For a long while did we remain within the healing energies of nature's benevolent power.

When the sharp edge of my empathy dulled and no longer

cut through to my heart, I raised my head and smiled up at my loving companion.

"I'm really sorry," I said. "I didn't mean to get so involved with it, but it was just so sad. I'm okay now."

"You sure, babe?"

"Yes. I can handle it now."

After several golden moments passed between us, I asked him if he had discovered anything during his own scanning.

He pointed over to two tall lodgepoles. "See those two pines—the real tall ones?"

"Uhuh."

"The man's going to materialize between them. That's where I felt him enter. And, over there," he said, moving his arm to the left, "by that boulder, that's where the graves were."

"Were?"

"Yeah. That's where he buried his family then killed himself. They're not there now, though."

"Do you think they got reburied in a churchyard?"

"I don't know. What makes you say that?"

I shrugged. "Because that's what I got. I guess somebody saw the fire and folks thought they deserved a decent burial."

Silence fell between us until Bill disturbed it.

"Babe?"

"Mmmm."

"Did you ever pick up anything dark?"

"No, did you?"

"No. So what's this hell-demon thing supposed to be?"

"I forgot about that. I don't know what it could be either because I'm sure there's no negative force around here."

"Me too. I never felt a thing and I was on guard for it."

I casually scanned the surround. "Do you think whatever it was is gone now?"

"Do you?" came the serious reply.

"No. If No-Eyes saw us finding out what it was. . .it must still be here."

"That was my thinking."

"Well," I sighed, getting to my feet and brushing off my jeans, "for some reason, I'm not really concerned about them. I'm just tired."

Bill stood to put his arm around me. "Let's get back and have a bit of something to eat before our rest. You'll feel a lot better after you've slept a while."

"I don't feel like eating," I said while heading back through the forest. "I just couldn't right now."

"Sure you could, you'll see. The walk back will make you feel more like eating."

I seriously doubted that, but I remained silent and just smiled up at my well-intentioned mate.

The walk back to the pickup did, in fact, generate somewhat of an appetite. Although I managed to eat a little, I did so mainly to soothe Bill's concern over me. He had a natural tendency toward overprotectiveness and worried if I didn't eat right or get enough rest. At times his doting nature could be frustrating, but I loved him deeply for it because I understood its source—our last lifetime together when he lost me far too soon. So now, because of his concern for my welfare, I managed to take a few bites of this and a few of that just to appease him.

After our portable supper had concluded, we repacked the leftovers, secured the back door of the makeshift camper and crawled into the raised bed. Bill lay on his back and stretched out his arm for me to rest in its crook. I held him tightly.

Now that my physical had been satisfied with the food, my mate was worried about my psyche.

"You feel any better about those impressions?"

"Yes. Now that they're not so vivid, the initial pain of them has faded. Now there's just a dull ache."

"Many Heart told you that you need to control that—temper it more."

"I know. It's not as easy as it sounds, though. Empathy isn't a learned emotion—it's natural, and when it arises, the pain has already surfaced. I'm doing quite a bit better with it, but I need time to experience more control. It's difficult to master."

"I imagine it is. Just don't give up trying, babe."

"I won't."

A shadow blanketed our bedroom as a thick bank of clouds drifted beneath the sun.

"Honey?" I said. "Shouldn't we talk about later? We need to have some kind of plan."

"Does it matter anymore? Seems to me, from our experiences so far, that the workable plans don't materialize until we're well into the encounter. They sort of present themselves as the specific circumstances dictate."

"I realize all that. What I guess I really meant was do you have any tentative ideas about this one?"

"Not the faintest."

Silence.

"So? What's got your mind grinding now?"

"It's not important, but since I know you won't rest until

you needle it out of me, I'll save you the effort. I was thinking that what we do could be real scary."

"Sometimes it is. Or at least it can be, considering the powerful energies we're dealing with."

"Well, that's not the aspect I was referring to. I was thinking about the fact that we go into these encounters cold. We place ourselves in possibly hazardous situations without having the slightest idea as to how we're going to resolve it. I think that could be very scary."

"Could be?"

"Yes, could be, because it's really not. Oh sure, initially going into one—the very beginning—gives me butterflies and anxiety, but once we're actively interacting, there's no fear of not knowing what to do."

He considered that fact. "Wasn't that what Many Heart meant when he first told you about this work? Didn't he say you'd get used to it after a while? I think this is what he meant. At first each case causes the nerves to act up on you, but then the mind and psyche take over and everything after that becomes so natural it's instinctive. Maybe there'll come a day when those initial nervous feelings also cease to come."

I smiled. "That would be nice, yet somehow I think I'll always get those butterflies. This is not your everyday job, you know. This job always presents the element of surprise."

A kiss came lightly on my cheek. "Eh, keeps your life interesting."

I groaned. "You keep it interesting enough, don't you think?"

He grinned. "I try, babe. I try."

And with that, we settled in beneath the comforter and finally drifted off to sleep.

The Night Spirit was compassionate, for I was not visited by the heart-rending visions of a mother and her twin babies dying in a blazing fire. My dreamscapes were soft and soothing. They were of No-Eyes.

When I awoke, darkness had descended upon Phantom Canyon. No starlight twinkled down. The sky was cloud-filled.

I closed my eyes in preparation for what was ahead.

"Honey? Wake up," Bill whispered.

"I'm already up. I was working."

Without saying another word, he too closed his eyes and began his own personal visualization process that led to the stage of increased energy and strength.

When we were finished, we slipped on our jackets, grabbed

the lantern and left for the woods. Now that we knew right where we were headed, the way was easier and we reached the clearing in less time. And, settling down behind the aspens, we waited.

The butterflies began to flutter in my stomach, for all around us was silence, and darkness, and this was the moment that always made me most nervous. The waiting was always tense and heavy with suspense.

Then. . .ignition. The sudden explosive flashpoint made my heart pound. What was darkness a moment ago had now flared into a blazing inferno. Before our eyes, the cabin ignited into a fiery mass. We watched in fascination as the fire consumed the building. The scene was chilling, for no reflected light from the curling flames could be seen, and no audio was heard. No crackling or roar from the fire. Only silence. Eerie silence. And it was like watching a silent movie.

Then the flames died. Embers glowed.

Bill whispered in my ear. "Now watch between those pines. He's going to be coming any minute."

I strained my eyes to watch for our target, and just as suspected, he raced out from between the trees and charged into the crumbled and smoking structure. With held breath, we saw the man scream soundless screams and dig through the rubble with his rifle butt. In agony did he pull out his family and begin to bury them.

I pulled on Bill's sleeve. "But he's *part* of the imprint!"

"I *see* that, dammit! He's *in* the imprint."

"Now what do we do?"

"Watch it an' go home, I guess."

Silence. This wasn't right, I thought. Something was very peculiar about this one.

Waiting.

Watching.

Thinking.

"Bill?" I whispered. "I've got an idea. I think he's going to do it all over again."

"You mean *after* the replay?"

"Yes! Just watch!"

When we returned our sights to the recorded action, the man's pistol had just soundlessly gone off. A puff of smoke could be discerned and he fell upon the fresh mound of grave earth.

Blackness engulfed us once again. The entire visual had vanished. The embers were no longer glowing. The charred rubble was gone. Nothing remained but the wildgrass in the clearing and the gentle breeze that blew across it. The replay was done.

"Now watch over there between the trees again," I said.

It was difficult to see in the darkness, but there was a rush of movement. When the man reached the clearing, he was closer—it was our target—the *real* spirit. We moved out from behind our cover.

Advancing toward the clearing, I was struck by the pitiful sadness of the scene. The man was unsuccessfully attempting to dig in the wildgrass that now covered the long-gone trapdoor. His efforts were fruitless.

As we neared, his breathless words were frantic.

"Gotta get 'em out! Gotta get 'em. Hold on Julia, I'm coming for ya."

By now we were toe to toe with the foundation stone. We stood mute and watched the man's exhausting efforts. Finally I couldn't stand it any longer, and, when I spoke, my voice was low.

"They're not down there."

Cussing. Digging. Calling.

"They're not down there," I repeated a bit louder.

The man halted a second, noticed two people and shouted at us, "Grab shovels! Help me!"

We didn't move.

The man went back to his labors of love, then froze. His face slowly raised. Eyes locked on ours in new curiosity.

"They're not down there," I softly stated again.

"The fire," he stuttered. "We gotta get 'em 'fore they suffocate."

"They're gone already," I said.

"Gone?"

"Yes. Your wife took both babies away from here. They're safe now."

The man's eyes narrowed as he looked us up and down.

"Say. You two ain't from around here. An' where'd you get them funny clothes?"

"No, we're not from around here," I said. "And our clothes don't matter. What matters is that we came to help you rejoin your family."

He squinted with deep suspicion. "Jist what're you talkin' 'bout?"

Bill recognized the beginnings of a threatening situation.

"Mister, we came to show you where your family is. They're safe and they're waiting for you."

Fire blazed in the man's eyes. "*You* got my *wife?* My *kids?*"

This was not working.

"Mister, please, hear me out," my partner said, trying another ploy. "Do you believe in God?"

Our target's fists clenched. "Why, you bold cur! You're tryin' to change the *subject!* You got my *wife!*"

In a flash, the man was on Bill. His rage had flared into action, and when his striking blow had no physical effect, the result did.

"Holy Mother of *God!*" he shouted in terror as he backed away. In shock, his wide eyes stared into Bill's, then mine.

"Please," I desperately pleaded. "Please listen to us. We. . ."

The man quickly slapped his hands over his ears and frantically backpedaled farther away from us. Eyes were rounded in terror-filled fright.

"Oh *God!*" he cried. "*Save* me from these *hell* demons!"

My scalp crawled then. We were the infamous demons.

"*Mister!*" Bill hollered while stepping closer. "Please! Let us *help* you. We're just *people!*"

"No! *Back,* I say. Back, back *away* from this God-fearin' soul!" He fell to his knees and hid his face from his imagined demons. "Lord *save* me from these silver-tongued devils! *Save* me, Lord!" came the hysterical pleading prayers. "*Deliver* me from these vile demons who come in sheep's clothing! Lord! Cast them *back* into their brimstone fire! Cast them *away* from me! Oh-h-h God, please *deliver* me! *Take* me into your almighty *kingdom! Take* my humble *soul,* God!"

The man bent lower and covered his eyes.

"The Lord is my Shepherd, the Lord is my Shepherd," he prayed.

"The Lord *will* deliver me. . .He *will* deliver me. . .*save* me. . .save. . ."

And, before our eyes, the man was delivered. Not from his imagined hell-demons, but from his own hell of self-imprisonment—from his own self-imposed exile.

Now, standing in the dark clearing, we were silent as our hands reached out to clutch together. It was a reverent time when we spent a couple golden moments in retrospective contemplation. It was time for our own silent prayers of thankfulness. And we each, in our own personal way, thanked God for continuing to give us the ability to help lost souls. We thanked Him for giving us the courage to carry it through, and we thanked Him for our continued success.

Together did we turn our backs on the clearing and begin our walk back through the forest.

Suddenly, the entire woods flashed with light.

We spun around.

Then, all was dark as before, and thunder rolled across the night sky.

Together we sighed a breath of relief, for the only flashes that came to Phantom Canyon now were those of natural causes. Lightning was evidence of the Thunder Beings' power. And they were well pleased.

It rained all of Saturday night and into Sunday. We were glad to get back home to the security of our cozy home, and the girls were overjoyed to see us—especially since it'd been storming so violently.

After dinner, as I was cleaning up, I caught a scent of something that sparked warning chills up my spine. I turned to the girls.

"Do you smell something?" I asked.

They sniffed the room air. No, nobody did.

I frowned. The peculiar odor bothered me, and while I washed up the dishes, I watched out the window above the sink at the falling rain. Sometimes I picked up a psychic scent that wasn't detectable in the physical. Was this one of those? No. It wasn't perceived in the same way. There was always a nebulous perceptual difference between sensing a physical scent and a psychic one. The lavender fragrance of Josephine in the Sweetwater Hotel was not brought by the same sensations I was now experiencing. My psyche was beeping wildly. Something was very wrong.

Rainbow sat by the back door and glared at me.

"It's pouring out, girl," I crooned to her. "You sure you need to go out?"

She cocked her head and whined.

"Okay, but don't say I didn't warn you."

I opened the door and immediately slammed it shut before the poor animal could get out.

"Oh my God! *Bill!*" I shouted, racing into the living room. "The whole neighborhood's full of *propane!*"

He shot from his chair. "Blow out that lantern. Make sure the furnace and hot water tank doesn't come on. Shut down the gas to all the pilots."

The shrill wailing of multiple sirens pierced the air and grew louder. Fire trucks turned off the highway and passed our house. The shrilling stopped abruptly.

We locked eyes for a fraction of a second, then ran to the back window. Fire trucks and police cars were jammed in the road near some cabins across the way from us. A sheriff car blocked the entrance to our road. People were being evacuated.

The next thing I knew, Bill was pulling on his jacket and going out the door.

"*Bill!*" I shouted. But it was too late; he was already racing to the scene.

The girls rushed to the window.

"Stay away from those windows," I ordered.

"But we wanna see daddy."

"Put on your coats," I said, getting the umbrella out. "We'll watch from the drive."

Once we were out in the pouring rain, we tried to get as close as we safely could. We stood at the end of our drive.

A policeman came up to us. "Sorry, ma'am, we've evacuated the area; you'll have to move on."

"I don't think so," I snapped in irritation. "We live here and my husband's over there. He works for the natural gas company."

"You mean Bill?"

"Yes."

"Okay, but it'd be better if you moved into your *front* yard."

We moved back only half the way.

Jenny huddled beside me. "I'm scared, mom. Why'd Daddy have to go over there?"

"Because that's what he does, honey."

"Is this what he does when the police or fire department calls him in the middle of the night?"

"Yes. They block traffic until he gets there and shuts off the gas or fixes the leak."

"Isn't that awful dangerous?" Sarah asked.

I squeezed her shoulder. "It can be, honey."

Silence.

Watching.

"Mom?" Sarah asked, "Is Daddy gonna blow up some day?"

Jesus, why'd she have to ask that now when propane hung like an iron curtain in the air.

"He knows what he's doing, honey. He's real good at it. That's why they call him."

"But they didn't call him this time."

"I know; he just went on his own."

"But he could blow up one of these times, couldn't he?"

Aimee shushed Sarah up in whispered tones. "Don't talk about that; can't you see how worried Mom is?"

I strained to see what was going on. Firemen were pulling on silver fire suits. Bill was down in the drain ditch with the fallen propane tank. A Colorado Springs TV news truck pulled up and the crew began filming.

"Mom?" Sarah said, still impatient for her answer.

"What!" I barked.

"Nothing, Mom." She patted my arm. "Daddy's gonna be all right. Don't worry."

I smiled down at her. "I'm sorry I barked at you, honey. Daddy's going to be just fine."

Then I noticed someone casually walking down the road toward the excitement. It was the manager of the propane company. So young. So inexperienced. So stupid, for he was lighting a cigarette.

A policeman shouted at him to put it out. And I was angry because my mate was risking his own life while the manager of the company stood around not knowing what to do.

Suddenly the hub of activity began dispersing. Firemen climbed back in their trucks. The police barricade was removed. And, soaked through to the bone, Daddy appeared and started walking across the road—toward home—in one piece.

Tears filled our eyes.

"You can turn the pilots back on now," he said.

We hugged the daylights out of him.

"What's the matter?" he grinned. "You girls all act like I was going to blow up or something."

The girls all cried that they were so scared for him, and why'd he have to go over there anyway when the police never called him?

"Could we go inside? I'm a little wet."

Once back in the house, we fawned over our hero. After he peeled off the sodden clothing and got into dry ones, the girls eagerly brought him hot coffee and a big piece of apple pie. They huddled around, anxious to ask their bursting questions.

"What happened?" was the first.

"Seems all this rain loosened the ground the propane tank sat on and the bank of the ditch started failing in. The tank finally toppled into the gully and the valve broke off. There was nothing to keep the gas from spewing out."

"But Daddy, you're not manager of that propane company anymore; why'd you have to go over there?" Sarah asked in childlike frustration.

"Honey, good thing I did, because they couldn't locate the manager. Emergencies are emergencies. If you know how to help—you do."

The girls were now old enough to fully realize that their dad's work was very dangerous. They worried about him just as much as I did every day he went off to work. And when those police or fire calls came in the middle of the night, they couldn't sleep until he was safe back home again. Sometimes a drunk had rammed his car into a gas meter—shearing it off at the ground. Sometimes a snow plow broke a meter. Or a main was hit by a construction or utility crew. No matter what the cause, he knew what to do, but knowledge wasn't a failsafe against Lady Destiny. . .and he tempted her patience daily.

Rainbow whined by the back door.

"Oh no," I groaned in sympathy, "she's still waiting."

Jenny ran to let the poor thing out. When she and the dog came back into the living room, her eyes brightened.

"Hey! Can we all stay up an' watch Daddy on the news?"

"Maybe they won't have it on until tomorrow," I said.

"Well, can we see?"

We watched the late news. Sure enough, they had the film. They showed the fire and police vehicles at the sight. They showed the barricades blocking both entrances to the road. They interviewed the fire chief and the manager of the gas company. And that was it.

Aimee frowned when it was over. "How come they didn't say anything about Daddy? They didn't even show him!"

Daddy chuckled. "They couldn't get close enough to the gully to film me, honey. The police wouldn't let them."

"Well, how come you didn't let them interview you when you got out?"

"Honey, after I finish one of those, all I want to do is get back home."

"But you were a hero!"

"Lots of people are heros, Aimee. You don't have to be on TV to prove anything."

That sounded familiar to all the girls, for we had always taught them to be good and helpful people just because it was the right thing to do, not for the honor or praise others would shed on you for it.

So the girls proudly hugged and kissed their hero and went to bed knowing their dad was safe. We soon followed their example.

Snuggling in close beneath the quilt, I quietly admonished my mate.

"I know you felt you had to rush over there, but do you know how many years I age every time you go out on those things?"

He kissed me. "At least it doesn't show."

"This is not funny. I'm serious."

"So am I."

I sighed. "This sure has been one hell of a weekend. First the suicide call, then the encounter, on top of that the whole neighborhood almost blows. I'm ready for that little cabin of mine. I'm getting too old for this."

His fingers stealthily crept up my bare arm like a spider. "Are you trying to tell me you're an old *woman*?" he slipped in.

"Goodnight, Bill."

"Sweet dreams, Grandma. We'll finish this little *discussion* in the morning."

"You'll forget it by then," I grinned.

"So remind me."

I smiled in the darkness of the bedroom, for I knew he never forgot to leave anything unfinished. And I drifted off to sleep, entering a golden dreamscape where two people were bathed in a warm and loving glow of shimmering sunlight. I slept long and sound. By morning I would be bright-eyed and bushy-tailed—full of frisky energy to finish that discussion. . .just in case he forgot.

Through Owl Eyes

Leaves flamed scarlet. Aspens quaked treasures of golden doubloons. Sky, splashed brilliant turquoise, held high the burnished disc of the bronze sun. Blood-red willows spiked tall beside blue streams. Living forests, supernatural in their glistening splendor, sang out their transcendental joy. The celebration had begun. The radiant raiments of autumn had enchanted the land, and whole mountainsides exploded in a dazzling symmetry of magic colors. Hearts quickened at the stunning sight. Minds swirled with the dizzying esoteric vision. And, once again, spirits yearned for a primordial union.

It was October.

Woodsmoke was in the air.

And we were off to our final encounter of the year.

Leaving Woodland Park, we headed west. At Buena Vista, a right turn brought us through town where we followed alongside the Arkansas River until we reached the highest incorporated town in the nation, Leadville, once more appropriately called Cloud City. It was a town that time forgot, a town where many a laboring miner became the silver barons of a time past. Although Doc Holliday's favorite hangout saloon is now a clothing store and Baby Doe Tabor's Opera House is straining to persevere, much of the original spirit remains alive enough to whisper its secrets to anyone who has the ear for them.

The older residential section still testified to the styles of the times. Most dwellings, built before 1888, were either tiny crib houses or elaborate two-story Victorians—all nestled shoulder to shoulder up the hilly streets and past the huge mounds of standing mine tailings. It was a town that some claimed was forty years behind the times because, they said, new industry was always shut out—there were those who wanted it to stay just as it was, just as it always was. It was a town of many secrets—then. . .and now.

So on this beautifully alive autumn morning, we pulled up in front of the Golden Burro Cafe. It was well into breakfast time. And as we leisurely enjoyed our meal, the beginnings of nervousness nuttered into my receiving psyche.

I glanced out the window to watch the traffic pass on Harrison Avenue. I was trying to disassociate my consciousness from the upcoming encounter so I could be free to sharpen receptivity of the nebulous sensations.

Nothing specific revealed itself.

"Want to come back to Leadville?" my partner said.

I turned to him. "Say what?"

"I asked you if you want to come back to Leadville. Obviously your mind's way out somewhere. What were you thinking about?"

"I was trying to get clear. Something's starting to nag."

"Something usually does at the beginning of these. It's got a name too. Nerves."

My smile was a weak one. "I know, but this time it's more than just the usual case of pre-encounter jitters. This time I feel something really strong underlying the event."

Bill's expression turned quickly from nonchalance to deep concern.

"Can you tell what this feeling is associated with?"

"Not yet. It's just a terrible inner nagging, like a pulling type of sensation."

"Do you think there's the possibility of danger?"

I shook my head. "Definitely not."

A brow rose in doubt. "That answer came awfully quick."

"That's because it's an answer I'm sure of. No, it's nothing from without, nothing exterior."

"Then it must be generated from within yourself. It must not only be a psychic sensation, but also a personal one. That'd create a pretty powerful punch to feel." He paused to give me one of his extra-hard eye-to-eye looks. "What exactly do you feel?"

"At odds with myself. I feel torn inside. Yeah, that's a good description. I feel torn."

"Torn *between* something?"

"Yes. I want to do this one, but on the other hand, I don't. I can't explain that either, so don't bother asking me what I mean by it." I sighed and glanced out the window to better collect my thoughts, my enigmatic feelings. When my eyes again locked onto Bill's, they were met by expectancy. "Could it just be possible that aspects about this one could have changed since No-Eyes told me about it?"

He pursed his lips. "Anything's possible. You know that. But what I want to know is why you'd think that."

I stared down into my coffee cup. I didn't have a solid response. I didn't have anything logical to back up my theory with, so I just shrugged.

"Then we're right back to what your feelings are," he wisely whispered. "If you think that the couple are no longer there then there's no reason for us to. . ."

"They're still there."

"Then you're not verbalizing what you're thinking. If they're still there, we need to help them; we still need to clear the area. You sure they're there?"

I nodded.

"So why the problem?"

I didn't know. And I didn't like that fact; I didn't like it at all. It was extremely unnerving for me.

"Well," he said softly, "then maybe we'll find out what this is all about when we get there. These types of glitches usually iron themselves out with our on-site impressions." He reached across the table to hold my hand. "If we can't sort it out now, we will then. Right?"

I smiled. "Right."

And during our ride out of Leadville, and all along Highway 24, I pushed aside the nebulous feeling in deference to the glorious scenery. More than likely, it wasn't a completely voluntary conscious effort; more than likely, nature wedged her usual bright way into my head to replace the darkness that had been crouching there.

When we crossed the arched girders of the Redcliff bridge that towered over the Eagle River, I knew we were just a few curving turns away from Gilman. Just as anticipated, the driver pulled off the road and we got out.

Standing on the precipice, we silently looked down on the dozens of frame homes that were perched so precariously on the mountain ledge—all empty. It was an eerie sight. So many whitewashed houses standing empty. A ghost town on the edge of a mountain ridge. Rumors had it that Vail bought the town to accommodate their workers—but no one would live there. Other rumors claimed the state condemned the place because it was determined unsafe due to the chasm it rested above. Then others swore the ghosts drove everyone away. Whatever rumor was true—if any were—we still found the site fascinating. Why leave it all so intact if nobody was allowed to inhabit it? Why not move the houses and make use of them?

So many homeless people and here were literally dozens of homes sitting idle. Secrets. More secrets. The mountains were full of them, and some, only the mountains could know, for they have been there to see which rumors were really true.

We left Gilman in the lonely silence we found it and continued over Battle Mountain to end up in Minturn where we picked up the Interstate west to Eagle. We didn't know it then, but three years later, our friend Robin would be managing the main convenience store there and our two daughters would be hired on full time—Eagle would be home for us for six months until our rental house was sold out from under us. It would seem that Lady Destiny held all the cards and would deal us a few bad hands. But now Eagle was a new hamlet for us to see.

Located on the western side of the Continental Divide, it was naturally a warmer and dryer climate. Scrub and piñon were more in evidence here rather than the tall conifers of the high country evergreen forests. Its setting was more of what folks think of when someone mentions the Old West.

We drove beneath a bridge. A freight train passed overhead. We drove over another where the Eagle River lazily meandered away from the town. Then up into the center of the business district that ended just after a couple blocks and turned into the residential section.

What impressed us most was the tidiness of it all. The town was squeaky clean and the folks were as friendly as friendly gets. Neat little homes with autumn decorations of Indian corn and dried flowers on doors lined the streets. In the road, golden leaves fluttered down across our path. Tranquil and serene. Eagle appeared to be a pleasant community to raise a family in.

We headed out Brush Creek Road toward Sylvan Lake. It was a rough dirt road that ascended into some magnificent mountain country. Rugged and virgin. The tall pines returned; so did the water. And, after a time, we finally reached our destination.

It had me enrapt.

Beside the surging river, Bill cut the engine and just looked over at me.

When my eyes met his, they were soft with contentment, for the welling within my heart and the recognition that struck my spirit had said it all—this was home.

"Do you feel it?" I reverently whispered.

He smiled wide.

I rested back in the seat and exhaled a long sigh.

"I can't believe it. After all this time. All those years of wondering and searching are finally over and I'm not even excited."

"It's relief, honey. Pure and simple relief. Now we know where home is."

I turned my gaze to the thick woods. I listened to the spirit-soothing voice of the rushing river as it spilled its torrents over and around the mossy boulders. My soul was basking within the surround of its newfound sacred ground, and it didn't want to move. It just wanted to settle down in and never leave. And my body reacted in a like manner. I felt drained and closed my eyes.

"Honey?" Bill said softly.

"Mmmm."

"I feel like I just ran a marathon."

"I know the feeling."

"If I didn't know better, I'd think this area was feeding off our energies."

"The unburdening is always tiring. Our new home is drawing out all the negatives of anxiety, worry, and frustration. We'll feel better in a few minutes."

We both gave in to the unburdening process and rested our heads back against the seats to close our eyes. The watercourse began to work its magic and soon we found ourselves dozing off. When we opened our eyes, the extreme exhaustion was gone. It had been replaced with the renewed energy that comes with the solid sense of purpose and finalization.

Bill unfolded our map and began studying it.

"What're you doing?" I inquired.

He flashed me an impish grin. "Just checking something."

"Checking what?"

Intent searching going on.

"Honey?" I nudged.

"Mmmm."

"What're you looking for?"

Then, "Ah-ha! There's one. And there's another!" he mumbled, moving his finger around the worn paper.

"Will you please tell me what. . ."

He then looked me square in the eye and shook his head.

"You're not going to believe how damned obvious this was. You're just not going to believe it. Remember what Many Heart said about our land? And how cryptic you thought it was?"

I nodded with growing interest.

"Yes. He said that beneath my feet will be a power point. At

310

my head will the mighty winged person fly. To the east the great water spirit will sing, and in the west, three rivers converge as one."

"Uh-huh. Get out."

Curiously I clambered out of the truck while my partner did the same. He ran around and took my arm. With a knowing grin, he positioned me behind the vehicle.

"Now," he explained, holding the map up before us, "you're facing north. Look down at that map and tell me what you see. We're right here," he informed, pointing on the spot of paper.

I tried real hard to see what he saw. I looked all around but made no connections. With frowning brows and a rather silly grin, I looked back at him.

"Give me a hint."

"You gotta be blind as a bat!" he laughed. "Just keep Many Heart's words in mind and look again."

Now he really had me wondering as I excitedly gave the map my full attention. As I studied it, I unconsciously shifted my position.

He turned me back. "You have to face north," he insisted.

I was still having trouble until I envisioned myself as a stick figure standing on the spot Bill had pointed to. Then everything around the crude figure fell neatly into place. The circle of the head rested just below Eagle County.

"North!" I flared, looking up into the landscape. "*Eagle's* north. . .at my *head!*"

Bill beamed. "That's clue Number One. At your head will the mighty winged person fly—the eagle—Eagle County! Now go on from there."

With a wildly pounding heart, I looked down at the map again. To the right of my imaginary figure rested Lake County.

"I can't believe this! *Lake* County? He said 'to the east the great water spirit will sing.' Of course! *Lake!*"

Bill couldn't contain himself any longer. He was too eager to help point out the rest.

"And. . .'beneath your feet will be a power point.' Right here! Where you're standing! And there," he said, indicating the three main Gold Medal fishing rivers, "how did his last hint go? 'And in the west, three rivers converge as one.' Look how they all end up in the Colorado River!"

"How could we have been so blind?" I cried in amazement. "Many Heart actually pinpointed our land!" I sighed and let the map drop to my side. "This is just incredible."

"There's something else too," Bill added.

"I don't think I can take anymore surprises right now."

"You're going to have to. Well. . .it may be nothing, but after I realized the connection, something else came to me. Remember when you were telling me about when No-Eyes revealed all these encounter locations?"

"Yes?"

Didn't you say that when she mentioned this specific one she seemed to have some kind of peculiar look—a twinkle in her eye?"

My eyes then narrowed at the remembrance. "Why that little minx!" I grinned. "She knew all along we'd discover our land when we came here to do this one. She *sent* us here!" I just stood there in shock and slowly shook my head.

Bill pulled me to his chest and hugged gently.

"So many hints—so many. And to think Many Heart actually gave you symbolic coordinates," he sighed.

"I feel like an idiot," I moaned. "A real fool."

"Nah, don't be silly. But I don't see how Many Heart could've said that and kept a straight face at the same time."

"I do. It's called control."

"I'd call it something else," he said.

"Oh?" I uttered, looking up into his eyes.

He smiled. "It's called compassion. His empathy's still there. . .at least for you it was."

My head rested back on to his chest. I didn't respond to my mate's last words, for we both knew he had spoken the truth of the matter. We felt wonderfully warm inside knowing my Dreamwalker had cared for us enough to show us the way, even though we weren't smart enough at the time to see it.

Together did we cling to each other for a long time while our feet were solidly anchored to our power point and the mighty eagle flew at our heads. Sounds of the river voice filled our hearts as she sang and sang, "Home. Home. You're *home!*"

Then, from within the virgin woods, another sound reached out to me.

My neck pricked at the sudden sound and I raised my head to scan the tree line. High on a golden aspen branch, an old owl blinked down at me. No-Eyes' words echoed through the chambers of my mind.

"Watch for the owl. Watch for the *owl*."

I grinned then.

Bill noticed. "What's so amusing?"

I inclined my head to the winged person. But when he looked, she was gone.

"What, babe?"

"Oh nothing. It's just so good to be back among friends again."

"Friends?"

"Yeah, *old* friends."

"You mean the nature of our sacred ground? All the life?"

I smiled softly. "Yeah, all the life. . .*all* the life that I ever loved."

He kissed my forehead and took my hand.

"Let's walk awhile."

And we did. We walked through the forest and then spent considerable time sitting beneath the soughing pines that edged the singing river. We passed several hours absorbing the peacefulness that our new land so eagerly offered us. We were emotionally riding the high of our new revelation, but, mentally, we had not forgotten about the purpose that had led us there. It was that issue that now began to come to the forefront of our consciousness to dominate the conversation. Bill was first to broach the subject.

"So now you know what your mysterious nagging feeling was all about."

It was a statement that was clearly supposed to claim itself as a resolution to my former inner conflict.

It didn't.

Now that we were back on the subject, I noticed that the queer sensation hadn't dissipated as was expected. It had hung on with a tight-fisted death grip. When his statement failed to elicit a confirming response from me, he peered around into my face.

My expression was not a sanctioning one.

His voice was solemnly heavy. "Then it didn't have anything to do with the discovery of our land."

I shook my head. "No, it's connected with the encounter."

"Let's go," he said, getting up. "We need to get to the bottom of this thing."

We got back in the truck and, as he eased the vehicle along the road, I silently intensified my inner perception of the woodland vibrations. Somewhere near, very near, the waters had drained the warm life force from the couple. And as my physical discomfort increased from the intensifying psychic sensations, I wondered how this could possibly be both the location of the tragic deaths and still be our sacred ground.

I subconsciously rubbed my stomach to ease the ill feelings.
The truck slowed.

"You sick?" asked the driver.

I shook my head and motioned him to continue forward.

Worriedly he continued and I was aware of how frequently
he glanced over at me. But still the physical discomfort persisted until I actually began feeling sick to my stomach.

"Here. Stop."

The vehicle eased off onto the grassy shoulder and Bill cut
the engine.

"What's the matter? Are you really feeling sick?"

"Yes and no because I think it's all in my head. I need to
walk around."

Hand in hand we picked our way through the tall wildgrass
to the high bank.

"This is the spot," I informed. "This is where they ended it
all."

We both stared down into the roaring whitewaters. Then I
couldn't help saying what was in my heart.

"Bill?" I began hesitantly.

He looked to me. "Babe?"

"I can't do it. I can't do this one."

My companion was silent for several moments before
responding. "They still around?"

I gazed up into the beautifully healthful trees. I looked far
into the woods past the river.

"Yes."

"Then we have a job to do."

"I can't." My soulful eyes met his. "I just can't."

"Then we're going to have to talk about this, honey. You're
going to have to make me see what it is you're feeling."

Silence.

Waiting.

Rushing river sounds. Wind soughing through trees.
Birdsong.

I stared down into the river.

His knuckle touched my cheek to stop a trailing tear.

"Hey, what's this?" he softly asked. "What's going on in that
head of yours? What're you getting?"

My gaze slowly raised to lock on his.

"They're happy. They're totally happy just the way they are.
I can't send them back."

"But we have to. We have to make them. . ."

I shook my head. "No we don't, Bill. We don't have to do

anything. I wish you could feel their contentment, their peace. . .their love. I just wish you could feel those things from them."

He released a weighted sigh. "Well maybe they are happy and content, but they're still not where they're supposed to be. They're both still wayward."

My look was gentle. "Are they?"

His fingers ran through his hair in a gesture of frustration. "What're you doing to me? What're you doing to yourself? Our purpose?"

"I don't know. All I know is that this isn't right. We can't interfere with this one."

My partner was at a loss for what to do or say next. Finally he led me over to some boulders by the bank and we sat beside the watercourse.

I knew I was being terribly difficult—even bad—but I couldn't ignore that which pulled at my heart. Reaching down to the ground, I picked up a fallen Aspen leaf and twirled it between my fingers.

"Put that back on the tree," my mate said suddenly.

"What?"

"I said for you to stick that leaf back on the tree."

"That's real dumb. I know you've got some high philosophy hidden somewhere in that directive so let's hear it."

His expression remained unchanged. "Put the leaf back where it belongs."

I dropped it into the churning waters.

"So why there and not on the tree?"

My smile was warm. "I know what you're trying to accomplish with all this symbolism, but the analogy isn't quite exact."

"Oh?" he muttered with a raised brow. "Aren't spirits just like the autumn leaves? When the lifetime has been lived and it's time to move on, they don their glorious robes for the transition journey from the tree/body—they break with their physical life support system to enter another phase of existence. And. . .the *wayward* ones are those that *refuse* to leave that physical life support reality—those are the sorry ones." He paused a moment before continuing. "Ever go woodswalking in the middle of winter and see a lone leaf clinging to the tree that can't support it any longer? Isn't it a sorry and forlorn thing? Isn't it solitary and alone not having followed the natural order of things—of life?"

"You're forgetting one thing in your analogy. These spirits

aren't forlorn and alone—they love each other. They have happiness and the love of each *other*. They've no need for the tree. They support themselves."

My poor mate sighed again.

"But their reality is a false one. It's self-created just like all the other spirits' existence was. Just because these two appear happy doesn't make it any less wrong."

"Does to me."

"Mary, they're *wayward*."

"Are they?"

"Yes!"

We listened to the river voice for a long while. We were at odds on this one and there didn't appear to be any happy median—none whatsoever—and it was frustrating for both of us. I hated the situation we found ourselves in. Always we were so in tune and of one mind on everything. This new dilemma was causing us both some painful heartache. Oh how I wished he could feel just a fraction of the emotions I was picking up from the Indian couple. What love! Yet I knew, as we sat here so together yet so separate, that he too was hurting inside over the confusion that had arisen so unexpectedly.

I reached for his hand. "I'm sorry, honey. I agree with your side of the dilemma, but I can't reconcile what I feel with it. Maybe after our rest I'll see more clearly."

He smiled. "It's worth a try."

We settled down on the camper bed and the rushing water sounds lulled us quickly to sleep. I dreamed of the Indian couple as they were—then and now.

On a green and grassy bank, sunlight glistening off long, ebony hair. Large dark eyes, smiling. Soft doeskin clothes, sparkling with the glint of intricate beadwork. Laughter. The two reclining together, so in love. Whispered endearments. Gentle touchings. Beautiful. Peaceful. Contentment filling their unified aura. Perfect for all eternity. But then. . .there in the tree line shadows stood a figure. Dark and ominous. Black robe and hood. Executioner's hood. The figure raised its hand to remove the hood. . .it was me.

"Oh God," I blurted, sitting up. "Oh no."

"What's wrong?" Bill flared, coming swiftly awake.

"*It's* wrong. It's *still* all wrong." And I told him all about the terrifying dream—the nightmare.

He tried to analyze it away. "Don't you think that that just symbolized your deep conscious fears for this one?"

"No."

"Are you rationalizing?"

I shook my head. "Honey, I'm really sorry, but I don't want to send these two back. I can't explain why not, but my gut feelings are just too strong. There's something really different here. Besides, No-Eyes always stressed the need to go with your feelings—to *always* listen to them."

He thought on that last fact. "But she also said that some feelings were false and that you had to logically consider them. Babe, these have got to be false feelings."

"But I've had them all day! That's got to mean something significant. I'm not frivolous. I just didn't up and decide I didn't want to clear this one. *Something's* different here!"

The sound of an owl hoot reached the camper.

We paused our debate to take notice.

"Honey?" I said. "No-Eyes talked about the owls and how they're connected to the spirit world. Remember that?"

He nodded, but didn't comment.

"She said that owls were the spirits' connective link to this world. They were frequently the forebearers of a spirit communication and also that they were the Omen Givers."

Silence.

"Do you remember all that?"

"Yes," he admitted thoughtfully.

"Bill. . .there's an owl out there tonight. Doesn't that seem to be a little more than coincidence to you? It does to me. Especially since none of my feelings can be reconciled to our purpose here. Especially since I can't bring myself to clearing them. I just know my feelings are right on the mark. I believe No-Eyes sent us here to discover what's so different about it."

After several quiet moments of in-depth consideration, he looked away to the window.

"Let's go then. Let's go see what's so different."

We hurriedly pulled on our jackets and left the secure warmth of the camper. Outside the moon shed its nightlight around through the forest. It played and danced on the river surface. And beside the waters, behind the boulders, we took up our routine vigil.

We waited twenty minutes. . .forty. . .sixty-five.

Nothing.

I started when the owl voiced one hoot above us.

Bill whispered to me. "Where are they?"

I shrugged. I was getting stiff from crouching and I altered my position.

"Maybe we're too early. Give it more time."

More time passed. Another twenty minutes soon stretched into another hour. . .two.

Bill finally rose and rubbed his back. "They're not here."

Stretching finally, I responded. "They're here. I can feel them. They're very powerful."

"So? Where are they then?"

"I just know they're here. Something's different. . .really different. Let's go warm up."

We left the bank as empty as we found it. The camper, once the heater was lit, felt wonderful. We talked.

"I know they're there somewhere," I repeated with conviction.

"Okay, so they're there. Question is, where is 'there'? And, how do we connect?"

"I've been thinking," I mused. "'There' is not here."

"That was brilliant. That was a good one. Every once in a while you come up with a real good one like that. Now what does it mean?"

I grinned. "Well?"

He smiled amusingly, "Well? Go on, I'm ready to listen to just about anything right about now."

"I think they're here as Earth Protectors. I think they're here, but not in the In-Between dimension like all the other wayward spirits. In other words, they don't manifest themselves. So. . .they're here, but they're not here. See?"

The strange look I got was skeptical.

"I'm serious, honey. It all fits! Think about it for a minute. Why would No-Eyes send us here if *no* spirits were around?"

"She wouldn't," he admitted quickly.

"Right. Now, why would I have that nagging feeling that some aspect was so different about this one if it wasn't?"

"I don't know. Maybe you finally went over the edge."

I flashed him a "be serious" look.

"Okay. Okay. I get the general drift," he corrected. "So then when your feelings urged you not to try to *clear* this place, you concluded they were *meant* to remain. . .with a *purpose*.

"Yes!" I beamed.

Silence.

"So?" I pushed. "What's the problem?"

"The problem is, why are we *here* then? Why are *they* still hanging around?"

My eyes rounded like full moons.

"Don't you get it? *They're* here as nature entities, Earth

Protectors, to ensure the area remains virgin—unspoiled. *We're* here to *commune* with them!"

My companion just stared at me. "Commune?"

"Yes!"

"Why?"

I shrugged.

"We were sent all the way over here to commune with these Earth Protector spirits and you don't know why?" he said.

I nodded then shook my head. "Don't have the foggiest."

"Uh-huh. This is just great."

"Isn't it!" I sparked in excitement.

"How do you plan on making this communion?"

"Mmmm," I frowned.

Silence hung between us as we each seriously considered the technique options we were familiar with.

"A spirit journey?" he offered.

I shook my head. "No good here."

"Joint meditation?"

"Nope."

"The Corridor?"

"We're not going anywhere but here," I reminded. "Besides, we've never done that one alone."

"Well, what else is there?"

"Projection?" I tried.

"No," he sighed. "We need the use of our full faculties for this."

"Mmmm."

Silence reigned again for several prolonged minutes of deeper thought.

I jumped up. "I know!"

"Jesus! Don't do that! One of these days you're going to give me a heart attack!"

"I'm sorry, but I've got it. We'll use *Intent!*"

"I've never done that."

"I have. . .with Many Heart. That's how I got myself to the top of that mesa, remember?"

He was doubtful. "I don't know, hon."

"Why not? It's the only way to meet them and still carry everything with us."

"How do we get back?"

"Same way we went. They'll help."

He wasn't at all as confident as I was.

"You sure? About their help, I mean?"

"No. But how'll we know if we don't at least try?"

"I don't know about this. You've had a lot more experience, but how many times have you journeyed by way of the Intent Path?"

I grinned with the answer. "Once."

"Ahuh. That's what I thought—a real pro."

"Oh c'mon. Please?"

Deep inner conflict going on.

"Stop debating with yourself," I teased. "That only gets you more mixed up."

And again the owl hooted at us.

He eyed me as if I was in cahoots with all of nature. "Oh, all right, but if anything goes wrong, I'll never. . ."

"Nothing's going to go wrong. Where's your faith anyway?"

He ignored that last question, switched off the heater, and turned out the lantern.

"Let's go commune. I think you have all the forces on your side tonight," he mumbled.

Once back by the river, we sat on the bank and crossed our legs in the fashion Many Heart had shown me. We each privately worked to clear our minds of everything extraneous. We replaced the new void with our new goal and soon found ourselves on the Path of Intent. Together did we succeed in traversing the Trail as a unified pair where we were eventually met by another—one dressed in resplendent doeskin and brilliant blue beads.

The meeting ultimately proved to be a highly private affair where we learned many enlightening factors that directly affected our physical sojourns, both for the present and for the future. We were made aware of the couple's spiritual purpose, for they truly were commissioned with the task of protecting and preserving that Earth Mother's region from those who would destroy it with poisons or greed. Much was revealed and shared with us while we were on the Intent Path that moonlit evening. And when all was said and done, we were gently eased down off the Path to find ourselves once again beside the rushing river waters.

To attempt a description of how we both felt upon returning to conscious awareness would turn out to be grossly inadequate. No words could adequately express the warmth we were filled with, nor the depth of love we felt for one another for many hours after that. So I will simply say that we returned to the camper and fell asleep holding one another—we held one another just as lovingly and as peacefully as our new home held us. It was the human embrace within the ultimate embrace of the Earth Mother, for after years and years of searching, we were now home—truly home within the welcoming arms of our new-found land. And we fell asleep that wonderful night listening to our twin hearts keep perfect rhythm with the great heart that beat beneath the sweet breast of our beautiful sacred ground.

When we got home that Sunday evening we were ecstatic to finally make the long-awaited pronouncement that we had found our land. Everyone was excited and, on Wednesday, when we proudly showed them photographs of it, they were pleading to move there right away. We made plans to save up—we would have to wait now until Lady Destiny dealt us all the right cards, and her partner, Time, deemed the right moment for us to go. In the meantime, we frequently found ourselves intently studying the photos and envisioning the day they'd become a living, loving reality.

The following Saturday, Bill and I took off once again. This time was not for the purpose of journeying to an encounter case, nor would we be gone overnight. This time was just for us.

During our frequent travels through the mountains, we'd happened upon a remote high lake. The lake had no name. We called it Spirit—just Spirit. And it was there we were headed this magnificent late autumn day.

We greeted Spirit and settled on the soft bank beside her wavering liquid arms. Behind us, the aspens were nearly bare now; colorful threads of their former glory garments lay all around us. Sky, so dazzling, the blueness reflected into Spirit like a celestial mirror. Birds, flocking overhead in a great vee, moved raucously through the high fabric of shimmering sapphire. Alpine air, clear and crisp, was scented with new portents that hinted of changes in the offing. The gears of the Grand Timepiece clicked into the Cusp of Seasons. And, looking out across the sun-touched surface of Spirit, we took note of all the living essence of nature and we saw that it was good. . .so good.

Snuggled down into the warmth of my mate's chest, his arms tightly wrapped around me, I felt a wonderful peacefulness radiate about us. We had experienced a difficult year, one that tried the strength of our purpose and the power of our dedication. Now, especially here in this secret little spot of ours, we could finally find rest and solace. A fish jumped and made a playful splash in the calm waters. I smiled with the warm realization that Spirit's people were spared the intrusion of fishermen.

My mate's voice whispered near my ear. "I wouldn't think of fishing here."

I patted his hand. "I know. This is like some primordial place, isn't it?"

He readily agreed. "Just like we too are the only people at the Dawning of Time—so peaceful, so quiet.

Then, for a long, long while, neither of us spoke. We remained together and simply allowed our receiving spirits to absorb the healing energies that the pristine power-point emitted. It felt so good, so rejuvenating.

Finally I softly spoke.

"Honey?"

"Mmmm."

"I still don't know if I'll write about the encounters."

"That's your decision, but why wouldn't you?"

Watching some wood ducks glide by, I pulled his arms tighter about me.

"Oh. . .same old reason, I guess. There's just not enough general belief in spirit existence."

"There're all sorts of books on ghosts and hauntings, even quite a few by the professional parapsychologists."

"This is not quite the same. Yes, there're hundreds of stories, but they don't enter actual encounters."

"What's the real reason for your doubts?"

I chuckled lightly. "Am I really that readable?"

"You are."

I sighed. "For the second same old reason."

"Uh-huh. You're concerned about public opinion—what folks'll think."

I nodded.

"Well, babe, the way I see it, the phantoms we work with are the least dangerous. There're all types of phantoms in the world. Those of greed and egotism are far more dangerous than ours. And what about the phantoms that lurk in secret research laboratories, or those that crouch in the dark corners of human minds?"

He had a point and I pondered it while he continued.

"In fact, the way people hide their secrets, whether they be hidden personalities, family skeletons, or private hypocritical thoughts, you could view nearly everyone as being walking phantoms of their real selves. What was that I saw in your private notebook about something like that? About people wearing masks?"

"It was based on my observations of people on the street, in the marketplace. I noticed how they pasted smiles over themselves, like masks, it seemed. And I wondered where all the people had gone."

"See there? You noticed they were like looking at phantoms of their real selves. There was no warmth to their personality; they appeared to you as shadows, cold and false."

"But we don't deal with those types. We work with the real phantoms."

"So?"

"So I don't know. Even No-Eyes foresaw this inner conflict I'd have over this issue."

"And did she also envision its resolution?"

"Yes, you know she did."

"Honey, what's important here is not the uniqueness of what we do, but only the fact of the matter. The spirit survives physical death so it can return to God when it's complete. Some spirits have a little trouble, that's all. It can't get any simpler than that. So we help them out a little. Maybe some Anglos have a hard time with that, but a great many people don't. Indians don't."

I grinned at that.

"No, they've been doing it for centuries. . .at least some of them have," I commented, thinking back on the warm learning days with my Dreamwalker mentors.

"So, what's the big deal?"

"How come you can always make everything come out so simple?"

"Not everything, honey, just the ones that *are* simple. What we do is beautiful. Nothing can change that."

I snuggled down deeper into the warmth of my mate's surrounding arms. My gaze was drawn skyward as the whooshing of owl wings captured my attention.

Bill raised his head. "See? Even the Spirit Messenger comes to give you the solace of its confirmation."

A soft smile tipped the corners of my mouth while I watched the symbol of the Spirit World alight on a distant pine branch.

A soft smile warmed within my heart as my eyes locked onto the unblinking orbs of the Night Spirit. Then, as if satisfied with our powerful moment of union, he blinked and settled down comfortably upon the limb.

I returned my gaze out across the rippling lake. And, as the sweet Wind Being gently sighed across the living waters of Spirit, its wisdom words did touch the core of my heart. Yes, we were okay. What we did was beautiful, because, listening to the Wind Spirit's confirming whispers. . .I knew that it was true. . .I knew, for all of nature said that it was so.

Afterword

I wrote these encounter histories during the winter following their conclusion. Four years later, after the first three books of the No-Eyes' series were published, and *Phantoms Afoot* was scheduled for book Number Four, I reviewed what I had written. Then the sleepless nights began. The book haunted me day and night, for something wasn't setting right with me about it. The old nagging began anew. Should I really include it in the series? No. Do I really need to reveal our private spiritual work? No.

So I sat down at my desk and proceeded to tear up the entire manuscript. I tore up the only copy I had.

For a few days afterward, I felt wonderfully relieved. I felt like a great weight had been lifted. Now Bill and I could continue our work with complete anonymity and no one would know the difference. No one would give us odd side-glance looks.

But the nagging began anew. The sleepless nights returned in earnest. The book had to be done. It was a natural follow-up to Dreamwalker because it continued with the resolution of my dilemma with Many Heart regarding my obligation to the wayward spirits. It brought out the fact that my own forgotten experiences with the unexplained was a valid fact, and not only of my own life. Most likely there were many other people who had also experienced much the same in their own lives. Didn't I owe them explanations to resolve their own occurrences? Yes. Wasn't it my spiritual duty to provide the facts of the universal truths regarding spirit manifestations? Yes. Shouldn't I include *all* aspects of spiritual realities so concepts could then be clarified? Yes. Yes!

And, there was one more solid factor that propelled me toward my final decision to go ahead with *Phantoms Afoot*.

As mentioned earlier, we'd had to move from our Eagle location due to the fact that the house we were renting was sold. The owners weren't going to tell us that little fact until everything was finalized and the new owners were ready to move in. This would've put us out of the house in January. It was a cruel thing not to tell us, for moving and driving a moving van around the mountains in the middle of bitter snow-country mountains was a dangerous venture. Needless to say, our inner senses warned us that something untoward was going on. And, since there were no more house rentals in Eagle, we looked at Leadville, where we found a house large enough for the eight of us at a fraction of our previous rent. Everyone who had Eagle jobs quit them. We moved into the Leadville house in November. We were supposed to pack the truck all day Friday and pull out Saturday morning. But I couldn't shake the urgings I felt. . .we had to make the entire move by nightfall.

So, as tired as we all were, we loaded the final item at dusk on Friday and pulled out of Eagle. Bill drove the Ryder, I followed, and the other two cars were behind me. Ascending the steep grade of Battle Mountain, I continually worked at visualizing the White Light around the van ahead of me. By now it was totally dark. Blackness engulfed the small convoy as it snaked along the twisting shelf road. And snowflakes began drifting across the headlight beams. I worked harder to keep us all safe during the hazardous journey.

When we reached the new house, Bill and I entered alone while the others waited for us to return. Upon entering the still house, we felt a presence. It was one that quickly responded to the White Light, for it didn't materialize and also didn't care much for our intrusion.

After calling everyone inside, we busied ourselves with the task of unloading. As soon as we had the bulk of it in the house, it snowed and snowed. If we had waited until Saturday morning, we never would've been able to make it over the steep mountain terrain.

Two months after we were well settled in our 1888 dwelling, Bill saw a movement out of the corner of his eye. When he looked, he received the clear impression of a woman in a long gown passing from the hall into the downstairs bathroom. He rushed in, but nothing was there.

One afternoon, when I was cleaning the same bathroom, I heard beautiful clear singing. I went into the living room and asked the others who was singing. They all looked at one another. I left them sitting dumbfounded and entered the kitchen to ask Sarah if she'd been singing. She too gave me a quizzical took. Nobody in the house had been singing. In fact, they hadn't even been talking, for they were all deeply engrossed in books at the time. So I returned to my chores in the bathroom, where all was now quiet.

At different times, several members of our household said

that they saw a shadow of some substance in the bathroom while they were showering. They could see the nebulous movement through the curtain. When they quickly looked, nothing was there.

Then there were times when the living room was dark at night and the lamp switch would click on. This occurred while everyone was asleep and I was doing writing by oil lamp in the kitchen. One such occasion was when one of our members came home from a night shift. I was in the kitchen as usual, and the rest of the house was dark. When he entered the dark hallway, the living room lamp clicked on. He hurried to my side.

"You do that?" he asked.

"Do what?"

"That lamp just turned on again."

"Don't worry, Mike, it's just the lady again."

"*Oh.*"

"Turn it off when you go to bed."

Poor Mike furtively entered the room, switched off the light and hurriedly went upstairs to bed. I think he liked having Rainbow sleep with him.

Then there were the frequent times when the dogs would be lying peacefully on the living room floor while we were all gathered around watching television or reading, and suddenly they both would begin looking up toward the ceiling at something. They'd nervously whimper and whine. Magic, the collie/coyote baby we adopted, would run for cover with her tail tightly tucked between her legs. Rainbow would growl fiercely. Sometimes Magic would just run for the safety of her hidey-hole spot beneath our bed while Rainbow, unmoving, rolled up her eyes at the ceiling and growled threateningly under her breath. Poor Magic was such a baby when this happened. One of the girls would invariably croon, "It's *baaaaack,*" then hurry to Magic's side to give comfort.

The on-going incidents became a private family joke. When the semi-solid shadow first began appearing in the bathroom during their showers, some wondered if this old house was relocated to where the "Bates Motel" once stood. The events were accepted as just another aspect of reality and its multi-dimensional manifestations.

And so it was that these continuing happenings served to reinforce my decision to do *Phantoms Afoot* after all.

And the rewrite began in earnest.

I'm glad of my decision now because the final draft turned

out so much better. It wasn't that I remembered more of each encounter, but rather that I now included many conversations that I had left out of the original version—conversations that I now realize were so important to the overall issue because of their explanatory nature.

I would also like to say here that the time-frame spanning each encounter took up considerably more actual time than would appear in the telling. Obviously, the business of communication and the eventual convincing frequently took several hours. The main point that is relevant to each case is that what the entity needed most was simply the strong desire to return. So simple in theory—yet not always so simple in application.

So during the work of rewriting this book, while all the family was abed, and I sat at the kitchen table with the oil lamp burning brightly, there were two occasions when a sudden movement in the shadowed hallway drew my attention. When I looked, all I'd catch was the trailing hem of a long skirt. And when I rushed into the darkened doorway, nothing would be there. I'd return to my work.

Although we tried several techniques to draw the mysterious occupant out, she'd have nothing to actively do with us. The lady wouldn't manifest herself before us. . .at least not in her totality. She didn't desire a face-to-face confrontation. Perhaps she likes having our company and shows her appreciation by being playfully evasive. We'd like to help her, but there is little we can do if we can't make the required connection contact. We pray that one day her shyness will evaporate and we will succeed in discovering why she's here and, hopefully, show our lady the way home.

There are other incidents that reinforced my decision to include this book in the series. When my daughter, Aimee, attended the Woodland Park school, she relayed to me that she'd been seeing a figure in one of her classrooms. It was that of an old-time preacher with a black parson's wide-brimmed hat. I questioned her thoroughly. How were the shadows in the room? How was the sunlight at that time of day? Did the figure seem connected with a specific teacher? Or just with the room? Did she see him in any other rooms of the building? All physical causal factors had to be examined.

The fact that the apparition held an open book before him, and that he was sometimes alone and sometimes standing before a seemingly penitent woman, discounted the idea that the vision was being generated by simple shadowplay. When

I tried to research the geographical locale, there was no historical evidence of a church or school once occupying that precise
piece of land. Yet when I then had no recourse but to question
our Advisor on the matter, I was informed that a missionary
building had indeed been erected on that exact location over
one hundred years ago.

Then, in our Leadville house, when Aimee entered her room
one night, she saw her bed on fire. It was a psychic flash. When
she told me of it she feared it was a premonition, and was
naturally afraid to go to bed. I told her to be sure no quilts or
wastebaskets were touching the wall heaters, and I'd check out
her vision as soon as I could.

What I found out was that our house had been originally
located in the center of Leadville during the mining days.
When the big fire of 1888 engulfed and razed the court house,
the blaze could be seen from that precise corner of her room.
She had picked up on a former event and psychically envisioned the flashpoint of the occurrence. Now that the house
was moved, and is presently located up on a hill overlooking
the town, the position could in no way be the same as it once
was, yet she saw it as if it happened yesterday from the
viewpoint of its former location.

So many enigmas our finite minds are just now discovering.
So many mysteries are becoming clear. So deep and vast are
the newly-revealed realities and their magnificent dimensions.
So wonderful that we are opening our eyes to the splendorous
wonders that lay before us, for the power of the spirit is indeed
limitless. . .its scope and reach, endless and forever eternal.

Upon surrendering all his land, on which the city of Seattle is now located, Chief Seattle gave a speech to Governor Isaac Stevens before dooming his people to reservation confinement. His noble words of the heart are relevant to the issue of this book.

My people are few. They resemble the scattering trees of a storm-swept plain. . .There was a time when our people covered the land as the waves of a wind-ruffled sea cover its shell-paved floor, but that time long since passed away with the greatness of tribes that are now but a mournful memory. . .

To us the ashes of our ancestors are sacred and their resting place is hallowed ground. You wander far from the graves of your ancestors and seemingly without regret. Your religion was written on tables of stone by the iron finger of your God so that you could not forget The Red Man could never comprehend nor remember it. Our religion is the traditions of our ancestors—the dreams of our old men, given them in the solemn hours of night by the Great Spirit; and the visions of our sachems, and is written in the hearts of our people.

Your dead cease to love you and the land of their nativity as soon as they pass the portals of the tomb and wander away beyond the stars. They are soon forgotten and never return. Our dead never forget the beautiful world that gave them being. . .

When the last Red Man shall have perished, and the memory of my tribe shall have become a myth among the white man, these shores will swarm with the invisible dead of my tribe, and when your children's children think themselves alone in the field, the store, the shop, or in the silence of the pathless woods, they will not be alone. . .At night when the streets of your cities and villages are silent and you think them deserted, they will throng with the returning hosts that once filled them and still love this beautiful land. The White Man will never be alone.

Let him be just and deal kindly with my people, for the dead are not powerless. Dead—I say? There is no death. Only a change of worlds.

About the Artist

The new cover painting of this 1993 Edition of *Phantoms AFoot* was created by Carole Bourdo, world-famous artist of Native American and Wildlife subjects. Ms. Bourdo's originals are sought by collectors worldwide, and her prints are becoming increasingly popular throughout the U.S.

Carole Bourdo's native heart was recognized and honored when her Native American Naming Ceremony was performed by Chief Earl Old Person on the land of her People of the Blackfeet Reservation in May of 1989.

In 1990, the artist and Mary Summer Rain met their destinies to blend their talents. Ms. Bourdo's captivating art first appeared on the author's book *Daybreak*, and Ms. Rain's readers began requesting more of the artist's work on future books. By the time the author has concluded her series of books, Ms. Bourdo's sensitive art creations will grace a total of ten covers.

Because of the public's high demand for Carole Bourdo's art, beginning in early 1993 her offerings will be expanded to include China Collector Plates. This has been the brainchild of the artist's imaginative daughter, Lauri, who will be totally involved in the creation of the plates to keep it a family operation. The plates that depict the art on Mary Summer Rain's book covers will also include the duo signatures of artist and author in 25K gold on the back of each plate. For more information on the collector plates or any of Carole's art, please write to: Bourdo Originals, P.O. Box 62522, Colorado Springs, CO 80962.